B.D. Dunn

Paul B. Dunn

GREAT DONALD ROSS GOLF COURSES YOU CAN PLAY

PAUL DUNN AND B.J.DUNN

THE DERRYDALE PRESS

LANHAM AND NEW YORK

THE DERRYDALE PRESS

Published in the United States of America
by The Derrydale Press
4720 Boston Way, Lanham, Maryland 20706

Distributed by NATIONAL BOOK NETWORK, INC.

British Library Cataloguing in Publication Information Available

Library of Congress Cataloging-in-Publication Data

Dunn, Paul R.
    Great Donald Ross golf courses you can play / Paul and B.J. Dunn
        p. cm.
    ISBN 1-58667-060-3 (cloth : alk. paper)
    1. Golf courses—United States—directories. 2. Ross, Donald J., 1872?-
1948. I. Dunn, B. J. (Betty Jane) II. Title.

GV981 .D86 2001
796.352'06'8—dc21   00-047559

CONTENTS

INTRODUCTION

At the heart of this book is the simple idea that the golf courses designed by Donald Ross, with their unique characteristics, deserve to be well-known to the golfing public and played with full enjoyment.

Our goal has been to tell you where they are, how to get to them and, where possible, to give you a bit of history and feel for the courses and their surroundings. Unfortunately, many courses have no early historic records still in existence. The number of old wooden clubhouses that have burned to the ground, records inside, tells a sad tale. But where histories are available, we have some fascinating stories to tell.

You will see what the courses look like now, and in some instances what they looked like years ago. This has been a close collaborative effort among the authors and the hundreds of folks who manage and play the golf courses.

The authors live in Pinehurst, North Carolina, the village where course architect and player, Donald Ross, spent most of his professional life supervising the making of clubs and the designing, building and managing of

hundreds of distinctive courses across the land that have their own Rossian personality.

Our interest in Ross was piqued just before the U.S. Open was sited at Pinehurst, and was heightened during the event as more and more writers and commentators described some of the famed Scot's remarkable achievements.

When Ross' courses are rated by sports writers, the private courses generally receive top billing. The public courses, in particular, get heavy play, making them much more difficult to maintain in pristine condition, but the typical player may find it difficult or impossible to play the courses that re-

Above: Reflections at The Broadmoor in Colorado Springs. The 18th hole, the clubhouse and, in the background, the tower of the famous resort.

Right: Early morning mist over hole three

Linville photo by Hugh Morton

Above: The 14th hole at Pinehurst No. 2

ceive the greatest praise. They are private and some are exceedingly exclusive. It's sort of, "Look, but you can't touch the merchandise!"

That is why, of over three hundred Donald Ross courses still in existence, those described in this book are all open to the public. We have identified and researched each one. All the facts have been reviewed with the course owner, manager or the golf professional. The dates shown on the upper right of the opening pages indicate the year that Ross *designed* the course. The courses are either public, resort or semi-private. Two are military; open to retired and active military and their guests. We included these because literally millions of American golfers meet their criteria for play, and many active and retired servicemen and women may not know where the Ross courses are, and that they are available for you to visit. They exist for your golfing pleasure.

Donald J. Ross is admired by those who play his courses. And, as some jokingly claim, he's hated, too, when those unpredictable greens receive a well-aimed shot and, like a stern father with a recalcitrant child, send it away from the targeted pin.

But the praise far outweighs the occasional gripe. His influence is still felt by both players and golf course designers, many of whom still imitate his work. And too, they are paid handsome fees to put his neglected works back into prime condition. As a frugal Scot, he would have been flabbergasted to see what large sums change hands these days for redoing his works. Indeed, a foursome of players pays more today to play a round at some of his courses than he was paid in his early days to design an entire course!

course design and in the game itself. Having completed so many quality layouts from Maine to Florida, in the era of rail travel vs. jet travel, is an amazing accomplishment, and exemplifies his dedication to perfection."

Some golfers who read this book may take exception to the title, *Great Donald Ross Golf Courses You Can Play*. Indeed, they may say, "But they're not all 'Great' courses!" That's where we, the authors, disagree. We think that each one, in its own way, has a certain greatness. They all possess just a touch of the magic that was Donald Ross. It is great, too, that they have survived the steady pressures for change. And it is a miracle that many didn't simply disappear off the face of the earth during the Great Depression and World War II, times that sorely tried the resources and endurance of those who loved the game and refused to let it die.

Some courses are in mint condition, and some are far from it. But they all represent a piece of the work of a great master architect. Just as some works by Michelangelo, Titan or Picasso are not masterpieces, the quality of Ross' work is not always uniform. They were works in progress, improving with age. So with Ross. He did what he could with what he had to work with, often very little in the way of funds, an inability to visit every site, and city officials or course committees who would "second guess" him and make changes he'd have preferred to reject.

But in the end, there remain hundreds and hundreds of fabulous fairways and compelling greens that inspire golfers to feel a little sense of Dornoch and Pinehurst when they approach that first tee.

Above: The Bethlehem Country Club in the White Mountains of New Hampshire

One prominent architect who was directly influenced by Ross was the great Robert Trent Jones. Here is what his son, Robert Trent Jones, Jr. told us, "During the building of Oak Hill in 1926, my father met Donald Ross of Pinehurst, North Carolina, the leading golf architect of the time. Through conversations with Ross and observance of his work, my dad decided on his career and he, in fact, actually started competing with Ross for projects after dad attended Cornell for three years as a special student specializing in a curriculum that would prepare him for his career. I grew up on a Donald Ross golf course."

Tom Clark of Ault, Clark and Associates, Ltd. sums it up nicely: "Donald Ross provided an inspiration to all modern day architects in his passion for golf

Above: Ross did most of design work in this home at 120 Midland Road, Pinehurst. (His summers were spent in Rhode Island at Little Compton.) From the backyard's traditional English garden, one may look out on his beloved Course No. 2.

We have included several courses that you will not find in other Ross course anthologies or listings. For example, when you read about the William J. Devine course in Franklin Park, Dorchester, Massachusetts, you will discover the reasons why it has been included. We have also given prominent attention to the just-built VinnyLinks at Shelby course in Nashville, Tennessee. We believe it has a particularly exciting course history, and an original and special goal.

The book includes Richmond Pines in North Carolina, a course cited as a Ross creation by Pete Jones, and by Cornish and Whitten in their '93 work, although Whitten does not include it in the '96 work, *Golf Has Never Failed Me*. The scorecard here reads, "A Donald Ross Course." It has the look and feel of Ross, but it should be noted that it is, at best, a course Ross only visited and counseled, and for which he was never paid an architect's fee.

Many that he did design for a fee have been so severely changed over the years by remodeling, bunker removals, tee box moves, etc. that

they are probably far less Rossian than this one. Although he only visited Richmond Pines briefly, perhaps for a day or two, as it is only a short distance from Pinehurst, he was able to give advice on how it should be properly laid out, and that advice was followed "to a tee." The course since then has been preserved lovingly by members and management. So we think it rates inclusion.

At his peak, he maintained offices in Illinois, Massachusetts, North Carolina and Pennsylvania, relying most heavily on his associates, Walter B. Hatch, James Harrison, Henry Hughes and J.B. McGovern.

These engineers were often on site when Ross was occupied with other projects, or with his course management responsibilities at Pinehurst. Another associate, Walter Irving Johnston, who was both a draftsman and engineer, created the finished plans, including detailed specifications for individual holes and fairways that were provided to the building foremen. Donald's brother, Aeneas, worked with him for ten years, returning to Dornoch in 1932. Pete Jones, in his "*A Directory of Golf Courses Designed by Donald Ross*," estimates the Ross team completed designs for 388 courses.

METHODOLOGY AND ACKNOWLEDGMENTS

Our methodology for researching the book followed this procedure: First we checked commonly known published references for Donald Ross courses. These included: W. Pete Jones' *A Directory of Golf Courses Designed by Donald J. Ross,* Martini Press, Raleigh, North Carolina; *Golf Has Never Failed Me, The lost commentaries of legendary golf architect Donald J. Ross,* by Ron Whitten, Sleeping Bear Press, Chelsea, Michigan; *The Architects of Golf* by Geoffrey S. Cornish and Ronald E. Whitten, HarperCollins, New York; and *Sandhills Classics,* by Lee Pace, Pine Needles.

We also searched old golf, sporting magazines and newspaper articles for word of American Ross courses, or of courses even suspected of being by Ross. His two courses done in Cuba no longer exist, although there is a move on to reopen one. Of the Canadian courses, only one is open to public play and, sad to say, it is no longer considered a Ross course, having been completely remodeled by a contemporary course architect.

We were kindly given the compact disk of *Golf Magazine - DRIVE!* (by Greengrass Software Corp.), which was very useful in locating Ross courses. We also used available websites and e-mail addresses, which made it easier to gather information in the cyber age. Yahoo's *Golf Magazine Golf Course Guide* pages were very useful, too.

We visited and played as many of the courses as possible, and were invariably received graciously.

Once we established that a course was one of the over 315 still in operation that Ross had worked on, we sent a detailed questionnaire, then gathered historic information on the course, spoke to the course professional and/or manager, members and players, and,

from that information, wrote a description of the course. All course information was then re-checked for verification before publication.

We regret any course we may have missed in our search. We invite anyone who plays a course the public can play that he or she believes to be by Ross, that is not found in this book, to please contact us at: 125 Lake Shore Drive, Pinehurst, NC 28374.

ACKNOWLEDGMENTS

Peter Dennis and Rand Jerris at the USGA provided valuable information to us as did Sean M. Fisher of the Metropolitan District Commission Archives in Boston and Jon Seamans of the Boston Parks and Recreation Department, who brought to our attention Alan Banks' scholarly paper, *Golf in the Pleasure Ground.* Khristine Januzik at the Tufts Archives Wing of the Given Library in Pinehurst was also helpful to us.

Thanks to Bill Black and Mike Shatzkin for sharing their publishing contacts, Stephen Driver and Jed Lyons of Derrydale Press, Craig Bowen for his artist's eye, Tom Greenwood and Ron Sutton for their photographs, Dennis Blow for his advice, Ed Murphy for the wonderful Tin Whistles pictures, Tim Gold of Burchfield's, Tom Stewart of Old Sport; Hugh Morton for his special cooperation and photographs; Tom Clark of Ault, Clark & Assoc., Ltd.; MDC Archives, Boston, MA; Veda O'Neil, Francestown, NH; Arthur Boufford, No. Swanzey, N.H. and all the golf professionals, sports writers, mayors' offices, historical societies and players who provided information and pictures. We couldn't have done it without you.

Many photographs found throughout the book were taken, and are copyrighted, by Bob Labbance. Bob is an editor, writer, photographer and president of Notown Communications of Montpelier, VT., specializing in public relations and editorial services in the world of golf. He is the author of eight books on golf. Having played dozens of Ross-designed courses, he appreciates the design style of Ross and has translated that understanding to film. Visit the Notown website at www.notowngolf.com.

COLORADO

THE BROADMOOR GOLF CLUB

WELLSHIRE GOLF CLUB

DIRECTIONS: FROM DENVER, TAKE I-25 SOUTH TO EXIT 138 WEST. TURN LEFT ON PORTALS TO CLUB.

Resort with private membership. One must stay at the 700-room hotel to play. Open 12 months of the year. Of the 54 holes, The East Course only was designed by Donald Ross. Rental clubs. Golf carts and caddies required on all courses prior to 3 PM between May 1 and October 1. Driving ranges. Also at The Broadmoor—the West Course by Robert Trent Jones, Sr. (1965) and the Mountain Course designed by Arnold Palmer and Ed Seay (1976).

One of the most beautiful courses in the country

Broadmoor East is a championship golf course in the true sense of the word. It possesses all of the necessary ingredients: great natural terrain; large, fast and undulating greens; strategically placed sand traps in the fairways and surrounding greens; water hazards; deep grassy rough from which it can be difficult to recover, and an abundance of trees, shrubbery and underbrush. All of these elements add up to a golf course of exceptional challenge and beauty.

Cheyenne Mountain forms a unique backdrop for the 385 yard par four first hole. The tee is elevated, and pine trees line both sides of the fairway to the landing area. The green is also elevated and bunkered to the right front and left side. This is a magnificent starting hole, and it is not as easy as it sounds. Hole number ten is another dramatic setting. The par four hole plays downhill from tee to green. It is a place to enjoy the great view of Colorado Springs and the prairie to the east from the dogleg point of this fairway.

The nine holes of the East Course that remain exactly as Ross designed them are: numbers one, two, three, four, five, six, sixteen, seventeen and eighteen.

The hotel has a distinguished history of major tournaments, including: PGA Cup Matches, U.S. Women's Open, Trans-Mississippi Championship, Western Amateur Championship, NCAA Championship, U.S. Amateur Championship, Curtis Cup Championship, U.S. Women's Amateur Championship, Broadmoor Men's and Women's Invitationals, World Seniors Golf Tournament and the United States Olympic Committee (USOC) Celebrity Tournament. Jack Nicklaus won the '59 U.S. Amateur at the 18th, which is now the 15th hole on the East Course; Annika Sorenstam won the '95 Women's Open.

Famous players of the East Course include: Dwight D. Eisenhower, Jack Nicklaus, Arnold Palmer, Corey Pavin, Fred Couples, Nancy Lopez, Annika Sorenstam, Julie Inkster, Jackie Gleason, Bill Romanowski, Reggie Jackson, Julius Irving, Dinah Shore, Bob Hope, Bob Costas and Bing Crosby.

The resort, which is one of the few to earn the Mobil Five-Star and AAA Five-

Diamond ratings, also provides the following amenities: Tennis Center with tennis pavilion and stadium court, 12 outdoor Plexi-pave courts, horseback riding, bicycles and paddleboats, a motion picture theater, The Carriage House Museum, 11 restaurants/lounges, 16 up-scale specialty shops and over 114,000 square feet of meeting and exhibition space.

There is a full service spa, café and spa salon, state-of-the-art fitness center, indoor heated pools and outdoor heated lap pool with Jacuzzi and saunas.

Above: The 590 yard, par five third, where a pond sits immediately in front of the green. Right This spectacular par three of 157 yards is all carry over water to a large green sloping toward the water and trapped on the left side.

Tees	Par	Yards	Slope	USGA
Blue	72	7119	127	73.0
White	72	6562	122	70.5
Red	72	5921	139	72.7

WELLSHIRE GOLF CLUB

3333 SOUTH COLORADO BOULEVARD, DENVER, CO 80222
(303) 757-1352 FAX: (303) 370-1561 E-MAIL: BWEST@CI.DENVER.CO.US
WEBSITE: WWW.DENVERGOV.ORG/CONTENT/TEMPLATE2345.ASP

DIRECTIONS: FROM I-25 TAKE HAMPTON EXIT, WEST TO THIRD LIGHT (COLORADO BLVD.) TURN RIGHT. CLUB IS FOUR BLOCKS AHEAD AT COLORADO AND HAMPDEN BLVDS.

Public. 18 holes. Open year round. Pro shop opens 6 AM. Driving range. Putting green. Chipping and sand practice areas. Rental gas, pullcarts and clubs. Pro on site. Two restaurants.

DENVER AND COLORADO HOSTS
TO THE

34th United States Golf Association
Public Links Championship

WELLSHIRE GOLF CLUB

July 13-18, 1959   **Denver, Colorado**

COLORADO
RUSH TO THE
ROCKIES
CENTENNIAL
1859   1959

**Celebrating Colorado's "Rush to the Rockies"
Centennial Year—1959**

OFFICIAL
PROGRAM

DENVER PUBLIC LINKS
GOLF ASSOCIATION

FREE

Although Ross designed this impressive facility in 1923, it was not completed and opened until 1927. It was built for a limited membership of 400 at a cost of $300,000. It became a public facility in 1936, when the city purchased the entire holdings for only $60,000.

Often voted "one of the best public facilities in the nation," Wellshire works hard to maintain its reputation. The bent grass course layout winds through mature trees to medium sized greens. A persistent creek and good sized pond come into play on six holes.

Hole seven is the signature hole at Wellshire and deservedly so. It is a 409-yard par four and the number one handicap. The challenges on holes 12 and 14, are called the *Amen Corner* by the locals.

Wellshire was the site of the National Public Links Championship in 1946 and again in 1959. Arnold Palmer, Tommy Jacobs and Howie Johnson have played here. Ben Hogan won the Denver Open here in 1947 and again the next year The story goes that he left the tournament in '48, thinking he hadn't won and headed for the railroad station to head for Salt Lake City where he was scheduled to play another tournament. The mayor caught him as he was about to board the train, and handed him his winning check. Denver was his sixth straight tournament win, but he didn't make it to seven. He lost in Salt Lake City.

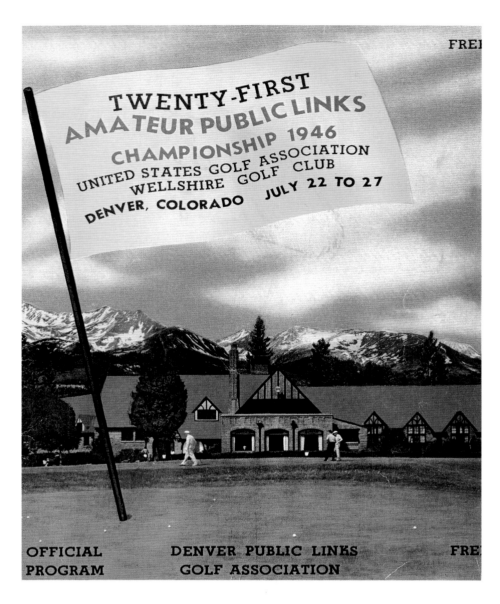

OFFICIAL
PROGRAM

DENVER PUBLIC LINKS
GOLF ASSOCIATION

FRE

Called a "Workingman's Competition," at the time, only four cities had held two such tournaments each: San Francisco, Indianapolis, Cleveland and Louisville. There were 192 entrants at Wellshire after sectional qualifying rounds at 39 locations, for a total of 3,586 players enrolled from 32 states, districts and territories in addition to Canada. The silver cup was donated by James D. Standish Jr.

The Wellshire Clubhouse and Inn. Modeled after an English Tudor manor, the clubhouse is built of red brick, with typical gables, ells and steep roofs. The dining room, lounge and grill are distinguished by rugged beams and great open hearths. The large windows facing west in the lounge face a vista of mountains said to be unsurpassed for grandeur anywhere in the world. Two shady porches face the 18th green and the ninth. Both are surrounded by hedges, shrubs, trees and flowers.

Tees	Par	Yards	Slope	USGA
Blue	71	6498	129	71.1
White	71	6232	127	70.0
Red	73	5720	129	71.2

5

Connecticut

Shennecossett Golf Club

SHENNECOSSETT GOLF CLUB

PLANT STREET, GROTON, CT 06340
(860) 445-0262

DIRECTIONS: FROM I-95 HEADING SOUTH, TAKE EXIT 87. TURN RIGHT AT SECOND LIGHT, MAKE IMMEDIATE LEFT AT NEXT LIGHT. HEAD OVER TO PLANT STREET AND TURN LEFT

Public. 18 holes. Open year round. Rental clubs, gas carts and pullcarts. Pro shop opens 6 AM. Putting green. Teaching pro. Restaurant and snack bar.

The clubhouse in the background. Wild grasses give the feel of Ross' native Scotland.

The year was 1898, and a businessman/farmer named Thomas W. Avery laid out a four-hole golf course in his home town of Groton. Since one of Connecticut's most prolific crops is rocks, Avery had to clear the land with horse-drawn weight cranes.

In 1905, Milton Plant, a socialite who lived nearby, bought the adjacent Griswold Hotel, which became associated with the golf course in future years. There were obstacles to Plant's takeover of the golf course, not the least of which were the ever present boulders. However, Plant was, first and foremost, a businessman who had built a $3,000,000 summer home in Groton, had franchised a baseball team, raced his yachts and overseen railroad interests along the East Coast, so he proceeded to purchase more than 60 acres, including Avery's four-hole course.

On May 5, 1914, the local newspaper quoted "Two big auto truckloads of furniture for the

A nuclear submarine rears its bow behind the flag on the par four number 16.

Shennecossett Golf Club have arrived. This is of wicker and is a pretty shade of robin-egg blue. All the work on the inside of the building has been completed, and the outside is nearly done. The windmill is being torn down, and there will be an electric well put in the place on the green in front of the clubhouse."

The clubhouse today retains its Spanish flavor, built of ivory stucco with blue trim. The roof is covered with blue shingles, and mosaics depicting arrowheads in red, white and blue reach along the archways over the verandas.

In 1916, Donald Ross was hired to redesign the 18-hole course. In 1919, he remodeled three of the holes to better suit his ideas of how the course should best be played. At the time, he was praised for "sculpturing his greens with a characteristic style that molded putting surface con-

The Independence Day celebration, with the Coast Guard's USS Eagle under sail on the left. She didn't deter this golfer from putting on the 16th hole.

tours into the existing terrain. His green sites nearly always put a premium on short recovery shots." Shennecossett is one of only five courses in Connecticut laid out by Ross during his career.

In 1945, the caddies went on strike to increase their fee from $1.25 to $2 per round, forming a picket line and threatening to draft bylaws to be filed with the Secretary of State in Hartford. Evidently, the caddies were divided into Class A and Class B. The tip for Class B was 60 cents and for Class A, it was from 75 cents to a dollar. The caddies won. In the early '50s, rumors abounded that housing developers were planning to absorb the course, but The Menlip Corp. decided to purchase it, along with the hotel, for $450,000. The fee for golf club membership at that time was only $75 per year. Chas. Pfizer & Co. bought the hotel in 1968, and the grand old resort was demolished.

In November of that year, despite some pressure to use the land for housing developments, the town of Groton, with help of a federal grant, was able to purchase the course and keep it open as a municipal facility. On opening day, April 10, 1969, 105 golfers teed off.

Ray W. Rancourt, in his book *Shenne-cossett—the History of a Golf Course,* wrote: "As a golfer walks toward the 18th green, he turns his back on Long Island Sound and the Thames River and confronts an open expanse of fairway with a trap on the left and a few trees on the right. One tree, a ginkgo, replaces a former large tree, a possi-

Tees	Par	Yards	Slope	USGA
Blue	71	6088	122	71.5
White	74	6142	121	69.1
Red	74	5571	122	72.4

ble headache to swingers who have a tendency to slice."

Today, the course has many of the characteristics of Ross' original design, a cross between a traditional and a Scottish links-style design. The fairways are mounded, lined with trees and rather narrow. The somewhat small greens are sloping and fast. The terrain is mostly rolling, with many uneven lies. Top golf writers have rated this course as the "7th Best Public Course in the State."

The copy from the Griswold Hotel folder, issued in the early 1900s, read: "The Shenecossett Country Club adjoining the hotel grounds, extends its privileges to Griswold patrons. It has a wonderful 18-hole golf course constructed by and under the care of a noted professional. The Club House with its afternoon teas and dancing and morning concerts, is a social center. Tennis courts, bathing beach, athletic field, fine motor roads, fireproof garage, beautiful walks affording matchless panoramas, ideal climate and accessibility, combine to give the utmost in pleasure and summer comfort. Situated halfway between New York and Boston, and with through express trains from Philadelphia and the South, it is most conveniently located."

Alex Smith, who won the U.S. Open in '06 and '09, was an early pro here. Glenna Collett was his pupil. She won the U.S. Open Women's Championship six times. Tommy Armour played "Shenny" often; he won the 1921 Men's Amateur. Harry Cooper, pro here, won the 1942 Bing Crosby Pro-Am.

Because of a well conceived land swap with Pfizer, many holes have been remodeled significantly by Mark Mungeam of Cornish, Silva and Mungeam, but good planning has preserved the true flavor of the course, and holes one, two, three, four, five, six, seven, ten (originally par four, then changed to three, then up to five, but now back to four), 11, 12, 13 and 14 remain as they were back in 1916-19.

In its heyday, the Griswold Hotel was plush, elaborate and catered to an elite crowd. Before the '29 crash, Walter Hagen, Bobby Jones and Babe Didrikson played exhibition rounds here to big crowds. Newly renovated, it will again be the scene of many important Connecticut tournaments.

Left: Standing on the fourth green, looking at the sixth green. At right is number seven and off in the right distance is the flag for number two.

FLORIDA

BELLEVIEW BILTMORE RESORT & SPA

THE BILTMORE

BOBBY JONES GOLF COMPLEX

DAYTONA BEACH GOLF CLUB, SOUTH COURSE

DELRAY BEACH GOLF CLUB

THE DUNEDIN COUNTRY CLUB

FORT MYERS COUNTRY CLUB

HYDE PARK GOLF CLUB

KEYSTONE GOLF & COUNTRY CLUB

MAYFAIR COUNTRY CLUB

NEW SMYRNA BEACH MUNICIPAL GOLF COURSE

PALATKA GOLF CLUB

PANAMA COUNTRY CLUB

PINECREST GOLF CLUB

PONCE DE LEON GOLF & CONFERENCE RESORT

PUNTA GORDA COUNTRY CLUB

BELLEVIEW BILTMORE RESORT & SPA

1925

25 Belleview Blvd., Clearwater, FL 33756
(800) 237-8947 Fax (727) 441-4173
Website: www. Belleviewbiltmore.com

Directions: From Hwy. 19 south, exit at East Bay Dr and go eight miles to Indian

Semi-private. 18 holes. Open year round. Metal spikes allowed. Rental clubs and carts. Practice range with putting and chipping greens. Fully stocked pro shop. PGA instructors. Sports World Bar and Grille. The clubhouse emulates the style of the hotel with a green gabled roof.

Built by railroad magnate, Henry Plant, Belleview Biltmore Hotel opened in 1897 and is currently listed on the *National Register of Historic Places*. It is reputed to be "the largest occupied wooden structure in the world." Its spectacular Tiffany Ballroom is 13,000 square feet with 30 foot ceilings. It offers 244 Victorian-style guest rooms. There is a well-equipped spa and fitness center, indoor and outdoor pools with cascading waterfalls and four red clay tennis courts.

It is strategically located between St. Petersburg and Clearwater, only 22 miles west of Tampa Airport. The property sits atop the scenic bluffs overlooking Clearwater Bay, seven miles from Clearwater Beach, which has been rated as one of the top ten beaches in the country.

The son of the founder, Morton Plant, was an avid golfer, and was determined to have a first class course at the resort. Unwilling to accept grasses that wouldn't survive Florida's sandy soil, he experi-

mented with different species, along with soils and fertilizers, bringing in trainloads of rich topsoil from Indiana and using it to replace six sand greens.

The course had been designed by Lancelot Cressy Servos, and by 1909, it was extended to 18 holes. Donald Ross was summoned in 1915 to

Above: The resort with Clearwater Bay in the background

12

design and oversee the construction of two 18-hole courses. He provided his typical small, undulating greens, hazards that punish the overly confident and the long fairways that were his signature.

Celebrities flocked to the Belleview, including: MacDonald Smith, Walter Hagen, Gene Sarazen, Francis Ouimet, Alex Smith, Betty Hicks, Virginia Van Wie and Grantland Rice. Ring Lardner and Rex Beach did some of their writing here, and Kennesaw Landis (the first baseball commissioner), Joe DiMaggio and Mickey Mantle were some of the sports greats who sought rest and relaxation.

The resort and spa was a popular destination for the rich and famous of the '20s and '30s, many of whom came down in their own private railroad cars. This was where the Vanderbilts, Pews, DuPonts and Studebakers vacationed for the winter. Many of these wealthy guests brought their servants with them. During the '20s, rooms rented for $4.

As we trace the history of these wonderful old courses, a pattern emerges. When World War II occupied the hearts and minds of Americans, little thought was given to preserving recreational facilities. The U.S. Army took over the resort, and without any care, the courses were soon hidden under a thick, knee-high growth of weeds and brambles. Even palmettos had sprung up in sand traps from lack of care. It was ten years before courses were reopened.

In 1946, investors from Detroit purchased the tired, old resort complex and managed to refurbish it in time for a gala 1947 opening. The west course was opened for the 1947 season; 11 holes of the east course were opened in 1949, and in 1957, both courses were finally completely renovated. Soon after, the Duke of Windsor was an enthusiastic golfer playing here.

Today, the course is a typical links style. Tiny greens demand accuracy, and the

lengthy fairways challenge short game players. The fifth hole is the number one handicap, a par four, 416 yard hole that requires a blind drive with an abrupt dogleg right over a water hazard. Try that one on for size! One must effectively fade the ball in order to conquer this tricky one. The author triple-bogied the hole when he played it!

Below: Tall palms frame the fairway on the 12th

Tees	Par	Yards	Slope	USGA
Blue	72	6695	118	70.7
White	72	6349	115	69.1
Red	74	5703	119	72.1

THE BILTMORE

1925

1210 Anastasia Avenue, Coral Gables, FL 33134
(305) 460-5364   Fax: (305) 460-5315

Directions: From Highway 95, head south to Highway 836 west. Go right on Le June Road south. Turn right on Anastasia Road into the club.

Public. 18 holes. Open year round. Rental clubs, carts and pullcarts Mat and grass driving range. Putting green. Chipping and sand practice areas. Teaching pro. Complete pro shop. Restaurant, snack bar and beverage cart.

A guest takes a lesson from the pro with The Biltmore in the background.

Nestled in the beautiful residential area adjacent to the National Historic Landmark Biltmore Hotel, the course is very generous off the tees, with pink bridges that cross over pools. In the early morning, The Biltmore Hotel's 15-story tower, which is modeled after the famed Geralda Tower in Seville, Spain, reflects on the still water, creating a picture-perfect setting.

In the '20s and '30s, this was absolutely "the place to play golf" in Florida. Some of the greatest golfers of many eras have teed off here, including: Bobby Jones, Gene Sarazen, Tommy Armour, Tommy Bolt, Arnold Palmer, Ben Hogan and Gary Player. The Coral Gables Open, the richest purse for its time, was featured here until 1962, the same year that Ray Floyd played his first professional tournament.

Motion picture stars Sylvester Stallone, Bill Murray, Robert Wagner and Dennis Quaid have all shown their skill (or lack of it), and President Clinton has played here many times. During the Summit of the Americas in 1994, Argentine President Carlos Menum discovered golf here and has returned again and again.

The number one handicap signature sixth hole, a 401 yard par four, may be picturesque, but it's also the most challenging of the front nine. Played into a prevailing wind, the ball must cross over the Gable Waterway, where manatees can sometimes be spotted. In all, seven holes challenge the golfer with "deep, dark, dank tern(s)" (Edgar Alan Poe's description of brackish water). Contrary to many of the Ross courses, the fairways here are fairly narrow, creating extra problems for the "Army" golfers (you know—left, right, left, right).

The four star, four diamond Biltmore

has hosted the Orange Bowl International Junior Championship each December, when young golfers who have been determined to be the top players in their countries are invited to participate. This tournament has been the launching ground for several PGA Tour professionals, including: Tiger Woods, Hal Sutton, Bob Tway, Willie Wood and Sergio Garcia.

The Biltmore's Head Professional, Bob Frier, tells the story about the time he was giving Robert Redford lessons while the actor was in town filming a motion picture. One lesson ran late in the afternoon, and it was so dark that Frier could only tell where Redford had hit by the sound of the balls landing on the turf. Redford was having so much fun that he didn't want to stop until it was too dark to see the ball at all.

This is a "serious" water course—just look at the photo. It's hard to "stay dry" for 18 holes.

Tees	Par	Yards	Slope	USGA
Blue	71	6624	119	71.5
White	71	6213	116	69.7
Red	73	5600	122	73.3
Gold	73	5292	115	70.1

Directions: From I-75, exit at 39, turn west and go three miles to Beneva Road. Turn north for one block and turn east on Circus Blvd. The club is less than one mile on the right.

Babe Ruth teeing off the number one tee around 1935. This hole is now hole number ten. The man in the blazer and sweater is George Jacobus, manager of Bobby Jones and president of the PGA at that time.

Public. Owned by the City of Sarasota. 45 holes. Two 18-hole courses and a nine hole executive course. Open year round. Rental carts, with ParView GPS System, pullcarts and clubs. Driving range. Putting green. Chipping and sand practice areas. Teaching pro. Restaurant, snack bar and beverage cart.

The original 18 holes were designed by Donald Ross in 1926 and dedicated by Robert Tyre Jones, Jr. on Sunday, February 13, 1927. Nine additional holes were built in 1952, and another nine were added in 1967. The nine-hole, par 30, John H. Gillespie Executive Course was completed in 1977.

In 1930, Bobby Jones accomplished one of the most amazing feats in sports history, the Grand Slam of golf. In honor of these great championships, the British Course front nine is named for his British Amateur victory at St. Andrews and the back nine for his British Open success at Hoylake. The American Course back nine holes, ten through 18 today, were Ross' original back nine, so it is possible to enjoy all 18 of his holes while playing at the Bobby Jones Golf Complex.

The American Course calls for accurate shotmaking, with water and trees seemingly around every turn. There was some redesigning in 1963 and again in 1988, but it is still typical Ross, with more out-of-bounds stakes than usual along the fairways.

The other 18-holer, called the British Course, is quite a bit more open, but makes up for the added play with a plethora of vexing sand bunkers that are frequently wide and often deeper than expected.

Large clubhouse signs welcome the visitor.

Paul Azinger won the Sarasota City Men's Championship in 1980 at Bobby Jones. In 1981 and '82, it was won by Scott Dunlap. Azinger set the British Course record of 62 in 1980. Over the years, the course has also challenged Walter Hagen, Tommy Armour and Gene Sarazen.

In 1940, the longest playoff for a PGA event was held both at Bobby Jones and nearby Sara Bay Country Club, when The PGA Seniors Championship Tournament needed 36 playoff holes before Otto Hackbarth bested Jock Hutchinson 294 to 295. Past LPGA greats, including Patty Berg, Babe Didrickson Zaharias and Louise Suggs, made the Jones a regular tour stop in the '50s.

July, 1926—Bobby Jones receives a new Pierce-Arrow sedan from Jules Brazil on behalf of the citizens of Sarasota upon completion of the new City of Sarasota course designed by Donald Ross. In those days taking money was not acceptable behavior for an amateur...but a spanking new auto was another story entirely!

Paul Azinger on the 17th green of the British course. This outstanding par three hole plays just 158 yards off the blues and is the number seventeen handicap at Bobby Jones. It was originally Ross' hole number eight.

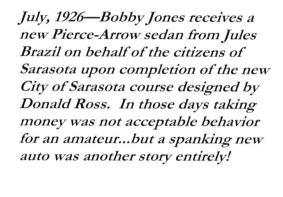

American

Tees	Par	Yards	Slope	USGA
Blue	71	6039	120	69.8
White	71	5496	109	67.6
Gold	71	4799	105	64.2
Red	71	4326	101	64.5

British

Tees	Par	Yards	Slope	USGA
Blue	72	6467	120	71.3
White	72	6184	118	70.0
Gold	72	5637	115	67.1
Red	72	5268	117	70.4

600 WILDER BLVD., DAYTONA BEACH, FL 32114
(904) 258-3119   FAX: (904) 239-6628
WEBSITE: WWW.CI.DAYTONABEACH.FL.US

DIRECTIONS: FROM I-95 SOUTH TAKE DAYTONA BEACH EXIT. TAKE HIGHWAY 92 EAST TO RIDGE-WOOD AVE. (US 1). TURN RIGHT GOING SOUTH TO WILDER.

Public. 36 holes. The South Course consists of 18 holes designed by Donald Ross, and the North Course 18 designed by Slim Deathridge. Open year round. Pro shop opens 6:30 AM. Electric, pullcart and club rental. Driving range. Chipping and putting green practice areas open from dawn to dusk. No club rentals. Snack bar. Teaching pro. The Clubhouse Restaurant is a delightful place to dine, offering breakfast, lunch and dinner. It is also available for weddings, banquets and parties for up to 200 people.

Above: The elevated green at the 184-yard par three 12th hole with "Ross Trademark" bunkers

The two 18-hole courses here are of almost equal length, but the Ross-designed South Course is more forgiving and open than the new Deathridge designed North, reopened in 1997. Much of the original design on the Ross South is still evident. It is considered a very "sporty" course, the tee shots being straightforward with open fairways, but approaches are very demanding if the golfer wants to get close to the stick for a birdie. Tall Florida oaks and pines with a little water are a beautiful feature. Water comes into play more often than you might expect or even want...on eight holes!

As for Daytona, it could be called the ultimate fun city. There are boardwalk amusement centers, Go-karts galore, mini golf at six locations, The Museum of Arts and Sciences, the Peabody Auditorium, the Seaside Music Theater with concerts, live performances of all kinds, four movie theaters and two ice skating rinks.

For lighthouse enthusiasts, there is the famous Ponce de Leon inlet lighthouse, located near the beach, which has been carefully restored and is open to the public.

Bike Week has become an international event, with bikers from throughout the country converging on Daytona. It is a long week, now running ten days every January.

In addition, the "World's Greatest Race," the Daytona 500, attracts the largest audience in motor sports. It is all in an enormous 480 acre complex. Two months of the year, all kinds of testing and development of race vehicles take place at the speed-way. It is open every day except Christmas. There are also amateur car races and antique and classic car shows throughout the year. And for the golfer, within a short driving distance, you will find 23 golf courses. Yes, 23! Few, however, have the wide fairways of Daytona—or the great history.

DAYTONA BEACH GOLF CLUB				SNEAD	NELSON	HOGAN	DEMERET
HOLE	YDS.	PAR	HDCP				
1	390	4	7	4	4	4	4
2	175	3	16	3	3	3	2
3	355	4	13	3	4	4	3
4	530	5	1	4	4	4	5
5	405	4	6	4	4	4	4
6	360	4	12	4	4	4	3
7	475	5	3	4	4	4	4
8	435	4	5	4	4	4	
9	155	3	17	3	3	3	3
OUT	3280	36		33	34	34	31

Record Demeret 63

HOLE	YDS.	PAR	HDCP	SNEAD	NELSON	HOGAN	DEMERET
10	475	5	4	4	4	4	4
11	376	4	10	5	4	4	4
12	186	3	15	3	3	3	3
13	370	4	11	4	4	4	4
14	482	5	2	4	5	4	4
15	142	3	18	4	3	3	3
16	275	4	14	3	4	4	2
17	387	4	8	4	4	4	3
18	406	4	9	3	4	3	5
IN	3099	36		34	35	33	32
OUT	3280	36		33	34	34	31
TOT	6379	72		67	69	67	63

PLAYER Sammy Snead
ATTESTED Byron Nelson
DATE Ben Hogan
Jimmy Demeret
HANDICAP
NET SCORE

This Card Measures Six Inches When Opened

Above: One of the treasures of the Daytona Beach Golf Club is this antique, March 13, 1947 scorecard. On that memorable date, Sam Snead, Byron Nelson, Ben Hogan and Jimmy Demeret competed. Jimmy set a course record of 63—a 32 on the front nine and a 31 on the back.

Left: The difficult (four handicap) par four tenth hole plays 394 yards with a faint dogleg right to a small, bunkered green.

Tees	Par	Yards	Slope	USGA
Blue	71	6229	118	69.8
White	71	5950	116	68.4
Red	71	5346	123	70.2

DELRAY BEACH GOLF CLUB

2200 HIGHLAND AVENUE
DELRAY BEACH, FL 33445
(561) 243-7380 FAX: (561) 243-7386 E-MAIL: DELRAYGC@AOL.COM
WEBSITE: WWW.AFFORDABLEGOLF.COM

DIRECTIONS: I-95 TO ATLANTIC AVENUE, WEST TO HOMEWOOD, SOUTH ON HOMEWOOD EAST ON HIGHLAND AVENUE TO CLUB.

Public. 18 holes. Tee times two days in advance. Open year round. Rental gas and pullcarts and clubs. Driving range. Putting, chipping and sand practice areas. LPGA, T&CP and PGA of America professionals on staff. Complete pro shop. Donald Ross Grille. Tommy Armour Lounge.

The large, comfortable clubhouse offers many amenities after a stimulating 18.

The City of Delray has an interesting history. In 1894 William S. Linton traveled by boat to this remote area to investigate the possibility of investment. With foresight, he purchased 160 acres for $25 per acre. Over the next few years, settlers began to arrive, and he established a town, which he named after himself. In 1896 the railroad came to Linton, the number of settlers increased, and a two-story hotel was built. In 1900, the name was changed to Delray. Telephones came in 1912, and a city electric and water plant in 1914.

As the years passed, more residents were attracted by the weather, and Donald Ross was hired to design the first nine holes at the new golf course. Today, five holes remain the same as when he created them: Numbers 10, 14, 15, 17 and 18. Robert Bruce Harris and Dick Wilson designed and built the second nine holes.

One of the reasons for Delray's success is the type of people who have been attracted to it over the years. In 1964, when the club was sold to a private owner, he asked a dinner meeting of players for money to put in an air conditioner in exchange for a ten-year membership. It is said that he was pledged $100,000 that night, and promptly put in a new bar in addition to the air conditioner!

Another great story about Delray is that of Bill Mudge, Inner Circle co-creator in 1952. Upon his death in 1970, his wake was held at the clubhouse and his ashes were scattered over the

18th fairway. Actually, two other golfers' ashes are in the greenside bunker at 18. A few players swear their ghosts have pushed their balls from the cup at the last minute.

The good news here is that this Palm Beach County course is very open. The bad news is that the elevated greens can be especially tricky, and there are four ponds that attract misdirected balls like magnets.

Water comes into play on holes two, six, 11 and 17. Hole number 12 is a beauty. It plays 561 off the gold tees and is the number two handicap hole on the course. The par five challenge calls for a careful approach shot to an elevated green. Rumor has it that the USGA considers this course to be one of the finest public courses in the nation.

In the years since the Bermuda grass course was opened, many of golf's all-time greats have played there, including: Tommy Armour, Betty Jameson, Jeff Gordon, Matt Blair, Sam Snead, Louise Suggs, Pete and Alice Dye, Glenna Collette Vare, Peggy Kirk Ball and Mickey Wright.

The visitor here will find a town that has been called the "Best Run Town in Florida." It features the USTA Delray Beach Tennis Center, where top-rated matches take place. Travel authorities rate its beach as "The best swimming beach in the Southeast." There has been an impressive downtown restoration. The Morikami Museum and Japanese Gardens and the historic Cason Cottage are sights to see. And in December visitors are treated to Delray's famous 100 foot Christmas tree—without the snow.

The Delray Beach course offers a great test for players of all skill levels. It's always preferable to boast accuracy off the tee, but that does not guarantee a good score. The trick is to get past those large bunkers that lurk in the fairways and protect the greens.

The course delights over 90,000 golfers each year, but good management keeps the greens in wonderful shape. The fourth hole is a dogleg left, par four, challenging 451 yards. The signature hole is the 561-yard, par five

12th, with water on the left and large bunkers on the right. A wide canal cuts across the fairway, so the golfer has to make a decision whether to cross it in two or play it safe and lay up.

For fifteen years, the master teacher, Tommy Armour, taught at Delray. During that time, the man and the legend inspired thousands of golf stories, among which was that, if he was bored with a lesson, he'd set his watch ahead, show it to the confused student and say, "See you next week."

The National Golf Foundation has awarded this course its Public Golf Achievement Award, and Director of Golf, Sandra Eriksson, was named National Professional of the Year by the Ladies Professional Golf Association Teaching & Club Professional Divison (LPGA T&CP) in 1999.

Ms. Eriksson is past director of research for the National Golf Foundation and regional sports director for the March of Dimes.

7th Annual Beth Daniel LPGA Golf Clinic held at the driving range in 2000

Tees	Par	Yards	Slope	USGA
Gold	72	6907	126	73.0
Blue	72	6360	119	70.2
Green	72	5788	114	67.6
White	72	5189	117	69.8

1050 Palm Boulevard, Dunedin, FL 34698
(727) 733-7836 Fax: (727) 734-0189

Directions: From Clearwater, Go north on U.S. Hwy 19. At Curlew Rd., go left (west). Proceed to Alt. 19 and go left (south). Go left again (east) on Palm Blvd.

Semi-private. 18 holes. Open year round. Pro shop opens 7:30 AM. Electric rental carts. Driving range. Putting green. Chipping and sand practice areas. Pro shop. Teaching pro. Restaurant. Snack bar. Call for tee time five days in advance.

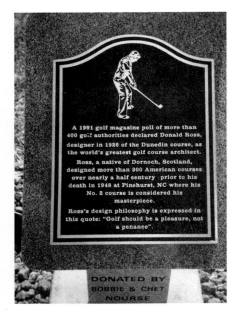

One of five markers placed around the course to emphasize that this is truly a historic venue

This venerable Tifdwarf grass course, located in Pinellas County on Clearwater Bay, was the former home of the Professional Golfers Association (PGA) from 1945 to 1962. During that time, the PGA removed about 60 of the original 114 bunkers to cut maintenance costs. Opening on New Year's Day, 1927, its original name was The Dunedin Isles Country Club.

Palm trees line good-sized fairways, and the greens are easily recognizable as the handiwork of Ross. Its greens are elevated and bunkered enough to cause the casual golfer no little trouble. Like many fine Florida courses Ross created in the '20s, here a golfer finds a water hazard when least expected—just waiting to entice his or her ball.

The hole layout retains the same old-fashioned look of 75 years ago, except for minor changes in lengths at numbers 12 and 13 to accommodate the installation of a water tower. Famous players include: Babe Ruth (who must have played every good course in America in his lifetime), Bobby Jones, Jimmy Demaret, Pal Runyan, Babe Zaharias, Ben Hogan and Sam Snead.

It took Ross' crew 296 days in 1926 to convert some orange groves into what is now one of the most historically rich golf courses in Florida. Two hundred and twenty six men using 68 horses and mules, 13 scrapers, five trucks, 16 wagons and carts, a grader and a roller accomplished the feat. It was to have been a drawing card for a multi-million dollar housing development, the dream of Detroit developer Ephraim Frischkorn, but by 1932 he was gone and the course in receivership. The city stepped in and leased it to the PGA for a dollar a year.

In 1945 the PGA Seniors' Championship was held here, and continued each year un-

A view over one of the ponds to the 14th, the signature hole

The home of the PGA in 1962

til 1962. In 1954, Teachers's Scotch put up $2000 in prize money and a winner's trip to Great Britain to compete in the British Seniors' Championship. Gene Sarazen tromped the field.

A frequently heard expression here at Dunedin is "I've been Rossed." Anyone who has played a Ross course knows that this means an approach shot hit just short of the green, and it either stayed there or rolled backward down the front of the elevation.

The most challenging hole, for long ball hitters, is 14. Ross laid it out as a relatively short par four, doglegged left around a small lake. The trick is to go for the green on one's drive. Of course, this requires a high, 250 yard drive over the lake and trees to a blind green.

The first four holes are considered probably the toughest in the Tampa Bay area. The back nine eases up a bit. Holes 12 and 13 each offer good birdie opportunities. Number 15 is a gambler's delight: 478 yards. If you can hug the edge of Curlew Creek with your drive, you can reach the green with a well-struck second shot.

Ross saved the best for last. Number 18 takes off out of a tree-lined chute. Then a well placed middle-to-long iron can put you on the green. But now the fun has just begun. With a 30-degree slope from back to front, this green makes putting a real

chore. PGA professional John Falcone says the course never plays the same because of the changing winds. The bad news: they can foul up your shots, but the good news is they keep the golfer cool.

History

A tattered and faded course layout blueprint made in 1926 by Donald Ross, along with his actual field notes, is now preserved at the Tufts Archives in Pinehurst, NC. A restored reproduction hangs in the clubhouse at Dunedin. Newspaper reports tell that Ross was on hand during the construction, which was not true of most of his courses.

Two months after the course was opened, the clubhouse was ready. Tommy Armour's initial reaction was very positive. "One of the finest courses I've ever played.

Tees	Par	Yards	Slope	USGA
Donald Ross	72	6565	123	71.1
Ben Hogan	72	6245	119	69.5
Gene Sarazen	72	5339	109	65.1
Babe Zaharias	73	5726	125	73.1
Patty Berg	73	5339	120	70.9

Another view of the signature hole

Photos by Mark Dremstedt

The layout's the thing. It's the best in Florida, perhaps in the country!"

During the earliest days, *Golfers' Magazine* in Chicago promoted a Dixie-Cuba Golf Pilgrimage to Dunedin. This involved 200 amateurs who would start in Chicago and travel south, playing en route at Asheville, Charleston, Savannah, St. Petersburg and Dunedin. Then they moved on to Havana for play on Cuban courses. On the way back, they played several more U.S. courses.

Frischkorn kept up the promotion drumbeat to sell land for homes, but then the unexpected happened. The Florida real estate market went into a tailspin.

By June of 1928, Dunedin properties were listed as being in arrears on mortgage payments. Properties were being auctioned off at ridiculously low prices. The new Hotel Fenway was threatened with foreclosure. Then came the 1929 market crash. Ironically, the course in 1930 was thriving, but this did Frisckorn no good. He had to sell his mansion on Buena Vista, with its 300 feet of bay frontage, 14 rooms, four bedrooms, three baths, two servant's rooms, and a two-car garage with a chauffeur's room and bath. The man with the $63 million dream was finished. Dunedin, the expected home to 50,000 people, was in for a rough time. He had personally dropped $5 million.

By 1938, the city was forced to take over the course. On May 11th of that year, President Roosevelt approved a request for WPA funds to restore the course, and by August 1, 1939, golf had returned to Dunedin. The Dunedin Golf Club leased the course from the city for $1 a year, and by 1940, tennis courts had been added and 1,400 spectators turned out to watch the number nine U.S. Men's Amateur and the number one Women's Amateur tennis teams play.

The course barely managed to operate during the war. In 1962, after the PGA's lease expired, the newly formed Dunedin Country Club leased the course.

Included in the course's noble history is perhaps its most famous foursome: Snead-Hogan-Nelson-McSpaden, there for their exhibition match in February, 1946. Snead set a course record of 66 off the blues. Milon Marusic shot a 64 in 1955, winning a Florida West Coast Golf Association match. And in 1998, Matt Mitchell shot a 62, a record that still stands.

The authors thank the club for providing Dunedin Dubs and Divots—A History of Golf in Dunedin 1925-1962.

THE SUNSHINE STATE OF FLORIDA WAS GOLDEN FOR DONALD ROSS

Palm Beach, Florida photo taken at night in November 1918 by Audrey Hanser, age 12 with a Brownie™ Box Camera. It was a time when a busy Donald Ross was working on The Palm Beach Country Club and The Country Club of Orlando.

There were many reasons for it of course, but once wealthy northerners got a good taste of Florida in the early 20th century they began to demand not only golf courses, but top quality courses to play on their winter vacations. And by then, Donald Ross' reputation had been well established. Good rail links to both East and West Coast locations made frequent visits by the architect practical and allowed him a way to be down when he had to, and to complete as many courses as he did. Even in those days it took very little time by rail from nearby Southern Pines to the Florida border.

Holly M. Hays claimed in *Travel Discoveries* that Ross designed 413 courses in America and 35 of them in Florida. Others have calculated a few more than that in Florida. But it is a good guess that he was on site for the design and construction of at least 16 courses and probably designed as many as 21 more that he never personally visited.

When working from Pinehurst, North Carolina and Little Compton, Rhode Island he was in constant touch with his supervising agents on site. Seven of his finished works never made it through to the 21st century. The precipitous collapse of Florida land values in the late twenties and throughout the thirties, closely followed by the war (and gasoline rationing) saw tourism and golf dry up. These difficult conditions dealt a death knell to the most financially fragile golf venues.

Although proud of his Florida achievements and profits, none gave him more pleasure or pride than the course at North Palm Beach, called Seminole Golf Club, which is not shown in this book because it is private.

Ross rarely sought out architectural commissions because he was busy enough without putting on sales pressure, but the Seminole commission was widely talked about, and several important architects were interviewed before the job was awarded. Ross wanted it badly and fought to get it. He pulled out all the stops and won out in the competition for the assignment.

It turned out to be an achievement of lasting beauty, situated along two distinct ridges near the Atlantic Ocean. Ross spent a great deal of time in the design phase and at the site itself to ensure that it would be done to perfection. It is ironic that it was done in the year of the stock market crash—1929, yet it somehow managed to survive and prosper. It has only improved with age and is considered his most successful achievement in the State of Florida.

FORT MYERS COUNTRY CLUB

3591 McGregor Blvd., Fort Myers, FL 33901
(941) 936-3126   Fax: (941) 278-7813

Directions: From I-75 going south, take exit 22 and go west six miles on Colonial Blvd. Go right on McGregor. Course is one mile on the right.

Public. 18 holes. Owned by the City of Fort Myers. Open year round. Pro shop opens 7 AM. Rental electric and pullcarts and clubs. Putting green. Chipping and sand practice areas. Teaching pro. Restaurant. Snack bar.

This wonderful old course is located in the middle of the town of Fort Myers, between US 1 and McGregor Boulevard, and boasts that all 18 holes are exactly as Ross designed them. It is the oldest course in southwest Florida and, in the early years, both Thomas Edison and Henry Ford played here, as Fort Myers was the winter home for both families.

The Ford and Edison residences are open to the public, and Edison's laboratory and gardens are popular tourist attractions. Each year the town celebrates Edison's memory with a *Festival of Light* featuring visiting high school bands and floats in a spectacular parade.

The Bermuda grass course is extremely popular. It is a classic Ross design, with four par threes, three par fives and 11 par fours. Club professional Richard Lamb told us, "The very small greens average only 5,000 square feet, with only 36 bunkers. It plays to 6,400 from the back tees. The course looks easy, but the small targets and undulations prove especially challenging." There are no homes on the course, which offers a relatively flat terrain. There are two ponds and a canal, providing water hazards that come into play on eight holes.

Some of the champions who have played the course are: Tommy Bolt, Bobby

Bobby Nichols putting on the ninth green

Nichols, Jim Albus, Nolan Henke (who went to school in Fort Myers and is now on the tour) and Tommy Tolles. Lee Janzen, who has won the U.S. Open twice, won a tournament here in 1988. Patty Berg and Terry Jo Meyers, both on the LPGA tour, are residents here.

Unlike many Ross-designed courses, the Fort Myers Country Club has in its possession the original Donald Ross architectural drawings of the course.

Above, right: The Hooters Girls
Above: Nolan Henke on the first tee

Tees	Par	Yards	Slope	USGA
Championship Blue	71	6414	118	70.5
Forward White	71	6066	115	68.8
Seniors Gold	71	5769	110	67.3
Ladies Red	72	5396	119	70.6
Ladies Pink	72	5760	117	69.1

HYDE PARK GOLF CLUB

6439 HYDE GROVE AVENUE, JACKSONVILLE, FL 32210
(904) 786-5410   FAX: (904) 786-2446 (CALL BEFORE DIALING)

DIRECTIONS: TAKE I-10 TO LANE AVENUE EXIT. TURN SOUTH TO HYDE GROVE AVENUE. TURN LEFT AND COURSE IS 1/2 MILE ON LEFT.

Semi-private. 18 holes. Open year round. Pro shop opens 7 AM. Rental electric carts and clubs. Driving range. Putting green. Chipping and sand practice areas. Pro shop. Teaching pro. Snack bar.

Above: Sam arrives in his Caddy—rarin' to go

Hyde Park is one of the truly historic courses in the State of Florida. The beautiful Donald Ross design is a favorite of all who play here. There are rolling hills, gorgeous Spanish oaks and towering southern pines.

During the '40s and '50s, Hyde Park was a tour stop for both the Men's and Ladies' PGA. The Jacksonville Open was graced by the presence of many of the game's legendary players, including Byron Nelson, Sam Snead, Ben Hogan, Babe Zaharias, Patty Berg and Louise Suggs. Mickey Wright won her first official pro tournament here in 1956.

Hole number six, a par three 140 yards, is called *Hogan's Alley*. It was at the 1947 Jacksonville Open when a local newspaper reporter came up with the nickname for the infamous hole. Gene Pullen, sports columnist for *The Florida Times-Union* of Jacksonville, tells the story that, at the Open, Ben Hogan hit his ball onto the edge of the water off the tee with a seven iron. He then took two shots trying to blast out. He finally lifted and dropped. Then Hogan flubbed the chip, sending it back into the pond, dropped on the other side, chipped on the green and two-putted for an embarrassing 11! Visitors who play the course always look forward to playing number six with high expectations and just a little fear that history may repeat itself.

In 1971, the course was purchased by former PGA touring professionals Billy Maxwell and Chris Blocker, who have successfully restored the old dowager to A-1 condition.

At this writing, Billy is 71 years of age and has been at Hyde Park since 1971. He holds the 1951 National Amateur Tournament title, winning four-three over Joseph Galiardi. This was a week-long event held at Saucon Valley Country Club, featuring Walker Cup members Frank Stranahan, Willie Turnesa and Charley Coe and defending champion Sam Urzetta, who were the favorites of fans and the media. Billy says life has never been the same since his famous win. "A million people have told me they were there and saw me win it!"

After college and a tour in the U.S. Army, Billy turned pro, winning his first professional tournament in Wilmington, North Carolina, the 1955 Azalea Open, by beating the great Mike Souchak. The Odessa Texan represented his country on the 1963 Ryder Cup team and continued to keep his name in the public eye on the Seniors Tour.

Tees	Par	Yards	Slope	USGA
Blue	72	6468	125	70.6
White	72	6153	121	69.0
Red	73	5558	122	71.0

Above: The number six hole, grandstanding with its spring azaleas

"I enjoyed every Donald Ross course I played; well designed with mainly small greens like I learned to play on in West Texas. Donald Ross made good chipping and bunker play necessary. Also, his doglegs made good tee shots mandatory. Donald Ross should be reincarnated. P.S. I still like to play when the PGA tour lets me."—Billy Maxwell

Left: The unmistakable Snead swagger. Note the small gallery.

The fabulous 15th

DIRECTIONS: TAKE HIGHWAY 26 EAST TO HIGHWAY 21 NORTH. TURN LEFT ON PONCE DE LEON STREET AND GO ONE MILE. COURSE IS ON THE RIGHT.

Semi-private. 18 holes. Open year round. Pro shop opens 7:30 AM. Tee time reservations: weekends and holidays. Rental electric and pullcarts and clubs. Driving range. Putting green. Chipping practice area. Teaching pro. Snack bar, banquet room and bar.

Right: Hole number 14— 175 yards from the whites—par three—plays 130 from the reds—an original Ross creation

As early as 1519, Spanish explorers were investigating this part of the Spanish Empire. Impressed by its fertile land, they returned to build missions, grow food and raise cattle to feed themselves and the Seminole Indian population.

The British were only here for 22 years, from 1763 to 1783, when Spain again achieved control and kept it until General Andrew Jackson occupied the area and overthrew the Spanish once and for all.

Over the years, thousands of visitors to Keystone find wonderful beaches in nearby Jacksonville, good golf here in Keystone, and for cultural activities, nearby Gainesville has it all—music, theatre and ballet.

This tourist Mecca is noted for its profusion of camellias. In Keystone, many members of the Gainesville Camellia Society have developed special flowers that are now world famous. You can see many of them in full color here or just pull up the Society on the internet to view their fabulous colors.

Donald Ross designed a nine hole Bermuda grass course for the wealthy residents of Keystone Heights. Originally known as the Keystone Heights Golf and Country Club, the club added nine more holes in 1959, which were designed by Albert Anderson.

Today, holes one, two, three, 13, 14, 15, 16, 17 and 18 remain essentially the same as when Ross created them. There are no water

Above: Hole number two—just as it was when Ross laid it out 84 years ago—a par three—a 169 yard beauty

Above: Hole 16—a Ross classic—a 331 yard, par four, a slight dogleg right to a good-sized putting area—number eight handicap hole

hazards at Keystone, but there are many strategically placed tall pine trees that can prove a headache to the golfer who fails to take them into account. The land on which Keystone was built is almost flat, with gentle rolls to its reasonably narrow fairways. The greens are typical examples of Ross at his best: quick and undulating, requiring a steady hand and an eye that can read the subtle breaks.

The back nine greens are all elevated and crowned, meaning that the ball hit too hard onto the dance floor will very often not hold and may fly by the pin. It is not uncommon to hit up and over, and then on the return chip go completely over the other side. It is the Pinehurst No. 2 phenomenon, but found in sunny Bradford County.

The Ross holes are much more open than the newer holes, which are laid out with fairways placed much closer together. The course starts off in the typical Ross manner, with a relatively easy 351 yard par four leading away from the clubhouse, followed by an achievable par three hole that plays 169 yards from the men's tee. The first par five on the course, hole three, plays to 505 yards off the whites, and is a sharp dogleg right. The only other par five hole put in by Ross is the final hole. Number 18 plays back toward the clubhouse and has a slight dogleg left—and as a ten handicap, it is a feasible par, offering players a good shot at a birdie if the approach shot is played with care.

Photos courtesy of Ben Walker, club president

Tees	Par	Yards	Slope	USGA
White	71	6128	118	68.7
Red	71	5289	117	70.7

3536 COUNTRY CLUB ROAD, SANFORD, FL 32771
(407) 322-2531   FAX: (407) 323-2759

DIRECTIONS: FROM I-4 EAST TAKE EXIT 50, TURN RIGHT ON LAKE MARY BLVD. AND GO EAST THREE MILES TO COUNTRY CLUB RD. TURN LEFT. ENTRANCE IS 1/2 MILE ON THE LEFT.

Semi-private. 18 holes. Open year round. Pro shop opens 7 AM. Rental gas carts. Grass driving range. Putting green. Chipping and bunker practice areas. Teaching professional. Clubhouse with locker rooms and showers. Restaurant and snack bar.

Mayfair is proud of its history.

Thanks in part to the creation of the Walt Disney properties south of here, this is now a very busy course in a bustling part of the State of Florida, with an estimated 50,000 plays every year.

It lies on land that has long been dominated by the history-rich Saint Johns River, which runs more than 200 miles. During the six year conflict with native Seminole Indians, the river provided water transportation for U.S. troops to the first white settlement established in 1836 on the southern shore of Lake Monroe.

It was the river that allowed agricultural products grown in this part of the state to be shipped to northern markets. From the 1850s, steamer traffic developed, carrying tourists as well as cargo. This was the start of recreational boating, which is now a big factor in the communities in and around Sanford.

The town was named after General Henry Sanford, who laid out the town in 1870 near Fort Mellon. Within 15 years, it was the largest citrus producing area in the world. By the late 1880s, rail came to Sanford and with it northerners seeking winter recreation—boating, fishing and ultimately—golf.

Today over those rails the Autotrain finds its southernmost terminus. In addition,

the Orlando Sanford Airport deposits hundreds of tourists each day during the season. With average temperatures year round of 72 degrees, and rarely topping 95, golf is a natural here.

Downtown Sanford is noted for its clock, which marks the center of town, and its historic walking tours, antique shops and a charming waterfront filled with yachts and vessels of all kinds.

Golf reared its head in 1920, when Donald Ross was commissioned by the city fathers to create a championship course on the site of

Mayfair offers the golfer wide fairways and a plethora of doglegs. Half the holes have no water to worry about, but the other nine can be trouble.

an orange grove. An early course record was established by Walter Hagen and Gene Sarazen in 1925, when they each shot a five under par 65. The 1926 four-day Florida Open was a 72-hole contest with prizes of $1,000 to $5,000—big money in those days. In '26, Johnny Farrell won over Hagen. In 1939, the city renovated the course, and soon thereafter green fees rose from 50 cents to $1.00!

The golfers who like their Ross course as undisturbed as possible may think they're in golfer heaven because only two holes have been changed numbers 10 and 12. Mr. Ross, however, may be looking down in distress, at players on number 12 because although a very scenic 428 yards off the blues, it now has water on both sides of the fairway, running across the course in front of the green. The canny Scot hated to see golfers lose their balls in the water, but was at the mercy of the topography in this virtual wetland. Indeed, water hazards come into play on nine holes.

The signature hole is number four, a 371 yard challenge with a straight fairway guarded by a very large live oak on the right.

In 1949, the New York Giants purchased the club lease from the City of Sanford while they held their annual spring training here. The course name was changed from Sanford Country Club to Mayfair Country Club, and it became a regular stop on the big PGA tour. When the Giants moved their training camp in 1959, the course became a stop on the North Florida PGA mini-tour for many years. Over the past few years, the present owners have upgraded the facility to the point where it is regarded as one of the premiere courses in central Florida.

In December, 1955, Al Banding defeated Mike Souchak and Ed Oliver by one stroke to win the $2,400 first place money in the first annual Mayfair Inn Open. Sam Snead was only six shots behind and took home $22. The total purse was $15,000. It attracted the biggest names in golf at the time: Tommy Bolt, Chick Harbet, Billy Maxwell, Doug Ford, Jay and Lionel Hebert, Don January, Dave Maar, Bob Toski and Gene Sarazen.

The next year Arnold Palmer, Mike Fetchick, Julius Boros, Doug Sanders, Porky Oliver, Bob Goalby, Tony Lema and Moe Norman would compete. Fetchick beat Frank Stranahan by 2 strokes, scoring 263.

Arnold Palmer's earnings for that PGA tour open event, held December, 13-16, 1956, was a grand total of just $528.00. He finished in a five-way tie for sixth place. That's the way it was during the "Golden Days" of golf, Tiger!

In 1992, Moe Norman, while playing hole number seven, called it the "Best par three hole in all of central Florida."

Above: the number one green looking back to the clubhouse—a 381 yard par four that plays to a five-handicap. It's an easy way to start, just the way Ross believed a game of golf should begin. It's picturesque, too, with the wide fairways lined with live oaks trailing Spanish moss. Water on the right.

Tees	Par	Yards	Slope	USGA
Blue	72	6382	117	69.7
White	72	5962	114	68.1
Red	74	5102	115	69.3

1000 WAYNE AVENUE, NEW SMYRNA BEACH, FL 32168
(904) 424-2192   FAX: (904) 424-2188

DIRECTIONS: FROM I-95, GO EAST ON HWY. 44. EXIT AT BUSINESS 44/RTE. 1 AND TURN LEFT ON RTE. 1. AFTER TWO LIGHTS, TURN LEFT ON WAYNE AVE. TO THE ENTRANCE ON THE RIGHT.

Public. 18 holes. Open year round. Tee times available 48 hours in advance. Rental carts, and clubs. Driving range. Putting green. Chipping and sand practice areas. Teaching pro. Restaurant, snack bar and beverage cart.

Below: The good-size clubhouse at New Smyrna Beach offers a comfortable respite from the Florida sun.

This is believed to be the last golf course designed by Donald Ross. His design fee was $3,500, a much higher sum than he received for most of his other designs, for by this time he had earned the reputation as the greatest course designer in the world.

When the pro Art Vogt resigned in July of 1953, records show that Marvin Harvey was hired by the City Commissioners as golf professional for a fee of $220 a month, to serve "at the pleasure of the City Commission."

The course is owned and operated by the City of New Smyrna Beach. It is open seven days a week from 6:30 AM until dusk, with the first tee time at 7:02 AM. The course has 800 members and plays 80,000 rounds a year. It is only closed on Christmas Day.

It is basically a flat course, with elevated tees and well-bunkered greens. There are fairway bunkers on the par five holes, with small, sloping greens at the front, back and sides—a Ross hallmark. There are splendid tree-lined fairways, and the greens are Bermuda grass. Water comes into play on several holes.

The Indian River Open has been held here on many occasions. Moe Norman, who won here in 1965 and 1968, advised players:

"Tight fairways, small greens and don't go over the greens!" New Smyrna is said to have some of the best greens in the state.

Donnie Hammond, Barney Thompson, Dave Rummalls, Nat Stark and Jay Delsing have played here, and Mark Calcavecchia won the Indian River in 1984. This has been the Host Course for the North Florida Section of the PGA (mini-tour) for 40 years. This tournament has more pro entries than any other stop on the winter tour. Charles Rymer won going away in 1993 with tremendous drives.

Ross purists will be pleased to learn that all the holes on the course are basically the same today as when he designed them. The only changes are new tee boxes, and bunkers have been added to the par five holes to make them even more difficult.

Above: A water bird stands watch at the large pond bordering the left side of the number two fairway. This is a 369 yard, par four hole (number five handicap)—dogleg left to two big bunkers.

From the City of New Smyrna Beach Commission Records

January 9, 1947

The City Manager reported he had met with a golf architect and Mr. William F. Tydings of Indian River Plantation and had thoroughly gone over the grounds that had been suggested for a golf course. All concerned had been very pleased with the general outlay. Mr. Ferris then read a letter from J.B. McGovern, Associate of the firm of Donald J. Ross, Golf Architect of Pinehurst, North Carolina. After consideration and discussion it was moved by Commissioner Sapp that the City Manager be authorized to have a topographical survey of the proposed golf course area as soon as a definite commitment was received from William F. Tydings, owner of the Indian River Plantation, for a ninety-nine year lease and a one-dollar rental.

January 23, 1947

The City Manager read a letter from William Tydings and G.E. Flora stating they would lease to the City for $1 a year land holdings necessary for the construction of an 18-hole golf course. This golf course is to be constructed at the expense of the City. Mr. Ferris also read a letter from J.B. McGovern, Associate of the firm of Donald J. Ross, requesting a topographical survey be made and maps submitted to a scale of 1" equals 100'.

Tees	Par	Yards	Slope	USGA
Blue	72	6377	117	70.2
White	72	6063	113	68.7
Gold	72	5457	109	65.7
Red	72	4817	115	67.4

Photos by Cindy Evans

PALATKA GOLF CLUB

1715 MOSELEY AVENUE, PALATKA, FL 32177
(904) 329-0141   FAX: (904) 329-0106   E-MAIL: INFO@MGGI.COM

DIRECTIONS: FROM JACKSONVILLE, TAKE HWY. 17 SOUTH 45 MILES INTO PALATKA. TURN RIGHT AT MOSELEY AVE. FOR ONE MILE.

Public municipal course. 18 holes. Open year round. Pro shop opens 7 AM. Rental electric carts, pullcarts and clubs. Shag tee. Putting and chipping practice areas. Restaurant, snack bar and lounge. Teaching pro.

Palatka is known as the "Gem City of the St. John's River" with good reason. The course here is classic Ross in every way, with its challenging turtleback greens guarded by bunkers, tall pines and huge live oaks.

Situated on the highest point in Palatka, just a short drive from historic and fun-to-visit St. Augustine, the layout is cut around Ravine State Gardens, creating scenic, but often dangerous shots into difficult-to-hold greens, with the likelihood of hitting into a sand trap being very strong indeed.

The course has a reputation for being meticulously maintained. Some think of it as being a far south version of Pinehurst number two in many respects, with lovely homes lining the course and no water hazards.

Its brochure asks the question, "How many oysters must you shell to find a pearl? How many municipal courses must you play to find a gem?" The answer, "Just one, if you tee it up first at Palatka Golf Club."

It is always a joy to find a course where 16 of the original 18 designed by Ross are still exactly as he designated; only numbers 15 and 16 have been modified. The push-up greens are standard here, with subtle and often frustrating breaks—just the way Ross liked them. The bunkers are shallow and strategically placed, coming into play on the narrow fairways just a little more often than comfortable. At just under 6,000 yards, the long ball hitter loses his usual advantage to the sharp, determined iron

The number one handicap hole, par four hole seven—405 yards and straight as an arrow

36

player who can get onto these tough-to-hold greens in regulation.

For a municipal course, you will find a very fine clubhouse, which features a restaurant that serves alcoholic beverages and offers a casual but excellent menu and a well-trained, professional staff.

Since 1958, Palatka has been the proud home of one of the oldest running tournaments in the state, the Florida Azalea Amateur. Past champions include Tommy Aaron and Dan Sikes in 1960 and '61 and Bob Murphy in 1965 and '66. The Ronnie Clark Pro-Am and the J.W. Reynolds Pro-Am are also featured here. Top players who have teed off at Palatka include: John Daly, Tom Lehman, Fuzzy Zoeller, Frank Conner, Jim McGovern, Gene Sauers and Barney Thompson. The course record is 60, re-

corded by Sean Pacetti and Tom Sykes.

The property adjacent to the golf club is home to the world famous Ravine State Gardens, and should not be missed. Built by the WPA in 1933, they lure visitors with a nature trail, which follows the paths of three ravines that drop to depths of 70 to 120 feet. The steep, lush banks are covered with cypress, cedar, live oak, southern magnolia and saw palmettos, while in a spring-fed stream, water lilies in shades of pinks and creams grow in profusion. Here the peak flowering season is springtime, when over 100,000 azaleas may be seen in bloom. Hiking and biking trails course through the property. One of the highlights of the garden is the Court of States, an impressive lawned area surrounded by tall trees and shrubs.

The par five hole number four plays 484 off the blues. It borders the resplendent Ravine Gardens on the right side of the fairway.

Tees	Par	Yards	Slope	USGA
Blue	70	5942	110	67.4
White	70	5700	115	67.0
Red	72	5217	118	69.2

PANAMA COUNTRY CLUB

100 COUNTRY CLUB DRIVE, LYNN HAVEN, FL 32444
(850) 265-2911   FAX: (850) 265-6144   WEBSITE: WWW.PANAMACC.COM

DIRECTIONS: GO NORTH ON HIGHWAY 77, TURN RIGHT ON 9TH STREET. COURSE IS A SHORT RIDE.

Semi-private. 18 holes. Limited times available for out-of-county guests on Tuesdays, Wednesdays and Thursdays. Open year round. Electric rental carts. Driving range. Pro shop opens 7:30 AM. Putting, chipping and sand practice areas. Swimming pool. Large clubhouse. Restaurant and snack bar.

Below: Saint Andrews Bay. Late tee times often give the players a sunset view with colors so dazzling, they hold up play.

Ponce de Leon, seeking waters that make "old men young again," called this Pascua Florida (Feast of Flowers). Now, almost 500 years later, 40 million tourists flock into Florida for its restorative elements: beaches, sun and golf.

Driving here along Route 98 from Pensacola provides views of a gorgeous sandy shore the color and consistency of granulated sugar. West of Tallahassee, the state capital, Apalachicola National Forest's 558,000 acres en-

tice visitors with lakes, rivers and trails—a veritable wildlife heaven.

One gets a sense of northern influence in this southern Gulf Coast area upon viewing the unusual Grand Army of the Republic Monument in Panama City. The only known memorial to a Yankee soldier standing in the home of rebellion, it was erected about the time Ross did his work here. In those days, the Civil war was still talked about and remembered, and northerners, coming down to vacation and play golf, welcomed the sight. The natives may have had other feelings, which they politely kept to themselves. Now the battles that are waged here between native and Yankee often take place on the links at Panama. The weapons of choice: Cobras®, Tight Lies® and Pings®.

The Panama Country Club was originally known as the St. Andrew Bay Golf Club. During the '50s and '60s, it hosted the "Little Tournament of Champions," which was a stopover on the PGA tour. The 72nd Sherman Invitational, one of the oldest running amateur tournaments in the south, has also been held at Panama.

The beauty of this old Tifdwarf grass course for Ross aficionados is the fact that eight of the original 18 holes remain unchanged from when Ross first created them. These holes are virgin: one, seven, 13, 14, 15, 16, 17 and 18. There are significant water hazards on seven, and behind two and nine greens.

The course has a flat surface throughout, with wider than average fairways approaching the kind of greens in which Ross specialized: small, fast and usually well bunkered. This is a course for straight shooters, or for guys and gals with lots of spare, old balls in their bags.

Hole number seven, a par three playing 153 yards from the Championship tee and only 134 from the Whites, is the course signature hole. The reason is easy to understand. The golfer faces a large threatening pond, and the small target green is backed by two tempting bunkers. Bring your camera; it's a beaut!

This is a course whose members are very nature-minded and environmentally sensitive. The bird life here is bountiful, due to generous feeds by members of corn, sunflower seeds and peanuts. Recently heard are bobwhite quail calling along the 12th fairway. The bluebird boxes scattered about the course are filled, and the beloved, beautiful quick flyers are seen in good numbers.

A recent "Chatter," the club newsletter, reports that the pro, Bubba Patrick, has promised to put up a hummingbird feeder in the flowerbed outside the pro shop. Members have been encouraged to put out garbage can covers filled with about an inch of water during the hot summertime, keeping them in the shade, changing the water every few days. They provide a drink to ground birds and "critters," among whom pesky squirrels are most prominent.

Photos courtesy John Benefield

Above: The front of the modern clubhouse

Tees	Par	Yards	Slope	USGA
Blue	72	6609	125	72.1
White	72	6298	122	70.6
Red	72	5283	123	70.8
Gold	72	5657	116	67.7

PINECREST GOLF CLUB

2250 SOUTH LITTLE LAKE BONNET RD., AVON PARK, FL 33825
(863) 453-7555   FAX: (863) 453-8242

DIRECTIONS: FROM US 27, TAKE COLLEGE DRIVE. FOLLOW TO MEMORIAL DRIVE ON THE LEFT.

Semi-private. 18 holes. Open year round. Rental carts. Driving range. Pro shop. Putting green. Chipping and sand practice areas. Teaching pro. Restaurant and snack bar. Any time for public play. Allow three days advance booking. Afternoon tee times generally available even during peak season.

The 154 yard, par three tenth hole

Pinecrest Country Club and Golf Course is a rare gem. The rich Spanish architecture of the former Pinecrest Hotel, although now a retreat center that is not connected to the course, still adds a unique beauty to its surroundings.

In the '20s, rich Chicagoans came down by train to escape the mean winters and be transported to the then popular Jacaranda Hotel by horse drawn wagons.

After World War II, Pinecrest's golf course was recognized as one of the finest in America. NBC television selected it as the site of its very first nationally televised golf matches in December 1959, *The World Championship of Golf.* Bob Crosby was the announcer Don January and Gardner Dickenson played, and Cary Middlecoff was the winner.

In the '70s the City of Avon took over the course and soon sold it to a group of local golfers who gradually built the membership to what it is today, owned by approximately 200 members. Many are snowbirds from Canada, New England and the Midwest.

The Haig and Haig Tournament was held here at Harder Hall resort from 1959 to 1963 and was played by Sam Snead, Fred Hawkins and Al Balding. The latter two still play the course, and Pinecrest sponsors The Fred Hawkins & Al Balding Invitational Tournament each year. In the '60s, most of the major touring

Just pretend the water isn't there!

pros, including: Arnold Palmer, Bob Goalby, Tommy Bolt, Mike Souchak, Julius Boros, Doug Sanders, Kathy Whitworth, Mickey Wright, Marlene Hagge and Big Momma Carner were all here.

Like many Ross courses, the layout seems easy. There are wide fairways and a few "blind shots" to the greens. A meandering swale that connects Lake Lotela and Little Lake Bonnet seems harmless enough—unless you hit into it. The beautifully manicured greens are large, and their surfaces provide plenty of challenge regardless of skill level. The often-present wind and a few local secrets, ("it will roll to the lake, laddie") add to the pleasure found here. The orange groves, when in bloom, make it one of Florida's loveliest courses to savor. The large trees deliver good news and bad news—shade from the Florida sun and obstructions to the errant golf ball.

Ross approached this course with his consummate respect for topography, retaining the natural beauty of the terrain. All earthmoving was done by horse, minimizing any changes to the pleasant landscape.

Legend has it that both comedians Burns and Allen and gangster Al Capone played Pinecrest—not at the same time, we suspect, but they would have made an interesting grouping, don't you think?

Above: The typical Ross elevated green surrounded by bunkers.

Tees	Par	Yards	Slope	USGA
Black	72	6572	122	71.1
Green	72	6252	119	69.6
White	72	5483	112	66.1
Red	72	5357	114	70.5

DIRECTIONS: FROM I-95 SOUTH, GO THROUGH JACKSONVILLE TO EXIT 98. GO SOUTH ON US1 FOR 20 MILES. ENTRANCE IS ON THE LEFT.

Resort. 18 holes. Open year round. Rental clubs and carts. Driving range. Putting green. Chipping and sand practice areas. Teaching pro. Golf school. Restaurant. Snack bar. Nine-hole pitch and putt course on the property.

Below: Blue skies, tall palms and wide open spaces

Florida has long been a winter playground for northerners, and most of the early courses were built for the wealthy Yankee tourists who came south. The first course, of only three holes, was located on the grounds of Fort Marion in St. Augustine. It was built by the St. Augustine Golf Club, which was organized in April of 1898. The Ponce de Leon Links, originally known as the St. Augustine Links Course, was opened here in 1916 by Henry Flagler and his Florida East Coast Hotel Company for the enjoyment of his guests. The original brochure quotes George Low, the Baltusrol professional as saying, "There are shots for every club in the bag." The brochure also says of Ross that he is "the architect who is already admitted to be entitled to first rank."

The course was originally 6,288 yards in length. When Ross completed his work at The Belleview Hotel in Clearwater, Florida, St. Augustine was next on his agenda. He created two 18-hole courses here, Links South and Links North. The North course, now the Ponce de Leon, was built for the munificent sum of $100,000. It was considered at that time to be the finest course in America and is still recognized as one of Florida's premiere links courses.

The Ponce de Leon has hosted many famous national and sectional tournaments. The first professional was Jimmy Farrell. Sam Snead, Byron Nelson and Gene Sarazen have competed here in men's events, and Babe Zaharias and Peggy Kirk Bell have been among the outstanding women to play.

For years, this course has hosted the National Championship of Golf Club Champions. In 1937, the prize money for the Third Annual National Amateur-Professional Best-Ball Match Play Championship was "increased to $3000, with $1000 to the winning pro." The silver Walter J. Travis Memorial Trophy went to the club whose member won the tournament.

It was at the Ponce de Leon that the

first Florida East Coast Women's tournament was held. The 1979 State of Florida Women's was a huge drawing card, as was the 1995 Florida State Seniors Tournament. Babe Ruth loved this course and played it often, and Jackie Gleason, an avid golfer, would play rounds with club pro Ronnie Ward in the '50s. It was said to be his favorite Florida venue.

Fortunately, the managers of this course valued the Ross tradition, and holes one, two, seven, eight, nine, ten, 15, 16, 17 and 18 are exactly the way Ross laid them out in 1916. Ross took full advantage of the waterfront location, placing the front nine in full view of the sea and the sailboats lazily catching the leeward breezes. The feeling is of a traditional Scottish "links-style" golf course within a magnificent Florida setting.

When players make the turn, it is on to a majestic, century-old, moss-laden live oak and magnolia-lined back nine, reminiscent of Tara and the old south.

Donald Ross designed 35 courses in the State of Florida during his working years. Despite the Depression and two World Wars, 27 still exist. Eleven of these are links courses that are open to the public. In many cases, he never was actually on site during the construction periods, and so was felt to have been paid an adequate sum, often only $500 to $1,000.

After 18 holes, the Mulligan's snack bar, Bogie Lounge and Fairway Grille are attractive options.

"Ross is the architect who is already admitted to be entitled to first rank."
From the original Ponce de Leon brochure

Tees	Par	Yards	Slope	USGA
Blue	72	6823	131	72.9
Gold	72	6399	127	71.1
White	72	5856	123	68.6
Red	72	5308	121	70.6

Water, water everywhere. That's the theme of Ponce de Leon—and the challenge too.

PUNTA GORDA COUNTRY CLUB

6100 Duncan Road, Punta Gorda, FL 33950
(941) 639-1494   Fax: (941) 639-8624
Website: www.puntagordacc@juno.com

DIRECTIONS: FROM I-75 NORTH TAKE EXIT 29 AND GO RIGHT ON HWY. 17. ENTRANCE IS ON THE RIGHT OFF DUNCAN ROAD.

Below: The signature par three seventh, its water and bunkers make it a visually intimidating hole. Wind plays an important role, so club selection is paramount. Don't be short!

Semi-private. 18 holes. Open year round. Rental electric carts and clubs. Driving range. Putting green. Teaching pro. Full service bar and restaurant. Pro shop opens 7 AM.

This is a classic Florida Ross course, with Bermuda grass on the greens. They are typically elevated, and the fairways are open but filled with challenges from water to vexing greens placed in often surprising and difficult-to-master places. The scorecard is uniquely helpful in that it marks the location of all large trees and identifies them by type: orange, twin palms, pine, Norfolk pine, Australian pine, melaleuca and eucalyptus. The greens will be a demanding test for the first time player, as they tend to be just sloped enough to provide too many close-but-not-in putts.

The original Punta Gorda Hotel was erected for wealthy sportsmen by the Florida Southern Railroad as its southernmost terminal in 1886. It declined as more luxurious resorts were built in southwest Florida. In 1925, Barron Collier bought the hotel and renamed it the Charlotte Harbor.

A nine hole public golf course had been established during the post World War I land boom at the location, and Collier bought it for use by his guests, remodeling the clubhouse to resemble the hotel's architecture. The original 174 acre tract had been purchased for $4,000, and the cost of building those first nine holes was $13,390. To clear the land of palmettos, workers were paid $2 per ten-hour day to hoe them out by hand.

Collier had made a fortune selling streetcar advertising in New York City, and he hired his uncle, John Law Kerr, as the architect of the hotel. The central tower was raised in height and covered with stucco with a Spanish motif. A huge swimming pool, tennis courts and a skeet range were built, and he later added nine more holes to the course.

Donald Ross was tapped to remodel all 18 holes in 1927, but the Depression made the operation chancy. For years, just the payment of local property taxes was a great chore for the facility, and it fell on hard times. In 1959, the hotel burned down, and the course was idle for several years. Then in 1966 it was reopened, and in 1996 the new clubhouse burned and was rebuilt.

Over the years, needed changes to the course have been carefully planned and executed. The old greens were rebuilt, and holes five, 11, 14, 17 and 18 have been renovated and enlarged. The number three green was moved to the right by about 40 feet. The practice green has been enlarged, a new irrigation system installed, and cart paths have been added. Today the course is in the best shape it has been in years.

Punta Gorda is truly a thing of beauty. The seventh hole (par three, 121 off the whites, 109 off the reds) is the signature hole, playing over water to a small green bunkered left and right. Wind can create odd surprises and club selection is key. Leave it short or right and you'll leave it wet.

Number 12 is a more difficult par three with a ten handicap, playing 215 off the whites and 169 off the reds. It takes both accuracy and skill to land on the narrow, 22 foot deep green, guarded by two bunkers and a threatening pond on the right. But the killer is the number one handicap hole, six. It plays 530 off the whites and 466 off the reds. A drive to the right is the pro's recommended shot, as trouble lurks to the left. Approach shots must be long to carry the bunkers guarding the greens. Slicers may find water on the right off the tee. Here, going up the fairway there are two large oaks on the right, out 250 and 86 yards, and twin palms on the left at 177.

For more than 25 years, the Powder Puff has been played here, and has become the largest women's golf invitational in the area. The Snowbird Couples and Turkey Tournaments are also popular. Members have a choice of five membership plans.

Above: This is the par four fifth from the 100 yard marker. It features a short, sharp dogleg to the right. If you have a long drive to the left, you can take a short iron to the green, but you must watch out for the water off the right side of the fairway.

Tees	Par	Yards	Slope	USGA
White	72	6117	117	69.5
Red	72	5613	120	71.7

Above: The 13th offers a still greater challenge after completing the difficult 12th. Even the big hitters will be left with a lengthy approach shot to this small, guarded green. There's water in front of the men's tees, and tall pines and palms line the fairways.

The par five number six from the 150 yard marker is the number one handicap—at 530 yards, the longest hole on the course.

Gary Player photographed at the 2000 Open Championship at St. Andrews, Scotland

TWO MEN FROM OVERSEAS WHO INFLUENCED THE WAY THE GAME OF GOLF IS PLAYED IN AMERICA...DONALD ROSS AND GARY PLAYER

There are many so-called legends of golf; too many to enumerate. But to the authors, who have "lived" with Donald Ross and his course achievements for the past two years, there is one man in golf today who seems to have those important traits of character that made Ross so great. That player of the game and designer of fine courses is Gary Player of Palm Beach, Florida, by way of Johannesburg, South Africa. He is noted for his extraordinary work ethic and conscientiousness in every task he undertakes. The "Black Knight's" motto is, "the harder I practice, the luckier I get!" Like Ross, who was a founder of the Village Chapel in Pinehurst, Gary has a strong religious belief. And like Ross, he is first and foremost a sportsman and was awarded the mantle of South Africa's Sportsman of the Century in 2000.

He has won, as of this writing, 160 titles worldwide, and is one of only five golfers (with Hogan, Sarazen, Nicklaus and Woods), to have triumphed in the Grand Slam (all four major championships). He was inducted into the Golf Hall of Fame in 1974. He is still competing, while having traveled more miles than any other sportsman in history. He is surely the "International Ambassador of Golf."

We recently asked Gary about the strong influence of Ross on the game of golf and golf architecture. Here is what he wrote about the son of Dornoch:

"Donald Ross had a profound effect on golf course design worldwide. We are fortunate to have the opportunity to visit and play his golf courses—a proud legacy he left behind for us to enjoy."

Gary Player

Georgia

Bacon Park Golf Course

Forest Hills Golf Club

Roosevelt Memorial Golf Course

Wilmington Island Club

BACON PARK GOLF COURSE

ONE SHORTY COOPER DRIVE, PO BOX 31406, SAVANNAH, GA 31406
(912) 354-2625   FAX: (912) 351-9758

DIRECTIONS: TAKE I-75 GOING SOUTH FROM ATLANTA TO I-16 EAST, GO PAST I-95 TO LYNNES PARKWAY, THEN SOUTH AND EAST TO SKIDAWAY. TURN RIGHT PAST ONE LIGHT. COURSE IS ON THE RIGHT.

Public. 27 holes. Open year round. Pro shop opens 7 AM. Rental clubs and carts. Lighted driving range. Pro shop. Putting green. Chipping and sand practice areas. Teaching pro. Golf school. Restaurant. Snack bar.

Right: The way the original scorecard looked...note the names given to the holes.

The Donald Ross Original Golf Course Scorecard

Name:_____

Date:_____

Hole	Name	Yards	Par	H'cap				
1	Getaway	405	4	3				
2	Hogback	379	4	11				
3	Lowland	368	4	9				
4	Overbrook	161	3	17				
5	Crooked Valley	419	4	5				
6	Blind Tom	351	4	13				
7	The Stretch	438	4	2				
8	Long View	476	5	7				
9	Dead Aim	203	3	15				
Out		3200	35	Total				

Hole	Name	Yards	Par	H'cap				
10	The Narrows	454	5	12				
11	No-Foolin	315	4	14				
12	Canal	382	4	4				
13	Sore Thumb	355	4	10				
14	Spitball	151	3	18				
15	Belly Acres	418	4	1				
16	Triangle	376	4	6				
17	The Oak	166/233	3	16				
18	Home	506	5	8				
In		3190	36	Total				
		6390	71	Total				

Scorer:_____

Attested By:_____

Bacon Park is conveniently located in midtown Savannah, just minutes from the downtown tourist area. Its setting is within one of the most magnificent bird sanctuaries in the region. It was not planned that way, but with the forested borders, the abundant water and deep grasses, the sound of birds attests to the natural attraction of the place to fowl of all kind. Muscovy ducks, mallards, pelicans, wood storks and egrets are seen here, and cormorants diving for fish are common sights.

On the sixth tee of Cypress, one may see a red-tail hawk or overhead a pair of ospreys swooping down in hope of a meal. White ibises with long curved bills are seen in formation as they graze a fairway. And like many courses, the Canada geese make the scene, too. Even yellowcrowned night heron make appearances with the great blues. For those who rarely get a "birdie," the course promises a chance to see hundreds of gorgeous natural ones while playing.

The course was originally designed by Donald Ross to play 18 holes. In 1985 it was ex-

Above: The 375 yard, par four number seven on Cypress protected by a typical Donald Ross bunker (formerly hole number 16)

panded into a 27-hole complex: The Live Oak, The Magnolia and The Cypress. All three of these nine-hole courses, in combinations, are par 72 and feature championship, regular, senior and ladies' tees. All are USGA and Slope rated.

When originally created, the course played to 6,390 yards for a par 71. Number 17, The Oak, could be played from two tee boxes for a distance of 166 yards or 233 yards.

The way the course is now set up, these holes are still in existence just the way Ross designed them: Live Oak's one, two, three, four and eight; Magnolia's two, three, four, five and seven; and Cypress' seven and nine.

In the early days, boxing champion Joe Louis, as well as Pete Cooper, Gene Sauers, Claude Harmon, Bert Yancey, Jim Dent, football great Jim Thorpe, and Felix Millan were seen at Bacon Park.

Each year the Savannah City Amateur Tournament is held here. This is considered the most prestigious tournament in the area and is set up so the players use only the 18-hole layout that as closely as possible constitutes the original Donald Ross design.

Under EDR Management Inc.'s vision, the course has recently experienced a real renaissance. Eleven tee boxes have been rebuilt; the practice putting green has been completely resurfaced. The driving range has been increased by 50 yards, and three holes have new putting surfaces.

Here the theme of EDR has been the preservation of the best of Donald Ross' design work, and the results have been outstanding. This course is a real treat for Donald Ross fans to visit.

Top: The 161 yard number four, elevated par three green looking back over water to the tee box on Live Oak

Bottom: A long bunker stands sentinel on Live Oak.

FOREST HILLS GOLF CLUB

1500 COMFORT ROAD, AUGUSTA, GA 30909
(706) 733-0001   FAX: (706) 667-0093

DIRECTIONS: TAKE EXIT 196A FROM I-20. GET OFF AT EXIT 2 AND TURN LEFT. GO TWO MILES AND TURN LEFT ON MAGNOLIA DRIVE, THEN ANOTHER LEFT AT COMFORT ROAD.

18 holes. Public with limited membership (150). Driving range. Putting, chipping and sand trap practice areas. Full pro shop. Changing rooms with shower. Full service dining room. Snack bar and beverage services.

The clubhouse with a long veranda, reflects its southern hospitality.

The history of Forest Hills goes back to 1917, when hundreds of army tents blanketed the area as part of Camp Hancock during World War I. In 1926, The Forest Hills-Ricker Hotel opened, attracting northerners with tennis, archery, golf and horseback riding. The golf course was designed by Donald Ross, enticing experienced players, and the Southeastern Open Tournament originated in 1929, with play being split between Augusta Country Club and Forest Hills.

The course was the delight of snow-weary northerners, with its sumptuous cathedral pines and dogwoods, and azaleas lining the course in the spring.

During the tournament of 1930, Bobby Jones beat Horton Smith by 13 shots, calling it "the best-played tournament I ever turned out in my life." He went on that year to win the envi-

Below: The 194 yard, par three sixteenth hole requires a nice, high shot over the lake onto a narrow fairway and a small green with bunkers on both sides.

able Grand Slam with victories in the U.S. Open at Interlachen, and the U.S. Amateur and British Open.

In 1938, Forest Hills was the scene of the Augusta Open. Tony Penna, Byron Nelson, Gene Sarazen, Ben Hogan and Tommy Armour competed for the then-grand amount of $5,000. The Forest Hills Invitational brought the distaff side to the course, and spectators were treated to the likes of Babe Didrikson Zaharias, Louise Suggs, Jane Cothran, Dorothy Kirby and Augusta's own Eileen Stulb.

The 1940s brought World War II, and the army commandeered the hotel, converting it into a hospital named Oliver General. Fortunately, the golf course survived, serving as a tool for the recuperation of the soldiers. The Veterans Administration retained the golf course after the war, but in 1977, declared it surplus.

Enter the Augusta Golf Association. Augusta State University's golf team lacked a home course, and in 1978, the property was transferred from the government to the Board of Regents. The Board of Regents turned it over to Augusta State University, which leased it to the AGA. (In return, the AGA donates revenue over operating expenses to the Augusta State University Athletic Association.)

A huge and expensive project lay ahead—replacing the weeds that had choked the Bermuda grass on the fairways and redoing the greens and bunkers. In addition, a new irrigation system had to be installed.

Today, over 70 years after the course was born, Donald Ross' aura still exists. Forest Hills is known as the home of the Augusta State University Jaguars, a Division One golf team that usually finishes as one of the top 25 collegiate teams in the nation. The Cleveland Golf-Augusta State University Invitational, a national intercollegiate tournament, is held here each year. Many of those college champions, winners at Forest Hills, have gone on to glory, including Phil Mickelson, Davis Love III, Jodie Mudd, Tim Herron and Justin Leonard. The Augusta City Amateur Championship is played during the third weekend in July each year

The list of famous golfers who have played Forest Hills would take up more space than is available here, but note that Tiger Woods did an exhibition at the driving range; Bing Crosby and Phil Harris played here during their heydays; and Ben Hogan, Sam Snead, Lloyd Mangrum, Al Watrous, Gene Sarazen and Denny Shute braved the hilly terrain and uneven lies.

These days, the fairways are wide, and a lake comes into play on two holes, 12 and 16. The signature hole is number three, a 575 yard, par five.

Below: Hole 14 (winter), par four, 410 yards off the blues

Tees	Par	Yards	Slope	USGA
Blue	72	6840	126	72.2
White	72	6403	123	69.9
Gold	72	5765	120	68.5
Red	72	4875	116	68.3

ROOSEVELT MEMORIAL GOLF COURSE 1926

HIGHWAYS 41 & 27A, WARM SPRINGS, GA 31830
(706) 655-5230 FAX: (706) 655-5581

DIRECTIONS: FROM HIGHWAY I-85 SOUTH GO PAST TOWN OF NEWNAN TO EXIT 41. TAKE 27A SOUTH, GO ABOUT 33 MILES AND LOOK FOR SIGNS TO THE ROOSEVELT INSTITUTE.

Public. 9 holes plays 18. Open year round. Rental gas and pullcarts and clubs. Pro shop opens 8 AM. Putting green. Teaching pro on staff. Snack bar.

Below: The clubhouse

A venerable bent grass course is located at world-famous Warm Springs, a health spa (turned treatment center) made famous by the visits of President Franklin Delano Roosevelt in the '30s and early '40s. It was here that the President died in 1945, while having his portrait painted.

Roosevelt had heard of Donald Ross and specifically requested that the noted architect do the course at Warm Springs. Roosevelt never played the course, but was an avid fan while here. The course's construction was a top priority for him, and he helped in the designing of the course, working closely with Ross.

It never grew beyond the original nine holes, but men's tees are set up to play 18. The terrain is hilly with small, well-bunkered greens. To hold them can be difficult as they tend to undulate and contain hidden breaks. A creek courses through the property and becomes a hazard on five holes. Fairways are lined with tall pines and oaks. It is unique in that one will not find another nine-hole Ross course in the State of Georgia.

It has changed little from the day it opened, but with the advances in the development of electric-powered personal mobility vehicles, it is possible for golfers with disabilities to play. The course owns three *Golf Xpress* prototype single-rider golf carts. One player who recently traded in his wheelchair for the powered unit said, "I enjoy being outdoors, and it's another sport in which I can take part." One vehicle user with a physical handicap quipped, "Besides, in golf, everybody has a handicap."

In the early years at the course, in keeping with Roosevelt's philosophy of democracy, there was always an eclectic mix of players. It

Above: Four young golfers in their plus fours pose before starting a tournament, circa 1930.

was one of the few courses where the caddies were encouraged to play. Every Monday caddies were seen swinging irons instead of carrying them for others.

Today, the course is open to staff, patients and students, and anyone who wishes to play is encouraged. For several years, until the present organization outgrew the accommodations, the Southern States Amputee tournaments were held in Warm Springs. The popular three-day events drew many eager participants and large crowds of curious spectators. Fifty years after FDR's death, a helicopter landed at the course, and another president who loves the game of golf descended from the aircraft; it was Bill Clinton.

The course has hosted its share of famous golfers, including Larry Nelson and Hugh Royer. Recently a former caddie informed the club manager that he had caddied for Bobby Jones here in the '40s.

It was here in these warm waters that

FDR discovered relief from the debilitating effects of polio and founded a treatment center for polio patients. It was designed for accessibility, and earned a reputation for the quality of service and innovation, which became a tradition here. Roosevelt Warm Springs Institute for Rehabilitation offers independence, choice and quality of life to people with disabilities dating from its very beginning in 1927. Here one finds a serene and beautiful campus providing an unmatched setting for recovery, learning and personal growth. There is a comprehensive medical care program, vocational rehabilitation and a center for therapeutic recreation, including a two-story, 72,000 square foot recreation building. Here is the Roosevelt Sports Training Center and Camp Dream, a 400-meter

Tees	Par	Yards	Slope	USGA
Blue/White	70	6198	122	68.7
Red	72	5272	117	69.2

track and twelve acre lake. The recreation building has a 25-meter pool, NCAA basketball court, bowling alley, fitness room, indoor track and racquetball court.

In Geoffrey Ward's book, *A First-Class Temperament,* he tells that in 1927 Paul Hasbrouch, a young polio patient from Poughkeepsie, arrived in Warm Springs in April. He noted, "the tremendous scale of operations in preparation of opening here this summer has amazed me. Workmen remodeling the cottages, the hotel, building a third swimming pool and laying out a nine-hole golf course to be enlarged later to 18 holes."

He went on to write, "It is further evidence of Eleanor's increasing distance from her husband that once, when asked to recall the psychological impact of his illness upon him, she replied that the only thing she had noticed was that she had never heard him speak of golf after he was stricken, although it had once been his fa-

vorite game. In fact, he spoke of it often at Warm Springs, where he helped design and supervise the laying out of the course with a network of roads and specially reinforced bridges so that those with polio, like himself, who could not play but liked to watch, as well as those who could play but could not walk long distances, could drive from hole to hole. After the course was completed, he liked to drive with Missy or the pretty young wife of a Warm Springs physician at his side, shouting bawdy advice to the players and carrying with him a silver pitcher of martinis with which to toast good shots and bad."

For years Warm Springs operated at a loss, and FDR personally covered the expenses. After the March of Dimes was founded to raise funds for the foundation to aid polio research nationally, he would be free of financial worries for the health center. Ten years after FDR's death, Dr. Jonas Salk developed the polio vaccine.

Photos Courtesy of Roosevelt Warm Springs Institute for Rehabilitation

Above: Players in an amputee tournament in the '60s.

Where Donald Ross got his lifelong course design inspiration: Royal Dornoch Golf Club, Dornoch, Scotland.

Photograph by Iain Lowe, St. Andrews Studio

SON OF SCOTLAND

The inspired motto of the Ross clan is "Spem Successus Alit"—Success Nourishes Hope. The most common tartan of the Ross clan features deep blood red and navy blue. Like most highland tartans, the Ross patterns and shades vary and go back centuries.

Unlike heraldry, tartans are not controlled by statute either in use or design. The only time tartans were involved in the law was when the Proscription act (1747-1782) banned them along with highland dress after the 1745 rebellion. Then, only the Black Watch tartan was legal, because it was worn by those regiments raised in Scotland that were loyal to the Crown.

Hunting tartans were traditionally more subdued in color, while the dress tartans were usually brighter. In the case of the Ross tartans, it seems to be the other way around, with the hunting tartan far brighter than the dress clan tartan, featuring light blues, greens, pink and pale yellows.

There are almost three thousand tartans registered in Scotland. To see illustrations of various historic Ross clan tartans one is invited to contact: info@tartans.Scotland.net.

Following the debacle of the ill-fated rebellion in Scotland of clansmen against the British Crown in 1745, Highlanders flocked from the land of the thistle to America in general and North Carolina in particular. That is why there were so many names like Aberdeen and Scotland County dotting the landscape near Pinehurst when Ross finally settled down in his adopted country.

The presence of so many MacDonalds, McDougals, McDowells, McEachens, McElligotts, McElreaths and McGaheys surely made the newcomer feel right at home. Today, that Scottish tradition continues. The phone book in Pinehurst's Moore County contains hundreds of Mc's and Mac's. Indeed, if you look at photos taken of Ross in his early years, you'll see him sporting a Harris Tweed jacket and a well-worn old country golfing tam. There is a large oil painting of the course master in the clubhouse at Pinehurst, dressed just that way.

At Pinehurst, the site of so much of Ross' creativity, one can walk in the footsteps of the true golfing greats his courses tempted to compete there: Oimet and Hagen in the '20s, Jones in the '30s, Hogan and Snead in the '40s, Middlecoff and Nelson in the '50s, Palmer and Nicklaus in the '70s, Azinger in the '80s, and most recently by the beloved man with the Scottish name: Payne Stewart, who beat Phil Mickelson and Tiger Woods among others at the '99 Open. Donald Ross would have loved that match!

WILMINGTON ISLAND CLUB

501 WILMINGTON ISLAND ROAD, SAVANNAH, GA 31410
(912) 897-1615 FAX: (912) 897-9075 E-MAIL: KGRWPR@AOL.COM

DIRECTIONS: FROM HIGHWAY 80, EXIT AT BRYANWOOD RD. TURN LEFT AT JOHNNY MERCER BLVD. AND RIGHT ON WILMINGTON ISLAND RD. TO COURSE.

Semi-private. 18 holes. Open year round. Closed Mondays. Tee times available Tuesday through Friday and holidays. Saturday and Sunday preferred tee times for members. Rental clubs and electric carts. Grass driving range. Restaurant and snack bar. Carts are mandatory. 25,000 sq. ft. clubhouse. Banquet facilities. Fitness center. 6 clay tennis courts. Swimming pool. Club now has 375 members.

This Chatham County Tufton Bermuda grass course was, in other days, called The General Oglethorpe Hotel & Golf Club and then the Sheraton Savannah Resort and Country Club. The elegant, pillared clubhouse attests to its former grandeur, and there is now talk of changing it to private club status.

Above: Front view of the clubhouse

Donald Ross designed the course in 1927, and in 1966 it was completely rebuilt by Willard Byrd of Atlanta with only slight modifications to Ross' original plans. Lakes were added, and the present number one hole was shortened from a par five to a par four. It begins with a drive over water, unusual for a Ross course where the designer usually liked to start off "easy" and then "give 'em a few nuts to crack!"

The course is maintained in strict accordance with USGA specifications. It gives true meaning to the phrase, water hazard. One glance at the scorecard shows the golfer water on 11 holes, including four lakes and several streams. The number one handicap hole, and deservedly so, is number eight, a par four that plays 435 off the blues with a stream coming in from the right and another running across to the left along most of the fairway. The ladies get a break here, as the red tees are placed in front of much of the threatening water.

The topography is typically Savannah, with lazy winding streams, full live oaks draped in Spanish moss, picturesque pines and palms adding to the natural scenic beauty. Native birds are abundant and colorful, and sometimes downright noisy.

This course provides a very fine and fair test of golf. It is not overly difficult, but, as with all Ross courses, requires sound concentration. Contoured fairways and raised greens, planted in Tifton Bermuda grass, are enhanced by the strategic placement of bunkers and those nasty water holes.

Here the 2000 Georgia State 4-Ball Tournament was held, and the Georgian Open was played here from the mid-'80s to the mid-'90s. Wilmington Island has drawn many of America's top names in golf over the years, including: Arnold Palmer, Davis Love, Jr. and Davis Love III, David Frost and Gene Sauers.

It's interesting to note that Donald Ross designed courses for nine venues in the State of Georgia. Three no longer exist, and four are open to public play.

Above: The 435 yard par four number eight hole. The fairway drive is wide, but the second shot plays to a small landing area backed by water.

Above: The par three number six signature hole—155 yards over water. A 17 handicap, here's where birdies are made with great frequency!

Tees	Par	Yards	Slope	USGA
Blue	71	6633	132	72.0
White	71	6266	129	70.4
Gold	71	5529	119	67.1
Red	71	5140	121	70.3

INDIANA

FAIRVIEW GOLF COURSE

FRENCH LICK SPRINGS RESORT & SPA, HILL COURSE

FAIRVIEW GOLF COURSE

7102 South Calhoun Road, Fort Wayne, IN 46807
(219) 744-9368 or (219) 745-7093   Fax: (219) 744-4369
Website: www.fairviewgolf.com

Directions: From I-69 north, exit on Lower Huntington Rd. and turn right. At Tillman Rd., turn right to course on left.

Public. 18 holes. Open March 1 to November 11. Tee times required weekends and holidays. Rental electric and pullcarts and clubs. Driving range. Three practice greens. Chipping and sand practice areas. Snack bar. Outside pavilion can seat 200.

Below: Hole 18, a slightly raised, flat, circular surface seen from the trap behind the pin. The number two handicap hole, a par five, it plays 549 yards, the longest hole on the back nine.

This bent grass Hoosier course, built in 1927 to Donald Ross specifications, is situated on typical Allen County flat terrain with many elevated greens. The West course nine was the only course until the late '50s, when the East nine holes were added.

Numbers 11, 12, 13, 14, 16, 17 and 18 are identical to the way Ross created them—reasonably flat with push-up greens. Number ten has been changed to a straight away par four from its former dogleg right. The number 15 green has been redone and moved back about 30 yards. Water hazards come into play on six holes: numbers two, three, four, five, six and eight.

The very popular public course does over 40,000 rounds a season, thanks to its excellent condition with modern irrigation and reasonable rates.

Here, unlike some Ross courses, the slope to the green is usually less daunting than one might expect. Getting one's low pitch shot to stay on the deck is the trick. They are medium to small and can be exasperating. The course is very playable and easy to walk. Management has added many new trees to the already fine mature ones lining the fairways, and changes in green elevations have added to the beauty and difficulty. With no homes built on the property, the view is unimpeded throughout the course.

From its ancient origins as a Miami Indian village, to a rough frontier fort, to a booming canal and railroad town, Fort Wayne has a rich heritage. To the golfer visiting Fort Wayne for the first time, there is much to see when not on the course: The Allen County/Fort Wayne Historical Museum, Lincoln Library Museum, Fort Wayne Museum of Art, Fort Wayne Zoo, Fort Wayne Philharmonic Orchestra, Performing Arts Center, Cathedral of the Immaculate Conception, Lakeside Rose Garden, Three Rivers Festival in July, and the Trappers' Rendezvous in October.

It may be easier than usual to get a tee time on Memorial Day, when everyone seems to be headed for Indianapolis to watch the famed Indy 500, an event that draws a third of a million people at the great speedway to watch 33 cars zoom past the starting flag in one of the world's most stirring automotive spectacles.

Above: The par three 12th seen from the tee box. It plays 184 from the blues, but only 135 from the whites. Although the easiest hole on the card, it can be deceptive with its small putting area and two sand bunkers lying in wait for the errant shot.

Between 1917 and 1927, Donald Ross created only three golf courses in the State of Indiana, a total of just 45 holes. Today, two of the three venues are open to public play. The third, Broadmoor Country Club in Indianapolis, is private.

Tees	Par	Yards	Slope	USGA
Blue	72	6621	118	70.2
White	72	6078	113	68.5
Green	72	5189	NA	NA
Red	72	5012	108	71.1

FRENCH LICK SPRINGS RESORT & SPA

Hill Course
8670 W. State Rd 56, French Lick, IN 47432
(800) 457-4042   Fax: (812) 936-2100   E-mail: dharner@boykin.com
Website: www.frenchlick.com

Directions: From Louisville, take I-64 west. At Hwy. 150, go west toward Paoli. Go south on 56, proceed ten miles to French Lick. Entrance on the right.

Resort. Semi-private. 18 holes. Open March 1 to Dec. 1. Rental carts and clubs. Putting green. Chipping and sand practice areas. Driving range at the resort. Teaching pro. Golf school. Complete pro shop. Snack bar. Beverage cart. A second course here was designed by Tom Bendelow.

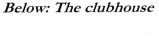

Below: The clubhouse

L*inks Magazine* has recognized this popular spot as one of the country's best historic resorts in its *Best of Golf 2000* issue. It boasts 30 activities for guests on its 2,300 acres, and the visitor has a choice of 471 rooms.

Located in the rolling hills of south central Indiana, the French Lick Springs Resort is "where the past is always present." This grand resort features 36 challenging holes of golf, indoor and outdoor tennis, a health spa, equestrian center, fine dining and great "Hoosier Hospitality."

The Valley Golf Links course is one of the oldest in the Midwest. As the resort grew in popularity, owner Thomas Taggart decided to commission another course—one challenging enough to attract a major tournament. In 1917, he asked Donald Ross to build a new course on 300 acres one mile south of French Lick. Thus, the French Lick Country Club, or "Hill Course" was born. It wasn't completed until 1920, perhaps due in part to World War I.

In 1924 the Seventh Annual PGA Championship, won by Walter Hagen, was played there. Hagen called it "a course where all 18 holes are uphill!"

The PGA returned in 1959 and '60, the Indiana Open in 1962, the Indiana Senior Open in 1984, the American Junior Golf Association Tour Group from 1982 to 1992, the Indiana PGA Match Play in 1993 and the Indiana Girls Championship in 1999.

For the Ross enthusiast, French Lick has great appeal, since only two of the original holes designed by the great golf architect have been modified. Holes one through thirteen, and sixteen through eighteen are the same today as they were back in 1920 when Ross performed his magic. And of course, there is enough water and pesky ravines for everyone. Indeed, according to PGA Professional Dave Harner, the terrain is "extremely hilly; the greens are undulating and treacherous, and there is a prevailing wind on most days."

For those who seek examples of Ross' finest works, French Lick ranks among the very best. It is kept in pristine condition, a true example of the art of golf design. Golf writer Ron Whitten has described it: "This is a step back in time, with only a few clusters of trees, bunkers still in original positions and terrific old-fashioned surface-drained greens. The greens are probably too steep these days, but who cares? French Lick is a classic."

The resort is said to be a favorite of basketball legend Larry Bird. The course is highlighted by the lake coming into play on three holes. *Golf Digest* has rated it as the "Tenth Best Public Course in the State."

Above: The 395-yard hole 14 (par four). Any tee shot 200 yards or more, placed between two giant white oaks, gives the player a magnificent view and an open shot at the largest green on Ross' Hill Course.

Tees	Par	Yards	Slope	USGA
Blue	70	6625	119	71.5
White	70	6291	116	70.0
Red	73	5422	111	72.2

Above: The elevated fifth hole on the older, 18-hole Valley Course at French Lick
Below: The deeply bunkered sixth hole on the Hill Course. The longest par three on the front nine requires 100% carry from tee to green into a usually prevailing south wind. Leave it short, and it won't bounce up onto the green. Plays 221 from the blues.

Above: The fourth hole, Hill Course—an uphill par three. The pros here recommend using an extra club. If you leave it short, you're in trouble due to the severe elevation. Plays 195 from the blues.

Donald Ross had only a brief connection with the Hoosier State. He did all his lasting work there within six short years, starting in 1917 at French Lick Country Club, where he designed the famed Hill Course. The country club evolved, of course, into the present French Lick Resort and Spa, whose slogan is: "Where the past is always present."

Ross, himself, described it as "a course with exceptional golfing terrain into which the greens and bunkers fit naturally."

One of the most talked-about holes in Indiana golf is the par four number eight. The hole is a perfect 90-degree dogleg. The ideal tee shot is toward a lone pine tree in the distance near the white 150 yard marker post. A drive 230 yards in that direction gets the player in perfect position to cross the deep ravine to the green, which slopes nine and a half feet from back to front. The player is advised to stay short of the pin on the approach or face many putts.

Ross' work here was followed up, four years later, with an important commission to do the Broadmoor Country Club (18 holes) in Indianapolis. His last design in the State would be the golfer-friendly Fairview Golf Club (nine holes) in Fort Wayne.

Maine

Biddeford Saco Country Club

Kebo Valley Club

Lake Kezar Country Club

Lucerne-in-Maine Golf Course

Northeast Harbor Golf Club

Penobscot Valley Country Club

Poland Spring Country Club

DIRECTIONS: FROM I-95 NORTH, TAKE EXIT 5 AND FOLLOW TO OLD ORCHARD ROAD.

Semi-private. 18 holes. Open April 1 to November 1. Rental gas and pullcarts and clubs. Driving range. Snack bar. Full pro shop that opens at 6 AM. Public may make tee times three days in advance. Teaching pro.

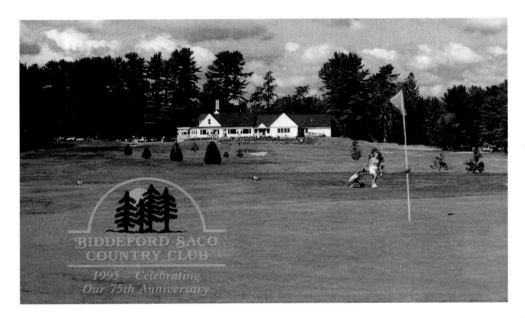

For centuries in pre-historic times, the dramatic falls of the Saco River, near where it now crosses Main Street, attracted summer visits from the Native Americans living in the area. Here they came to hunt and fish. By the early 17th century, the safe harbor and abundant natural resources drew European settlers.

The area was slow to develop because of the devastation of frequent wars between the natives and the French. Then in 1716, William Pepperell, a young merchant from Kittery, purchased 5,000 acres and timber rights to 4,500 more on the east side of the Saco River. He sold off parts of his holdings to millwright Nathaniel Weare and mariner Humphrey Scamman to expedite his lumbering operations. Main Street, Portland, Buxton and Ferry Roads were all laid out in 1718.

History buffs will thoroughly enjoy Saco, with nine properties listed on the *National Register of*

Historic Places. Area highlights include: York Institute Museum, Dyer Library, Sidewalk Art Festival, and La Kermesse Celebration and Fireworks.

There are world-famous ocean and bay beaches as well as a unique estuarine resource and one of the few raised bogs in the world. When you stand on the 14th tee, the vista takes in a vast marshland looking out toward Saco Bay.

Between 1913 and 1930, Donald Ross designed golf courses at 13 venues in the State of Maine. Seven remain open to public play. He loved new England because so much of it reminded him of Scotland, and he was totally enamored by the State of Maine where so many great holes give testimony to his course creativity.

In the beginning there was a temptation not to build a golf course because the Old Orchard Beach Country Club was right down the street, and their club offered BSCC members the privilege of using their golf course for a mere $15 a year. At a meeting of the BSCC on March 21, 1921, that generous offer was rejected, and a decision was made to build their own course. By April 11, the golf

Tees	Par	Yards	Slope	USGA
Gold	71	6196	123	69.6
Blue	71	5845	114	68.5
White	72	5433	117	71.4
Red	72	5053	110	69.2

Of the Ross holes, numbers eight and nine are tougher than they look. Eight, a par three, calls for a shot over a small brook to an undersized green 172 yards off the gold tees. Number nine, the number one handicap hole, is a straight 438 yards of narrow fairway to a tiny green protected by bunkers on two sides. Despite its many challenges, one player claims it's the "nicest course to women in Maine."

committee had contacted Donald Ross and found out that the cost of building the course would be $5,000 for the first four holes and $10,500 for the five additional holes to complete the front nine, with the back nine put "on hold." The trustees voted to approve the proposal. Membership grew through the sixties when a decision was made to add the back nine. The architectural firm of Cornish and Silva was hired to lay out the specifications for the remainder of the course. In 1992, membership was officially limited to just 500 active players.

Of the original Ross-designed holes, nine remain exactly as he designed them, following his old routing plan. Tim Angis, course pro, describes it as "truly fun to play." It is a bent grass course known for its narrow fairways and challenging greens. There are no homes to distract from the stunning views, and in the fall the color is spectacular. Fairways are heavily wooded, providing deep shade in late afternoons. The front nine has a difficult terrain to master, with seven pronounced gullies and water hazards on two holes. *Golf Digest* has rated Biddeford Saco as the ninth "Best Public Course in the State."

The city of Saco lies between Boston and Portland. With long stretches of beach, bustling fishing harbors and the historic shopping district, it is an ideal vacation spot. From north to south, the beaches are: Fortunes Rocks, Hills, Camp Ellis, Ferry, Bayview, Kinney Shores, Ocean Park, Old Orchard, Surfside, Grand and Pine Point. They all look out seaward to the famous Wood Island Lighthouse. If you like lobster and golf, this is your town! And if you don't find what you want when shopping here, you can always head up the road a piece to *L.L. Bean.*

KEBO VALLEY CLUB

ROUTE 233, EAGLE LAKE ROAD (BOX 583), BAR HARBOR, ME 04609
(207) 288-3000   FAX: (207) 288-3378

DIRECTIONS: TAKE ROUTE 3 FROM ELLSWORTH TO BAR HARBOR. TURN RIGHT TO 233 AND COURSE IS 1/4 MILE ON LEFT.

Semi-private. 18 holes. Professionally staffed full service golf shop. Open May 15 to October 31. Restaurant and lounge facility serving lunch daily from 11 AM to 3 PM. Complete meeting, banquet and reception planning available with accommodations for up to 150 people. Rental carts.

Below: The beautiful, modern clubhouse with KEBO spelled out in flowers. Since the first two clubhouses burned to the ground, this one has been heavily fireproofed!

Surrounded by the mountains of Acadia National Park, Kebo Valley Golf Club is the eighth oldest course in the nation. In a picturesque setting, Albino deer are seen frequently around the grounds. The view of the mountains is breathtakingly beautiful, particularly in the fall when the leaves change color. Just minutes from downtown Bar Harbor, it was originally designed by Herbert C. Leeds in 1888 and modestly remodeled by Donald Ross in 1926.

Most of Ross' work centered around the rebuilding of hole number three's green. He had recommended, in a letter to the club written while at Kebo, that "new tees and bunkers on number four hole also be built... and improvements to the fairways." The cost was stated to be not less than $4,000 and might amount to $6,000, depending entirely on whether or not ledge would be struck in the foundation of this new number three green. He also recommended that "the course would be improved by the addition of a few new bunkers and the remodeling of a number of the greens. But none of this work is as important as the care and improvement of fairways."

The authors join other golf writers in ranking Kebo among America's best 100 public golf courses. It was organized at a time when the social elite of the nation's larger cities summered in Bar Harbor. In this golden age, large mansions and "cottages" with elaborate grounds were summer playgrounds for the wealthy and powerful, rivaling Newport as the country's most socially desirable resort.

The Kebo stock corporation stated these purposes on April 27, 1888: *The business of purchasing real estate and erecting buildings and otherwise putting the property in suitable condition for the promotion and cultivation of athletic sports and furnishing innocent amusement for the public for reasonable compensation, including the erection and maintenance of a casino, which may include conveniences for dramatic and theatrical and musical entertainments under the name of Kebo Valley Club of Bar Harbor, Maine.*

In the beginning, the grounds offered a race track, baseball diamond and tennis, which was popular here until it was eliminated in 1938. Golf made its debut in 1891, when a "golf grounds" was laid out— six holes around the race track. By 1896, nine holes had been finished, with a length of 2,500 yards. Kebo joined the USGA in 1901. In an early tournament, open to all amateurs who had anted up $1, a cup was presented by Mr. Howard Hinkle. In 1922, Walter Hagan played two rounds with famous trick shot artist, Joe Kirkwood, and set the course record of 67, broken many years later by a local golf pro named Lewis Hershey. His 65 is yet to be surpassed.

In 1947, a great fire destroyed Kebo's second clubhouse; the first had burned down the day it was completed in July of 1899. The third opened July 1, 1948

Today young golfers are encour-aged at Kebo with free weekly clinics for boys and girls, and the Mt. Desert Island High School practices and plays here.

Ross' Singular Lasting Contribution to Kebo Valley—Hole Three

This par four is 335 yards. You drive from a flat tee to flat and relatively narrow landing area with a grass bunker bordering the right side for some 200 yards and out of bounds on the left side. The green is elevated, with deep grass bunkers on the right and back. A small green makes the hole a lot tougher than the yardage would indicate.

Number three was originally played as a sharp dogleg to the left, with the green on top at Bunker Hill, now a popular sliding area in winter. The tee for number four was near the third green at the top of the hill, and players hit down to the next green. Ross recommended number three be rebuilt because an approach shot failing to reach the lofty summit would "ignominiously roll back down hill past the luckless golfer." The climb to what members called "Shangri-la," was eliminated in the remodeling. In those pre-golfcart days, the climb up was just too much for most players.

Historic Note: President William Howard Taft shot a 17 on the 17th hole in 1911—another course "record."

Tees	Par	Yards	Slope	USGA
Blue	70	6131	130	69.0
White	70	5933	130	69.0
Red	72	5440	121	72.0

LAKE KEZAR COUNTRY CLUB

ROUTE 5, BOX 95, LOVELL, ME 04051
(207) 925-2462

1923

DIRECTIONS: TAKE RTE. 302 FROM PORTLAND NORTHWEST TO RTE. 93 NORTH. COURSE IS 12 MILES AWAY. (PRO SUGGESTS YOU CALL FOR DETAILED DRIVING INSTRUCTIONS.)

Semi-private. 18 holes. Open April 1 to November 1. Pro shop opens at 7 AM. Rental gas and pullcarts. Driving range. Snack bar. Putting green. Chipping and sand practice areas. Snack bar.

Above: The fourth fairway from the ladies' fifth tee—a par four, 297-yard hole (from the blues) with four bunkers inhibiting easy access to the dance floor

In the history books, they say that the Lake Kezar region of Maine was once occupied by the Red Paint People, a mysterious race whose archeological findings suggest they were in this part of North America over 10,000 years ago. They were followed by the Pequawket tribe of the Abenaki nation. When the white men came to this part of Maine, they petitioned the King of England that the area be deeded to the man who had mastered the Indians in battle. His name was Captain John Lovewell.

Another mysterious race now occupies this colorful land; its members are called tourists. And among the fiercest of this breed are the golfers. Armed with warlike clubs of many shapes and sizes, they, too, come in many shapes and sizes, but they have in common their determination to master this battleground. Moose are often observed watching the golfers with amused looks on their dour countenances.

This truly rustic Oxford County golf course was originally a Ross-designed, nine-hole facility. In 1998, it was redesigned by course superintendent, Brian Merrill, to become a full 18 holes. This was no easy task; it took over five years just to get the permits, as state, local and federal environmental agencies had to sign off on the project. Merrill says, "The members wanted to keep the layout they had, or at least change it as little as possible."

Only three holes remain exactly as Ross designed them. Number one, an easy opener, is a par four hole, playing 297 yards off both the white and blue tees. Number seven is a long and demanding par three, playing over water from the blue and white tees, and number eight, the longest hole on the front nine, plays 505 yards off the blues and 490 off the whites for the only par five on the front nine. Deep woods line the right side of the fairway.

The original nine are obviously Ross designs, but there have been modest changes made over the years. An abandoned tee next to the number two ladies' tee is still visible, but it is not possible to know which hole it served. There is also an abandoned tee adjacent to the

74

Above: The second hole, a par four, 310 yards off the blues

third green, which once served either the fourth or fifth hole, but no one knows for sure. The green on the par four sixth hole has been moved back to the right of its original location. Merrill has a good description for the grass found on the old nine fairways: "Heinz 57—it's quite a variety over there."

Pinehurst resident John Derr, the well-known television announcer, is a longtime member of Lake Kezar Country Club. He has personally contributed, over the years, to the modification of at least three of the holes, making recommendations about the positioning of the ladies' tees. John has played courses all over the world, as described colorfully in his books, *Uphill Is Easier* and *Don't Forget to Wind the Clock*, yet finds few as personally rewarding as his White Mountain summer retreat. Notables seen here also include: Monty Hall of *The Price Is Right*; Richard King of the King Ranch in Texas and Stephen King, the author.

As you might expect from a mountain course, the greens tend to be fast and uneven. The new course follows in the Ross tradition with narrow fairways requiring careful shot placement to score well. A meandering stream crosses these Ross creations— numbers two and seven fairways, and water also comes into play on holes four and five.

The authors asked CBS golf telecaster John Derr to give us some of his thoughts about Lake Kezar. He writes: "Lying along the flatlands that border the lower portion of 11-mile long glacial Lake Kezar, this land must have favorably pleased Donald Ross when he came there to create the Lake Kezar Country Club. Why? Because he was given land that did not require the removal of large outcroppings of rock that had challenged him at many New England courses.

"Ross found relatively flat land (the remnants of an abandoned apple orchard), the rows of which are ghostly visible, but a bouncing factor for anyone driving too fast in a golf cart.

"Four of his holes, including the first, are flat. Ponds, streams and gorges dot the other five holes. None require heroic drives, location being more helpful than distance, although one par three reaches 200 yards.

"Greens were not large by today's standards, and almost all were originally crowned to assist drainage from early or late snows. (It is New England, remember?)

"Gene Sarazen and Francis Ouimet were a part of the opening day ceremonies, and both are said to have personally congratulated Ross on his handiwork.

"By the time Lake Kezar was added, New England was dotted with Ross courses. These two stalwarts expected a good course at Lake Kezar— and they got it!"

Tees	Par	Yards	Slope	USGA
Blue	72	5961	117	67.3
White	72	5585	111	65.7
Red	72	5088	114	68.8
Gold	72	4661	108	66.9

LUCERNE-IN-MAINE GOLF COURSE

ROUTE 1A, EAST HOLDEN, ME 04429
(207) 843-6282   WEBSITE: WWW.INFO@LUCERNEINN.COM
INN RESERVATIONS: 1-800-325-5123

DIRECTIONS: FROM I-395, HEAD TO CITY OF BRUER. IT WILL CHANGE TO RTE. 1A. CONTINUE UNTIL
YOU REACH COURSE.

Public. 18 holes. Open May 1 to October 31. Pro shop open 7 AM. Rental electric and pullcarts and clubs. Driving range. Snack bar. At the inn, rooms, dining and outdoor swimming pool.

Below: The clubhouse in fall

The original nine bent grass holes, designed by Donald Ross, are divided by Route 1A. A new tunnel under the roadway provides easy access. Course designers Cornish, Silva and Mungeam have recently added a back nine and extended the length of the front nine hole course by a few hundred yards.

When originally built, this nine-hole course, located between Ellsworth and Bangor, was part of The Lucerne Inn, where the pro shop and clubhouse were located. Currently the 200-year-old inn is not part of the course operation. The present-day inn and course management cooperates to pro-

mote this outstanding golf/vacation site. The location is excellent, just 55 minutes from Mt. Desert Island, the location of Bar Harbor and Acadia National Park.

In the summer, cool lake breezes refresh the golfer, and the woodlands are lush with floral beauty. Whitetailed deer can often be seen meandering across the fairways. In the fall, gold, red and orange leaves attract visitors from around the world.

The inn, built in 1814, is a striking white clapboard mansion, nestled in the mountains and overlooking Phillips Lake. In 1934, when it was part of a 5,200 acre, 13 square mile property, two polo fields were kept busy. One of the property's movers and shakers was Robert E. Graham, whose Biltmore and other hotels were famous in Los Angeles and Florida.

In December, 1934, the local newspaper wrote: "Behind the announcement made by the officials of the company (Graham) yesterday is a story packed with romance for the thousands of people interested in the development of this beautiful resort and ringing with possibilities for the State of Maine, the like of which have not been experienced by the present generation."

That year, an invitation golf tournament was held on July 4th. The newspaper reported that there would be medal play, open to players from all parts of the state, and a big field would be expected.

Noted aviatrix Amelia Earhart flew in and stayed in the governor's suite of the then-famed Log Lodge. Socialites from all over the country came to view the event.

Today the Inn is truly one of the most spectacular places to stay in New England. The scenery is truly breathtaking when the setting sun shines on the quiet lake in full view of the dining room and every guest room. Food is elegant gourmet fare.

The new nine holes have been designed to be similar to those Ross might have designed were he here today. Because modern day conditions differ from 75 years ago, when Ross did his work, the course's look reflects the fact that today's practical irrigation is at work. With today's constantly improving equipment and balls, drives and fairway shots, even by some duffers, tend to cover more ground than in Ross' day, so the course now is set up to play a bit longer than it had been designed in the '20s.

Above: A rolling fairway ringed by heavily wooded mountains

Above: A typical Ross elevated green in the shade of a mature oak

Tees	Par	Yards	Slope	USGA
Blue	72	6540	119	70.6
White	72	5780	119	67.4
Red	72	5210	116	69.5

NORTHEAST HARBOR GOLF CLUB

SARGENT DRIVE, BOX 647, NORTHEAST HARBOR, ME 04662
(207) 276-5335   FAX: (207) 276-3866

DIRECTIONS: UPON ENTERING MT. DESERT ISLAND, FOLLOW SIGNS TOWARD NORTHEAST HARBOR, BEAR RIGHT AT THE LIGHT AND FOLLOW RTE. 198 SOUTH TO SCENIC SARGENT DRIVE. GO RIGHT ON SARGENT 3 MILES TO CLUB ON LEFT.

Semi-private. 18 holes. Open May 1 to November 1. Rental carts. Driving range for members. No restaurant.

Below: The par four number five hole plays 305 yards off the blues.

Nine holes at Northeast Harbor were built in 1895 by J.G. Thorpe, along the shores of Somes Sound. Golf pro Rob Gardner identifies Thorpe as a "pretty good player and runner-up in one of the amateurs of the time." The course was redesigned in 1898. Eighteen years later, the course moved inland, and these nine holes were redesigned by Donald Ross. As far as anyone knows, holes three through six and 13 through 15 remain the same today as when Ross created them. The back nine were designed by Herbert Strong in 1925.

The spruce tree shown on the club's coat of arms and scorecard had its origins in the first ever international match held at Hoy Lake, near Edinburgh, Scotland. This 1681 match was between two English noblemen and the Duke of York against a local shoemaker, John Patersone. The match, won by the Scot, settled a debate about whether golf was an English or Scottish game. Patersone won enough on the match to purchase a home and placed a coat of arms on the door reading "Far and Sure." That motto appears on the club's logo.

The task of removing huge trees and boulders attests to the determination of the early members to create a course on this hard property adjacent to imposing Norumba Mountain. Thick forests had to be cleared, and teams of men and horses worked long and hard to remove massive stones that had been locked for eons in the tough Maine soil.

During the second world war, the outside nine fell into disrepair. When Class A PGA professional and golf historian Rob Gardner arrived in 1976, membership had fallen to just 58 loyal members, and the course was in terrible shape. Since then the course has been brought back to life and its original rugged beauty, and membership is now over 400.

Above: The par three number three hole should be an easy par.

Holes 16, 17 and 18 were reopened in the late 1980s. At that time, members actually brought chainsaws and axes to help restore the course. (That's dedication.) Hole 16 had a ledge blasted away, the fairway and green reshaped and is now in tiptop condition.

Much work has been done here to restore Northeast to its past glory. The work was aided by the contribution of old photos that had been treasured by the grandson of Nate Smallidge, a longtime greens superintendent. The pictures helped guide the workmen as the restoration work was done.

In the book, *The Maine Golf Guide*, written by B. Labbance and D. Cornwell and published by New England Golf Specialists, Stockbridge, VT in 1991, Labbance writes of Northeast Harbor Golf Club in these glowing terms: "It's hard to be objective about Northeast Harbor Golf Club because it's my favorite in Maine. For me it has the elements of the Country Club (in Brookline, Massachusetts), Pine Valley (in Clementon, New Jersey) and Sugarloaf, but on a friendlier level. Immaculately conditioned fairways weave through enchanting forests and across a low links-like field bisected by the Mill Brook." The authors cite hole number five (shown on the opposite page), a classic Ross design, as "Maine's finest short par four."

Gardner says of the course, "Of the 18 holes, Northeast presents to the golfer the best of all worlds—13 magnificent wooded holes, surrounded by thousand of trees, and five traditional links-style holes, severe elevation changes, very small greens and unrivaled beauty."

Tees	Par	Yards	Slope	USGA
Blue	69	5430	120	67.8
White	69	5278	118	66.7
Red	71	4530	116	67.3

366 MAIN STREET, ORONO, ME 04473
(207) 866-2423   FAX: (207) 866-0442

DIRECTIONS: FROM I-95 TAKE EXIT 50. TURN RIGHT ON MAIN. COURSE ENTRANCE IS ON LEFT.

Semi-private, four visits per year only. 18 holes. Open April 15 to October 15. Pro shop opens 7 AM. Rental gas and pullcarts. Driving range. Putting and chipping practice areas. Restaurant and snack bar. 75 foot swimming pool. Banquet facilities can handle up to 200 guests with excellent cuisine and great scenic views.

Penobscot's bent grass course has hosted Bobby Locke, Tom Watson, Doug Sanders, "Champagne" Tony Lema, Bob Lee, and of recent vintage, tennis great Ivan Lendl.

In the pro shop hangs a proud picture of the king—Arnold Palmer. Arnold has played Penobscot and claimed that the par three 16th, playing 201 from the blues, was his favorite hole on the course. Need we add, he birdied it?

Penobscot has undergone restoration work by architect Ron Forse to retain the integrity of Donald Ross' original design. The new fairway bunkers are now blended perfectly with the Ross creations that are still in place; all has been gently molded back to Ross' original vision with considerate hands. Sixteen of the original holes are intact.

Ross did his design work in 1923, and the course was constructed under his direct supervision, on site, in 1924 at a time when Ross and his engineering associates were at their busiest. At that time, he sometimes had over 3,000 men at work on his various course projects around the nation. Architect Ron Forse has said that Ross only visited

Top: Sun and long shadows with mountains in the background
Bottom: An aerial view of Penobscot

about 45% of the courses to which his name is ascribed.

Ross' fee here was $20,000, paid by the Penobscot Realty Company in 1921. (This was one of his highest fees on record, and he did a grand job for his money.) After selling shares of stock to prospective members, the Penobscot Valley Country Club opened its doors. The company had acquired $150,000 for the sale of stock, purchased a piece of land called the McNulty Farm, and then proceeded to spend $100,000 on the renovation of the farmhouse and the construction of the course.

In the '30s, it was described in a promotional booklet as follows: "As you pass along the driveway, attractive lawns, flower beds profuse with perennials and handsome trees, typical alone of Maine, please your vision. The olden time portico, beneathe which we will be delighted to welcome you, will take your fancy. You know—even before entering, that here is one of those spacious, cozy Maine homesteads that say, 'Glad to see you!'"

Penobscot maintains its special back country charm to this day, almost resembling a motion picture set with its dramatic backdrop of the majestic eastern skyline of the Dedham and Holden mountains.

The course has undergone very few changes over its more than 75 year history. It provides the golfer a fair test of his game amid spectacular scenery. President Jimmy Carter, not thought of as a golfing president, played here, as have Sandy Koufax and Ted Williams of baseball fame. The first time Arnold Palmer tested the course, he had three pars and six birdies on just the front nine for a 30! He'd come to practice before flying down to win a Westchester, New York tournament.

The visiting golfer will find small-sized greens that are well protected with bunkers. The naturally rolling land virtually guarantees that the player will be hitting from an uneven lie. One of the most interesting holes is the ninth, a 392 yard, uphill par four that plays more like a 475 yard hole, with its strongly elevated green. It slopes from back to front, as many Ross holes of this type do, providing a real test at the close of the front nine. Then Palmer's choice, the par three, 16th hole is another long shot; stretching from the back tees to the cup for about 200

yards, making it a tough shot so late in the game. Birdies are rare on this hole, and a par is usually greeted with a loud sigh of relief.

In 1996, *Golf Digest* named this the "Fifth Best Public Course" in the State; this rating was later upgraded to *Fourth Best* in 1998. The State Amateur was played here in 1992 and the Women's State Amateur in 2001. The greens and fairways are maintained in excellent condition, aided by a state-of-the-art watering system, installed in 1992.

Under a sensitive management, over 40 bluebird houses have been erected on the course. Weeds are handpicked out of the tees, greens and approaches instead of using deadly chemicals. And pesticides are kept to a bare minimum. Purple Martin houses have also been set up, and bat houses are being planned—all in order to keep notorious black flies and mosquitoes at bay. This is a wildlife haven, and golfers often spy deer, bald eagles, blue heron, ducks, foxes, coyote and turtles as lazy hawks circle above.

Below: The turn toward the clubhouse—that mean-looking sand bunker has many cousins along the various fairways and greens here. This old white clubhouse at Orono is, sad to say, being torn down to make place for a new one. Progress!

Photo courtesy of Dr. Patrick R. McMullen, PhD, Auburn University

Tees	Par	Yards	Slope	USGA
Blue	72	6445	128	71.2
White	72	6301	126	70.5
Red	74	5796	128	73.9

POLAND SPRING COUNTRY CLUB

41 RICKER ROAD, POLAND SPRING, ME 04274
(207) 998-6002 FAX: (207) 998-2811 E-MAIL: POLANDSPRG@AOL.COM
WEBSITE: WWW.POLANDSPRINGINNS.COM

DIRECTIONS: MAINE TURNPIKE TO EXIT 11. TURN RIGHT AND TAKE THE FIRST LEFT, RTE. 26 NORTH. GO 10 MILES TO THE RESORT.

The Poland Spring Country Club, established in 1893, is a resort course. Members have priority from 6 AM to 9 AM. Its course was originally laid out by Arthur H. Fenn as nine holes. It was redesigned by Donald Ross in 1913 to its present 18 holes. Open from May 1 to October 30. Rental carts and clubs. Grass tennis courts. Entertainment every night. Swimming pool. Bocci. Shuffle-board. Horseshoes. Concerts under the stars.

The authors' favorite hole here: number six—a 163-yard par three. This tricky hole goes over a pond. Water is in the foreground to the right, so you're never sure where the wind will carry your ball. The bunkers are to the left and back of the green. An accurate shot to the green can yield that well-deserved score, but hit left or right, and you can count on a double-bogey.

This is reported to be the oldest resort course built in America. The wonderful, wooden, 300-room Poland Spring House, which was famous for the medicinal effects of its waters, no longer exists. In its place are Victorian-era design inns and cottages, with a large motor inn, collectively known as *The Inns at Poland Spring.* Interestingly (at least to one of the authors), it was the first course he ever played in Maine, back in 1963.

Poland Springs can best be described as scenic and hilly. "The Window," the 416 yard par four fourth, is typical of the challenge—the golfer is compelled to negotiate the narrow, tree-lined fairway downhill all the way to the green. It looks down to Lower Range Pond, as though offering a view out a picture window. Tall pines (80 feet) line the left side, while hardwoods march down the right.

Most of the rest of the course is open, and its typical Donald Ross sloping greens makes it a great test of putting control. The player gets plenty of chances to show off bump and run skills, and there is a plethora of sandy bunkers to snatch the errant ball.

The views during fall foliage time, bright with fiery reds, breathtaking yellows and brilliant golds, can distract the most avid golfer.

The Maine Golf Association's first Maine Open was won here by Arthur Fenn. Charles Lindberg; President John Kennedy's father, Joseph; Teddy Roosevelt and the great Babe Ruth all played the Springs in its heyday. When Jeff and Jim Gallagher, Jr. and Sr., played here, they agreed it had "some of the most picturesque holes we've ever seen."

Above: The fifth green—a 319-yard par four. The approach along the left side is wooded, the tee box is set to the right, and the left side of the green is banked eight feet with a large bunker carved into it. Proceed with caution!

Above: The fourth fairway—"the window"—looking down to the lower pond, a 401 yard par four beauty. It takes a 240 yards or better drive to see the green!

WHEN THE BABE PLAYED POLAND SPRING

Tom Turley wrote in his moving article, Babe in the Woods, *in the June, 1993 issue of* Yankee Magazine, *that when he caddied for the Babe in 1940, Ruth "approached me and handed me a small, square, unlabeled bottle filled with a brown liquid. 'This is medicine,' he said. 'Be careful of it.' I tucked it into the golf bag between some clean woolen socks, and we walked to the first tee.*

"Throughout the afternoon," Turley wrote, "the Babe, a lefty, hit towering arcs off every tee. But with almost every shot, he let loose a string of profanities in the most unexpected sequence. He was dangerously wild. We spent a lot of time in the woods and in the rough looking for his rockets. Even then, I lost three balls. On the fourth hole, we were crashing through the woods alone, when he asked for the medicine. I handed him the bottle and he took a long swig. I sniffed it; it smelled suspiciously like rum. At the 11th he bought soft drinks for everyone, including the four caddies. He summoned me for more medicine to mix with his Coke. He looked out over the mountains. 'Gee,' he whispered in that gravelly voice, 'this is beautiful. So peaceful and quiet. Isn't it wonderful?' He finished in the mid 80s. 75 cents was the going caddy fee. He tipped me $5, a monumental sum. Then he gave me a short wave goodbye and disappeared into the clubhouse. Later the Babe posed for photos with his fans. The Bambino was back on stage. The quiet moment we shared on the 12th hole seemed forgotten. Then he spotted me in the crowd and winked."

Reprinted with permission, Yankee Magazine, *June 1993*

Tees	Par	Yards	Slope	USGA
Blue	71	6200	119	68.2
White	71	5854	117	67.2
Red	74	5097	110	68.6

Massachusetts

Bass River Golf Course

Ellinwood Country Club

George Wright Golf Course

Greenock Country Club

Merrimack Golf Course

New Sandy Burr Country Club

Newton Commonwealth Golf Course

Petersham Country Club

Plymouth Country Club

Ponkapoag Golf Course

Tekoa Country Club

Wachusett Country Club

Whaling City Golf Club

William J. Devine Golf Course at Franklin Park

The Winchendon School Country Club

BASS RIVER GOLF COURSE

62 HIGH BANK ROAD, SOUTH YARMOUTH, MA 02664
(508) 398-9079   WEBSITE: WWW.SUNSOL.COM\BASSRIVERGOLF

DIRECTIONS: FROM BOSTON, TAKE ROUTE 6 SOUTH, GET OFF AT EXIT 8 (STATION AVE.), TURN RIGHT, GO PAST FIRST TWO LIGHTS TO REGIONAL AVE., TURN RIGHT AND FOLLOW TO COURSE.

Municipal. 18 holes. Open year round. Pro shop opens 7 AM. Rental electric and pull-carts and clubs. Putting green. Chipping and sand practice areas. Teaching pro. The snack bar offers a "million dollar view" of the Bass River as it winds to the ocean. Breakfast and lunch are served, and cookouts and catered meals can be arranged.

Below: The "photogenic" sixth hole—par three over water—only 155 yards from the whites—the number one handicap. This is the signature hole at Bass River. Pro Walter Hewins says he can use a four iron or a three wood here depending on the wind.

Two hundred and seventy five years after the Pilgrims founded this mid-Cape Cod community, golf was finally introduced. (They were in no hurry for golf's fun and games.) During the 19th century, the great age of sail, South Yarmouth became known as the "greatest nursery of seamen in North America." The experience of those world traveling seamen can be seen in the Greek Revival, French Second Empire and Gothic style architecture in the community.

The modern day visitor has much to do here: sailing, canoeing, kayaking, windsurfing, fishing and harbor cruising. Antiquing has been raised to a high art here, and local crafts are abundant. The John F. Kennedy Museum and Kennedy family compound are near. The Cape Cod Melody Tent and Playhouse feature theatre and outdoor concerts. There's bird watching, lighthouses—a great place to visit while here to play.

Although only ninety minutes from either Boston or Providence, there are 15 salt and fresh water beaches nearby, and for the golf nut, 11 nearby courses provide for all levels of play. For the golfer who likes tennis, there are 18 public courts in the area.

Bass River, the first municipal course on Cape Cod, was founded in 1900. Ross was called in 1914 to remodel nine holes and add another nine, developing what is one of Cape Cod's most dramatic courses, with breathtaking views of the Bass River. The narrow fairways are not easy; requiring careful ball placement because water comes into play on 11 holes. The greens are typical Ross creations, elevated, often hard-to-read and small in size.

Because the course is on a highlands above the Bass River, and is built on sandy soil, the drainage is excellent. Pro Don Deay says, "We can have an inch of water in an hour and be open for play 90 minutes later." Cool breezes make hot summer days pleasant, and the warming influence of the sea makes it playable 12 months of the year. The front nine is "short and tight, the back long and open," according to Deay. The front nine is still mostly a Ross course with several of the greens just as he designed them. Promoter Tom Marrin, who provided the photos here says, "The golfer who overshoots is dead meat here." Tom is a former Bass River caddy whose *Little Black Book of Golf* gives good insights into all Cape courses.

Walter Hewins, club pro from '67 to '93, who has played the course regularly since '56, loves the course. He says, "A lot reminds me of a course done in the early 1900s, when accuracy rather than distance was in demand. The shortness of the course, the smallness of the greens and the strong winds can make this tough going."

When the tide is high, the walk along the river holes (four, five and six) is so spectacular that sometimes it's dificult to keep one's eye on the ball. Hewins claims the course can be a tyrant or friendly, depending mostly on the weather and the tricky winds that can come into play. In season, tee times can be scarce, and a round is no longer 25 cents, but more like fifty bucks—but hey, that's progress. Or is it?

When a breeze whips the Bass River in the winter, it can be pretty raw—but loyalists here grin and bear it. This photo was shot from the tee box of the number one hole, the second easiest on the front nine—a par three.

Photos courtesy of Tom Martin, Publisher, The Little Black Book of Golf

A Short Bass River History

1900—Bass River Golf Club established on pasture land leased from two local families, Kelleys and Croswells. Green fees were 25 cents for nine holes, and caddies were paid 25 cents as well.

1914—Donald Ross remodels course on 105 acres.

1920—The Club buys the leased property plus 11 adjoining acres. Total cost—$11,386.

1921—James Shepherd, Jr.—first pro; 145 members; Green fees—$1.50.

1944—Hurricane devastates course.

1953—Town of Yarmouth buys course from the Charles Davis estate for $85,000.

1957—Clubhouse burns and is replaced. Holes are realigned.

1959—Don Deay, Director of Golf, started caddying here, age ten.

1969—Automatic sprinklers installed.

1971—Membership reaches 710. New members limited to Yarmouth residents and tax payers.

Tees	Par	Yards	Slope	USGA
Blue	72	6129	115	68.5
White	72	5734	107	66.5
Red	72	5343	115	69.9

ELLINWOOD COUNTRY CLUB

1928 PLEASANT AVENUE, ATHOL, MA 01331
(978) 249-7460   FAX: (978) 249-8978

DIRECTIONS: FROM ROUTE 2, TAKE EXIT 17. TURN RIGHT AND GO 1/2 MILE TO WOODLAWN ROAD. TAKE WOODLAWN ONE MILE TO COURSE.

Semi-private. 18 holes. Open April 15 to November 1. Cart and pullcart rental. Pro shop. Putting green. Chipping practice area. Snack bar.

"Golfers used to be made on the golf courses; now they're made in the machine shops."

Donald Ross

Welcome to Ellinwood

Cornish has integrated the remaining holes extremely well, adding to the total golf experience.

Interestingly, no two holes are precisely side by side, and each hole has its own unique character. The par four signature hole, number 11, measures 311 yards from the blues. From an elevated tee, you hit to a wide landing area. However, the key to this hole is the approach. The green slopes toward the water, and the ball is nearly impossible to stop, once it gets rolling on the dance floor.

Ellinwood has been called by a newspaper reporter, "A gem that shimmers." An hour away from Worcester, it is well worth the drive to experience nine of Ross' finest along with the other nine by designer Jeffrey Cornish in 1969, who took his cue from Ross. Holes one, two, three, seven, eight, nine, ten, 11 and 13 are just as Ross designed them, and

Your only chance is to play it below or parallel to the hole; if you're above the pin, it's big trouble. Thank you, Mr. Ross!

The 175 yard, par three eighth features a two-tiered green, measuring 18 yards across by 15 deep. It is surrounded by three bunkers, and the visually intimidating 416 yard, par four 15th hole challenges the intrepid golfer to lay up in front of a pond and hit a blind second shot that goes straight downhill to the putting surface.

This part of Massachusetts was originally named Pequoiag by the settlers after the name of the Indians who lived here. It acquired its present name when John Murray, one of the early proprietors of the land, chose the name because it reminded him of his ancestral home in Blair-Atholl, Scotland. Over the centuries, this town of 33 square miles has changed from primarily agricultural to a center of manufacturing.

In 1919, it was said to be "a clean, thriving, hustling manufacturing town of 12,000 people—and growing. Beautifully located in the valley through which winds the Millers River, in a country abounding with gently sloping hills, the town is 570 feet above sea level."

At that time, there were 18 manufacturing firms in the town, giving work to more than 3,700 people. It had four newspapers, three hospitals and six hotels. It was certainly time for a golf course, when Donald Ross was hired in 1920 to design nine holes.

In a recent article in the *Telegram & Gazette,* the reporter stated that the tees were in great shape, and that you will not find greens in better condition. He commented that they are, in typical Ross mode: "Small, well-protected, kitchen-floor-fast greens, some of which are crowned." Surprisingly, only the 13th fairway is sand bunkered.

A meandering stream on the par four number 11 signature hole can cause trouble here. The good news—no bunkers on this hole; the bad news—large rocks one hundred yards from the flag in the middle of the fairway.

Tees	Par	Yards	Slope	USGA
Blue	71	6207	123	69.5
White	71	5737	119	68.8
Red	72	5047	118	69.1

DIRECTIONS: FROM BOSTON, TAKE RTE. 93 SOUTH. AT EXIT 10 GO SOUTH TO MILTON ST., TURN LEFT. TURN AT BROOK RD. AND GO 2.5 MILES TO MATTIPAN SQUARE. TURN LEFT ONTO RIVER ST. AND GO TWO MILES TO WEST ST. TURN RIGHT AND ENTRANCE IS ON RIGHT.

Public with members. 18 holes. Open year round. Weekdays—first come, first served. Tee times may be reserved; call Tues. for Sat. and Wed. for Sun. Pro shop opens 6 AM. Rental gas and pullcarts and clubs. Snack bar. Putting green. Chipping and sand practice areas. Teaching pro. Snack bar.

Below: Few public courses in America can match the beauty and natural grandeur of George Wright.

1931 City of Boston Park Department contract to carry out Donald Ross' plan, reveals the magnitude of the construction project. Here are just some of the engineer's specifications:
1. Trees and stumps to be removed—2000
2. Various sizes of pipe for drains, culverts, water—41,552 linear feet
3. Earth excavation—29,000 cu. yds
4. Stone and ledge excavation—15,000 cu. yds
5. Rock, fill and loam quantities—129,800 cu. yds
6. Fairways to be prepared for loam and seeded—5 acres.

I t is a pleasure to find a mature public facility as well preserved as George Wright. A venerable bent grass course with inviting, mature tree-lined fairways, the particularly small greens demand carefully executed approach shots. *Golfweek*'s "America's Best Courses" ranks George Wright 11th in the nation of best municipal courses. Also on a list of 30 are Mark Twain and Mill Park, South Course—all by Donald Ross.

George Wright was one of the federal government's WPA project courses, built during the height of the Depression. A look at the 45-page,

Ross laid it out with water hazards on four of the back nine: number 12 where a stream is positioned just in front of the green; 17, a short par three, where the water is directly in front of the tees; 16, where the stream is tucked just behind the hole; and 18, where a stream meanders across the fairway starting on the right side about 60 yards out and ending up close to the left side of the green. A small pond between the 12th and 13th fairways captures an occasional mis-hit Titleist.®

Attesting to its quality is the fact that the 1999 USGA Public Links Qualifying was held here.

It was a page for the history books, as two new course records were established on the same day— a 64 and then a 63!

Who Was George Wright?

There are two Donald Ross courses named after famous baseball players: Rogell in Detroit, named after the World Series winning Detroit Tigers shortstop ('30 to '39), Billy Rogell, and George Wright, honoring the diminutive fellow (he stood only 5 foot 9 and weighed 150 pounds, but was a dreaded slugger) who played shortstop for the Cincinnati Red Stockings and later the Boston Red Stockings. From the 1860s to the '70s, he was undoubtedly the best player in the nation, consistently on championship teams and even managing one. His lifetime career totals tell the story: batting average—.256, with 59 home runs hit with the undefeated Red Stockings of 1869.

He founded Wright and Ditson, a successful sporting goods equipment manufacturer, and was instrumental both in making tennis popular in the States and in introducing Canadian ice hockey to this country. The National League issued him Pass No. 1, and he was a frequent guest at major league games after his retirement. He was named to the Baseball Hall of Fame and died in 1937 at the age of 90.

The City of Boston honored him by naming the golf course after this great athlete who generously donated this land to the city "for recreational purposes."

Photo by Bob Labbance

A golf writer dubbed this "Pinehurst North." Those are serious bunkers!

George Wright

Photo courtesy National Baseball Hall of Fame Library, Cooperstown, NY

Tees	Par	Yards	Slope	USGA
Blue	70	6440	126	69.5
White	70	6096	123	68.6
Red	69	5131	115	70.3

A large, inviting green in pristine condition awaits the George Wright player.

The built-to-last clubhouse at George Wright

Photo by Bob Labbance

Pinehurst, No. Carolina,
February 14, 1931.

Mr. W. F. Rogers,
Transcript Office,
324 Washington St.,
Boston, Mass.

Dear Mr. Rogers:-

      This will acknowledge receipt of your letter of February 6th.

      With reference to the proposed 18 hole golf course on the Redman Farm at Blue Hills Reservation, I should be very glad indeed to layout and design the course. My usual charge for such work is $2,500.00 but I will agree to do this work for $2,000.00.

      I will require a general plan of the property on a scale of one inch equals one hundred feet and contours at five foot intervals to be supplied by the Commonwealth of Massachusetts. After the course is laid out I will submit a general plan of the whole layout and also individual plans and specifications for each hole. It would be necessary for me to visit the property and make a study on the field and I should be glad to do this at anytime you wish.

      Mr. Walter B. Hatch, my Associate, who is located at North Amherst, Mass., expects to call on you and he will be very glad to give you any advice you may desire.

      Thanking you for writing me and trusting I can be of service.

Yours very truly,

Donald Ross.

DJR/N

THE WRITTEN RECORD

Fortunately for the golf historian, literally reams of Donald Ross' business and personal correspondence have been preserved and are in the possession and safekeeping of the Tufts Archives. This is located in a separate wing of the quaint Given Memorial Library, located on the Village Green at Pinehurst. It rests on land generously provided to Pinehurst by the Tufts family. Nearby is Ross' beloved Village Chapel.

Typed on a manual typewriter, often with grammatical errors and misspellings, these letters and hand-written notes provide an accurate insight into the business acumen and personal foibles of the pioneer of golf architecture. They reveal his high sense of business ethics, love of the game of golf and his concepts of good sportsmanship.

They picture his love of family and deep loyalty to his employers, the Tufts family members, with whom he worked for so many years in creating what is today the so-called "Golf Capital of the World." They show the reader what his day-to-day activities were like.

One day he might be writing a proposal for a new course, the next he'd be sending detailed and often pointed instructions to his on-site staff, the next he'd be specifying a mixture of seed for a newly constructed fairway. He'd not only describe the variety of seed he wanted used, but he'd give specific information on suppliers and prices. The same for fertilizers. No detail was too tiny to miss his attention. The letter shown here from February 14, 1931 is typical of his businesslike writing style and precise content. His fee here: $2,000 to layout and design Ponkapoag!

Often he'd involve himself in club management matters, like the time he recommended to Mr. Tufts, (he never called him by his first name!) that a priest, Father Sheedy, be removed from the membership roles at Mid Pines. Why? Seems the good father cheated on his tournament score cards.

The authors have also been generously provided with extensive Ross correspondence files from several public courses in Boston and Elmira. They consistently reveal his careful attention to the minutiae of the golf business. The result of this passion for perfection and a conscientious attention to every element is now to be seen on over 300 courses still here for the playing.

Source: Commonwealth of Massachusetts Metropolitan District Commission

DIRECTIONS: FROM MASS PIKE, TAKE EXIT 2 ONTO RTE. 20. TURNS INTO W. PARK ST. PASS STOP SIGN AND GO 1/2 MILE TO COURSE ON RIGHT.

Semi-private. Nine holes. Plays to 18. Open April 15 to October 15. Rental gas and pullcarts. Tee times, two days in advance. Member tee times, five days in advance. Pro shop opens 7 AM. Putting green. Chipping practice area.. Teaching pro. Two clay tennis courts. 19th hole and banquet facilities.

Below: The par three, 184 yard seventh hole, with four lethal bunkers around the green, seen from the elevated tee box

The quaint New England town of Lee, listed in the *National Register of Historic Places*, is located in the heart of the Berkshire Mountains. In its early history, with its factories, it was known as a "working man's town."

There is lots going on in Lee, including activities at scenic Laurel Lake and the October Mountain State Forest. For the family member who likes to shop, Lee offers a 65-store Prime Outlets operation.

Each year the town celebrates its birthday with a gala event during the first week of October. *Founders Weekend* is alive with music, living history, contests and a parade—a great time for the fall golfer to schedule several rounds here.

Although only nine holes, Greenock carries with it great prestige. The bent grass course was recently rated the number one nine-hole course in the state by the Massachusetts Golf Association. According to the USGA, it is one of the first one hundred clubs established in the United States.

Seven of Ross' original holes remain intact and are only slightly hilly. Holes one and seven have new tees, and all the bunkers are exactly as Ross placed them. The well-manicured greens are elevated and undulating. There are no homes on the course, so the mountain views are uninhibited. In the fall, when the Berkshires are alive with color, Greenock is at its very best.

The fact that Greenock remains as a nine hole course attests to the sentiment Ross expressed that "Some tracts are admirable for nine holes, but make abominable 18 hole courses."

The par three second hole, 168 yards off the men's, 157 off the ladies'

The view from the par four number eight tees...the number five handicap hole. A well bunkered dance floor beckons.

Tees	Par	Yards	Slope	USGA
Men's	70	6027	120	68.9
Ladies	74	5686	123	72.2

MERRIMACK GOLF COURSE

210 HOWE STREET, METHUEN, MA 01844
(978) 685-9717 FAX: (978) 725-3699 E-MAIL: KATTAR@MEDIAONE.NET

DIRECTIONS: ROUTE 93 NORTH TO ROUTE 213. TAKE EXIT 3, PLEASANT STREET. TURN LEFT TO HOWE STREET. TURN LEFT TO COURSE, ABOUT 3/4 MILES.

Semi-private. 18 holes. Pro shop opens 6 AM. Open April 1 to November 30. Rental gas, pullcarts and clubs. Putting green. Chipping and sand practice areas. Snack bar.

The par three, 213 yard seventh—the longest and narrowest par three hole at Merrimack

Most towns and cities have namesakes somewhere in the world, but no one has ever found another town besides this one that is called Methuen. It was named for Lord Methuen, an English noble friend of Colonial Governor Dummer. In its long history, its most famous resident was Robert Rogers, who gained recognition as the leader of Rogers' Rangers. Once spilling over into both Massachusetts and New Hampshire, its borders now are limited to just Massachusetts. Shaped like a butterfly, the town covers 22 square miles of gentle rolling hillsides, covered with picturesque farms and orchards.

The bent grass course, located in Essex County in the beautiful Merrimack Valley, has been host to the YMCA annual golf tournament for several years. It is also a revolving host of the Lawrence Eagle Tribune Rogers Tournament for the best amateurs in the area. Nearby golfers from New Hampshire join their Bay State neighbors in utilizing the fine facilities found here, which feature fairways with mature tree growth and a minimum amount of water on holes one, ten, 11 and 12.

From the clubhouse, the golfer has fine views of all or parts of 14 holes, and no two holes are the same. All of the holes with the exception of one, 11 and 18 are unchanged from when Ross put them in.

Around 1930, Walter Hagen, who had been paid to play for the crowd, lost a match by two strokes to the club pro, David Hackenney. Always a good sport, Hagen commented afterwards, "I would love to play here all the time. The scenery was magnificent." And it still is.

Most recent famous players include Willie Nelson, Bill Russell and Phil Esposito. Many of the Celtics and Bruins play here regularly.

The seventh hole, 213 yards off the blues to a small green, is surrounded by woods on the left, a 20 yard fairway approach, two banked slopes and water on the right. (A prayer to the golf gods may—or may not—help on this one.) Several golf magazines have named it one of the toughest par threes in America.

Tom Clarke, one of the oldest members, relates that when the club began, the pro wasn't allowed in the clubhouse; he could only go in if invited. He further recalls that when he caddied (1931 to 1935 at the height of the Depression) Class A caddies were paid 85 cents a round; Class B received 75 cents and Class C, 65 cents. For one bag, 18 holes. No tipping was allowed.

In those days, the fairways were only about 75 yards wide with very high rough. There were 125 caddies every day at the course. A membership in 1953 was $67 a year with $10 increases thereafter. In the '50s, caddies were allowed to play on Mon-

From the 11th tee, overlooking the first fairway to the number six, par four, 417 yard challenge. This is the number one handicap here. The drive must stay left for a long iron shot to a small green with two good-sized front bunkers.

day until noon, at which time many of the Massachusetts pros played the course in the afternoon.

In 1937, lightning struck the fifth fairway and it burned for two years. It is said that you could walk on it and feel the heat of the earth below. The fairway fell two to three feet. The clubhouse burned down in 1969, and in 1971 George and Phyllis Kattar bought the club at auction. Their family has run it ever since.

Tees	Par	Yards	Slope	USGA
Blue	71	6220	120	69.3
White	71	5871	117	67.7
Red	73	5151	116	72.3

TWO "GENTLE" MEN OF GOLF:
DONALD ROSS AND FRANCIS OUIMET

Francis de sales Ouimet won the U.S. Open at age 20, (accompanied by 10-year-old caddie, Eddie Lowery). He was America's first golf hero, having won the British Open by defeating Britons Harry Vardon and Ted Ray. To many it was the turning point for U.S. golf. Two years later, in 1915 he is shown in the above photo standing next to Alec Ross, (fourth from the left) with fellow Tin Whistle members, McLeod, Sullivan, Clark, and Shannon. Ouimet is second from Donald Ross on the far right. Ross and Ouimet remained lifelong friends.

Ross admired Ouimet's commitment to amateur golf. Francis won two U.S. Amateur titles in 1914 and 1931 and was runner up in 1920 and semi-finalist on six other occasions. He earned eight Walker Cup caps (1922-34), and was four times Walker Cup non-playing captain, ('36-'49). Few today recall that the USGA banned Ouimet from amateur competition in '16 because he had operated a sports goods business in Boston where golfing equipment was sold! The more tolerant Western Golfing Association thumbed its nose at the stuffy USGA and invited Francis to compete in its '17 Amateur Championship. He won and was soon drafted into the Army. He never felt animosity toward the USGA, joining the American Walker Cup Team in '22, and was a player and captain for 27 years. In 1951 he became the first of our countrymen elected Captain of the Royal and Ancient Golf Club of St. Andrews. He was elected to the Golf Hall of Fame, and is one of only three golfers to be featured on a U.S. commemorative postage stamp. The U.S. Senior Trophy is named after him.

In 1949, a group of his friends started the Francis Ouimet Caddie Scholarship Fund. At the time of this writing it has helped 3,600 needy caddies and course employees go to college, and this year it will award $800,000.

It is nice to note that its benefit golf outings are often held on Donald Ross courses: Belmont, Essex, Longmeadow, Newport, Oyster Harbors, Salem, Tedesco, Ridge, Weston, Vesper and Worcester. Like Ross he was self-effacing, believing the caddie fund to be his greatest honor. He died on September 2, 1967 at the age of 74.

Photo courtesy of The Tin Whistles, Pinehurst, NC

NEW SANDY BURR COUNTRY CLUB

103 Cochituate Road, Wayland, MA 01778
(508) 358-7211   Fax: (508) 358-2359   E-Mail: kmk88@aol.com
Website: www.sandyburr.com

Directions: From Boston, take 128 south. Take exit 26 (rte. 220) west. Turn left on Rte. 27. Course is 1/2 mile on the right.

Semi-private. 18 holes. Open April 1 to November 15. Public play limited to after 12:46 on weekends. Pro shop opens 6 AM. Rental gas and pullcarts. Putting green. Teaching pro. Restaurant. Golfers Lounge. Barbara Room. Snack bar. Fireside Room. Banquet facilities.

Thousands of mature trees are a hallmark of the course

Originally called Sandy Burr Country Club, this Middlesex County bent grass course lies on land that is rolling and inviting to play, with aged trees along the fairways and good sized greens. Giving the course an almost English countryside feel is the large and well-constructed Tudor clubhouse, which can seat 250 guests.

The great early American golfer, Francis Ouimet, Walter Hagen and Gene Sarazen were frequent players here. The 1935 Massachusetts Open was played at Sandy Burr. As the aerial photograph attests, the well-maintained, wide open fairways are lined with mature trees.

The modern courses rarely ascribe special names to the holes, but many of the older courses manage to entertain the golfer with quaint names. The holes at New Sandy Burr were known as: Down and Out, River Bound, Air Line, The Saucer, Spoon Carry, Trap Hill, Triangle, Old Elbow, Round Top, The Scoop, Rocking Chair, Sudbury Shore, Trouble Inlet, Lone Tree, Apple Hollow, The Narrows, String Bean and Hillside—almost descriptive enough to replace photos.

The course was host to the New England Professional Golfers' Association championship, in July of 1924, when an international return match between Archie Compston (called "Britain's leading professional" at the time) and Walter C. Hagen ("The British Open Champion and American Professional Champion") received widespread publicity. (The cover of the souvenir program is shown here.) The second 36 holes of the Compston-Hagen match was held at the Westchester-Biltmore course in Rye, New York. Bob

Dunbar, in his newspaper column at the time, called the match the "Battle of the Century."

Several years before, Johnny Farrell played Lagerblade and Stait in a match entitled, "New England Vs. the World." It was for 36 holes, and New England won. Then, two years later, Hagen and Ouimet were brought together in a memorable encounter in which they played 18 holes on each of two consecutive afternoons with Ouimet winning handily seven and five.

In 1921, Sandy Burr originated the New England Left Hand Championship, after the course had been designated by the Massachusetts Golf Association as one of the few courses in the state "best suited for championship events."

There are few golf course water views in New England to match this.

"Caddies wanted an increase in standard pay, something like a dime more to the 50 cent, double fee. The oldest caddie approached Ross, who was standing on the clubhouse steps with his ever-present seven iron in hand. The question was begged; Ross asked what the alternative could be. The caddie replied that the crew would strike. Ross then hit him on the head with the golf club and declared. 'The strike is over!' True? One never knows about these things. A tight man with a nickle—he might have been even tighter with a dime."—Dick Taylor, Golf World, June, 1989

Tees	Par	Yards	Slope	USGA
Blue	72	6412	125	70.8
White	72	6229	122	69.9
Red	69	4561	110	66.2

Above: It's a bit hilly, but a walk will do you good! A Ross course, like a fine wine, improves with age.

Wide fairways and glorious fairways beckon at New Sandy Burr Country Club

Photos by Bob Labbance

212 KENRICK STREET, NEWTON, MA 02458
(617) 630-1971   FAX: (617) 969-8756
E-MAIL: INFO@STERLINGGOLF.COM   WEBSITE: WWW.STERLINGGOLF.COM

DIRECTIONS: FROM ROUTE 128 BOSTON, TAKE EXIT 23 COMMONWEALTH AVE. WEST. TURN LEFT ON LAKE STREET TO FOURTH LEFT ON KENRICK. ENTRANCE IS 1/2 MILE ON LEFT.

Public. 18 holes. Open year round. Rental drive and pullcarts and clubs. Locker rooms. Snack bar. Public starting time 4 days in advance. Pro shop open 6 AM. Teaching pro. Putting green. Managed by Sterling Golf Management and owned by the City of Newton.

Below: The par four, 378 yard (from the blues) 13th hole from the green looking toward the elevated tee. On the opposite page, you'll see the water awaiting the short fairway shot. This number four handicap green has water on three sides and a bunker on the fourth—steady as she goes!

This was, in its early years, the home course of Donald Ross. It was originally organized as a nine-hole course called the Commonwealth Club, and was a spin-off of the old Allston Golf Club. Annual dues were $20, and a round of golf was 25 cents! Ross, who lived in nearby Newton Centre, redesigned it into an 18-hole course in 1920.

In its over 100 year history, Babe Ruth, Ty Cobb and Sam Snead were among the hundreds of famous golfers to attack the course.

Today, as then, Newton is a rare diamond of a bent grass course, narrow with small greens. It is always in top condition, and the player will find that holes two, five, seven and 13 are exactly as Ross designed them. In recent years, Sterling Golf Management has added many upgrades and taken significant beautifica-

Above: The number two hole from the green looking toward the tee. This is a par five hole, playing 533 off the blues, with a pond to the right of the tee box—don't slice! It's the number one handicap hole at Newton Commonwealth—and deservedly so.

tion steps to make it a fabulous public facility. Many tees have been rebuilt and bunkers renovated. There are water hazards to keep it interesting. It has been chosen as the site of the Ladies State Public Links Qualifier Tournament.

The number two hole is a beaut, measuring 476 yards off the whites. A frightening tee shot awaits here. Out-of-bounds runs tightly along the left, while a pushed tee shot will invariably find the pond on the right. If the golfer finds the fairway, the second shot is usually from a downhill, sidehill lie. A stream running diagonally must now be negotiated. Once safely in the fairway for the third shot (this hole is reachable in two by only the longest hitters), the golfer is faced with an uphill shot to a quick, canted green. Certain pin placements put a strain on the very best of short games. This is obviously the number one handicap hole, and a bogey here, early in your round, can make recovery difficult. A birdie can produce an early boost of confidence, and par is considered excellent on this killer hole.

Number 14 is no picnic either. From the blues, this is the toughest driving hole on the course. Tall trees protect the out-of-bounds line on the right, and two ponds lay directly in front of the tee. A stream connects the second pond with yet another pond about 220 yards from the tee. A straight, long tee ball is imperative to success. Once again, there is sufficient trouble behind the green to snare the golfer who lets down his guard on this number two handicap hole.

Final warning: many a tournament has been won or lost on number 17, a short-to-medium par three. The problem here is two-fold: out-of-bounds squeezes the left fairway, and anything even remotely right will go down a very severe slope onto the 15th fairway behind some evergreens. Play this hole with care and caution.

Tees	Par	Yards	Slope	USGA
Blue	70	5336	125	67.0
White	70	5009	122	66.0
Red	70	4349	118	69.4

PETERSHAM COUNTRY CLUB

1922

240 North Main Street, PO Box 35, Petersham, MA 01366
(978) 724-3388   Fax: (978) 724-0265   E-mail: PETERSHAMCC@YAHOO

Directions: Take Route 2. Exit at #17 and turn right onto Route 32. Club is just two miles on the left.

Semi-private. Nine holes. Plays to 18. Open seven days a week. Tee times 24 hours in advance. Open April 1 to November 1. Rental gas and pullcarts. Clubhouse. Lockers. Showers. Putting green. Chipping and sand practice areas. Teaching pro. Snack bar.

Above: Wide fairways grace the approach to the 438 yard number four. The large bunker on the right can usually be avoided. Don't slice here.

Petersham Country Club is a fine Ross bent grass course in a beautiful part of Massachusetts. It boasts a long history of distinguished golfers, including J. R. Starrett, the motion pictures' Durango Kid.

Holes fours, five, six and eight are exactly the way Ross designed them, although greens on holes one, two, three and seven have been modified. The second green was moved back, and the third green was reshaped in 1972 and again in 1993. The seventh green was reshaped in 1995 and in 1997. Nine has been moved about 100 yards toward the clubhouse, after the barn that formerly housed the locker rooms was razed. But the feel of the course is Ross all the way. Only on hole two (the seven handicap hole, a par three that plays from 164 yards to 209 yards), does the player find water to contend with, and here Ross placed it right in front of the green across the entire fairway. Although situated in a heavily wooded area, the fairways are not encumbered by trees, with only a few exceptions. Most of the fairways are rela-tively straight with slight doglegs on five (the only par five hole on the course) and six.

The clubhouse has been remodeled over the years, with major improvements to the kitchen and locker rooms.

construction payroll—$7,563; construction supplies—$240.74; *golf architect—$470.22.* The grand total came to only $8,274.72

Work was resumed the next spring, and in October construction was completed. The farmhouse had been remodeled for a clubhouse and had been fitted with plumbing and showers. Lockers could be rented for $2 a day, and in February, 1924, a house was built for the greenkeeper; the rooms he had been using were turned into a members' club room. The course was formally opened on July 4, 1924. On that Independence Day, a tournament was played, and a pro was hired. Greens fees for members were $2 a day or $10 a week. At the time, any person, though not accompanied by a member, who could satisfy the clerk that his residence was within 20 miles from the Petersham Town Hall, upon signing the register book at the first tee and paying $3, could play for the day.

In a letter dated February 18, 1925 from President John Woolsey, the members were informed that annual receipts were $12,095.68 and disbursements were the same. The letter also informed members that $3,000 would have to be borrowed to maintain the club.

Clubs that had their start in the '20s, particularly those with small memberships, had great difficulty surviving. Petersham was no exception, but fortunately its members persevered through the Depression and war, and the club managed to stay alive. Today it remains a small classic.

History

In 1922, Petersham Country Club Corporators were formed, with shares selling for $100 each. Total shares were 105, for a total of $10,500. Donald Ross was hired to design the course, with Walter B. Hatch as his site engineer. The original course layout was to be located on both sides of Route 32, but a land swap was made with a Mrs. Wilder so the nine holes could be built on the east side of the road so golfers wouldn't have to cross in front of speeding Model T Fords.

There was an average of 20 men and six teams of horses on the job between October 1 and November 25, when work had to stop because of the weather. All the greens with adjacent bunkers were built and graded, ready for topsoil and seeding. Trees and brush were cut on all fairways. Most of the stone walls were moved, and the greater part of the boulders were blasted away. The main expenses to January, 1923 were:

Above left: The only water on the course is on hole number two, a 209 yard par three from the blues.

Tee	Par	Yards	Slope	USGA
White/Blue	70	6007	68.4	118
White/Yellow	70	5486	64.6	114
Red/Yellow	72	5053	64.4	112

PLYMOUTH COUNTRY CLUB

WARREN AVENUE, PO BOX 3447, PLYMOUTH, MA 10261
(508) 746-780 FAX: (508) 746-9875
WEBSITE: WWW.GEOCITIES.COM/PLYMOUTHCC

DIRECTIONS: FROM BOSTON, TAKE RTE. 3 SOUTH. TURN LEFT AT EXIT 4. GO RIGHT ON WARREN AVE. THE COURSE IS AT THIS INTERSECTION.

18 holes. Semi-private. Open May 1 to October 31. Electric and pullcart rental. Clubhouse. Pro shop. Restaurant. Snack bar. Putting green. Chipping and sand practice areas.

Below: The seventh hole is tree lined with out-of-bounds to the left and one of the most difficult greens to putt since there are no flat areas anywhere. Anything long or left is trouble. Although this is the tenth handicap, it is one of the most challenging, measuring 344 yards from the gold tees.

An old-timer, Mr. John P. English, waxes poetic about the course as he played it when a child in the early 1900s. He says, "As a little tyke of about ten years, I started taking lessons three mornings a week from a very fine player, Donald Vinton, who, in spite of his tiny stature, won the state Open in 1926. Another active player of the era was Judge Webster Thayer, who achieved prominence through his handling of the Sacco-Vanzetti case. Judge Thayer encouraged all of us neophyte golfers and gave me the first four golf clubs that were truly mine and not borrowed.

"A small golf shop sat beside the first tee, and it had some distinguished occupants such as the Picard brothers. Henry Picard eventually joined the early PGA tour and won both the PGA Championship and the Masters Tournament in 1938."

Today, the 180 acre course is situated among rolling hills and tree-lined fairways, with 46 bunkers and greens averaging 3,000 to 4,000 square feet. Each June golfers gather to watch the prestigious Hornblower Memorial tournament.

Here is a course Ross would have been proud to call one of his own, as it exists today. Serious Ross enthusiasts feel a sense of awe, combined with just a bit of intimidation, as they realize that the overall course is 85 to 90% untouched—just as he designed it. Indeed, Allen Tassinari, Green Chairman, estimates holes four through 18 are original Ross.

He did his initial work here in 1927, and additional work seven years later. Ross' original training as a greenkeeper is reflected in the natural look of the roughs and plantings of shrubs and native new England grasses. The emblem of the Audubon Cooperative System is prominently displayed, evidence of management's and board's dedication to preserving the environment in this earth-friendly place.

A member of the Donald Ross Society, upon playing here, commented, "I would recommend that the Board of Governors draft an amendment to the by-laws of the Plymouth Country Club that any alternation to the course be restored to the Ross design." He felt that any updating or modernization would only detract from the authenticity of this classic.

Above: This long, sweeping "roller coaster" fairway with the green in the distance is the signature hole, number 12. The longest par four (449 yards off the gold tees), it is surrounded by tall pines and oaks. The sloping green brings woe to many a putter hoping for a par. The authors do not rate Ross courses, but if they did, this would have to be in their top ten for its sheer beauty.

"Plymouth is a course which should serve to make you play splendid shots. I consider it one of the best 18-hole courses in New England. The last nine holes of the course are better than the first nine and call for an exhibition of skill that is not excelled in any other course. The only weak hole in the last nine, to my way of thinking, is the 17th and possibly the 18th green. I do not care for holes that have greens sloping away from your shot. Such holes call for too much luck and too little skill."

Francis D. Ouimet
Brighton, MA

Tees	Par	Yards	Slope	USGA
Gold	69	6228	125	70.0
Blue	69	5887	121	68.6
Women's White	71	5299	125	71.1

PONKAPOAG GOLF COURSE

2167 WASHINGTON STREET, CANTON, MA 02021
(781) 575-1001   FAX: (781) 828-1526

DIRECTIONS: GO NORTH ON RTE. 128. TAKE EXIT 2A AND GO SOUTH FOR 3/4 MILE. ENTRANCE ON THE LEFT.

Public. 36 holes. Open April 1 to Nov. 15. Rental gas, pullcarts and clubs. Driving range. Putting green. Chipping practice area. Pro shop. Teaching pro. Restaurant.

Below: The 18th hole on Course One

Boston is a city of enlightenment, and one of its brightest lights is its Metropolitan Park System. Created in 1893, it was the first regional system of public open space established in America. It was a response to the turn-of-the-century regional land use concerns, explosive and unfettered metropolitan growth and the social issues related to that growth. In the words of Charles Eliot, landscape architect and driving force of the park system, it was created to preserve and manage "the rockhills, stream banks, bay and seashore for present and future generations. It is now managed by the MDC, the Metropolitan District Commission. It includes ocean beach, island, rivers, parkways, the Hatch Shell, bike paths, ski area, tennis courts, rinks, pools, playgrounds and let's not forget—golf courses.

In 1931, a year when Arthur Fiedler was directing 23 Boston Pops Concerts on the Esplanade, a special act was passed authorizing the construction of an 18-hole golf course with locker facilities. The MDC voted to name it Ponkapoag Golf Course.

In June of 1931, Donald Ross was hired by the MDC to lay out, design and supervise construction of an 18-hole course at Redman Farm in Blue Hills Reservation. The entire cost for the facility: $80,000. The first nine holes opened for play in July, 1932.

The Redman Farm consisted of 155 acres, with deeds dating back to pre-Revolutionary times, and the land had been under cultivation for nearly 250 years. In a letter to the MDC dated May 28, 1932, Ross wrote, "It is one of the most attractive courses in New England, both from a scenic and golfing standpoint. It is not too difficult for the high handicap player, and it has such a variety of golf shots that the better class of players will always enjoy playing over it. My belief is that it will prove to be very successful and enjoyable." On November 22, 1935, the Commission advised Ross that it was "authorized to accept his proposal of an additional nine-hole course layout for the sum of $1,000."

It was very popular, with 18,000 rounds of golf played that season. On July 1, 1933, the second nine holes opened for play. In that year, 27,000 rounds were played. In those days, a seasonal membership cost $20.

That same year, MDC records show "Request of Reverend R.B. Setup that clergymen be allowed to play golf without charge." This was deemed "inadvisable."

Donald Ross also designed a nine-hole pitch and putt course, or as he called it a "caddies' playground." It was never constructed. Ross had wanted it included because, as a report in the *Boston Evening Transcript* reported: "He believed in looking after the interests of the younger generation, of trying to do things which will keep the boys interested and which will tend to elevate them. He considers the caddie playground idea is one of the best mediums. It will give the bag toters something to occupy their minds and employ their hands while waiting for a job. He doesn't want them shooting craps or indulging in other time-wasting pursuits of no elevating order."

In 1935, Ross designed an additional nine holes, and it was constructed by labor supplied by the WPA. In 1936, play had risen to 38,700 rounds.

From 1938 to 1940 a second WPA project was begun to install a complete fairway and greens watering system for the entire 27 holes.

The final nine holes were laid out by William S. Mitchell, creating two separate 18-hole courses. This was built in 1956-57 at a cost of $134,062. In 1961, five greens were reconstructed, and in 1997, the 13th tee was reconstructed.

This was the eighth public course Ross had built. He agreed to design Ponkapoag for $2,000. Later he agreed to revise the agreement to "lay out and design the 18-hole golf course and supervise its construction for the sum of $4,000." The MDC is now a diverse network of 32 interconnected parks and reservations embracing almost 20,000 acres in 37 of the cities and towns that compose the Boston metropolitan region.

Ponkapoag Today

In an article in the September 28, 2000 *Boston Globe,* by staff reporter Paul Harber, he claims that much of the famed course here is currently in bad condition. Harber writes that "many of the holes are simply unplayable." He attributes much of the deterioration of the course to "years of neglect by the state." Unfortunately, this is often the fate of public courses which have to compete with finely kept nearby private courses for player approbation or condemnation.

The article was prompted by the fact that a golfer contingent from the Walpole Country Club was so disturbed by the conditions at Ponkapoag that it cancelled a scheduled event at the course. The reporter points to the lower holes as being in the worst condition they've been in twenty years. He goes on to state that the "tees were playable and the greens a lot better than they were several years ago when we found dandelions growing on the green."

His assessment is that only major capital improvements, "such as rebuilding many of the fairways and adding water retention areas will improve things."

He points to the fact that "three days after a recent storm, the third hole was nearly under water. This is a Mona Lisa covered by mud. Yet," he adds, "if this course ever had financing equal to major private clubs, it would be among the best golf courses in America, public or private."

Below: The locker building/clubhouse in 1934. The professional building is in the rear.

Photo Courtesy MDC Archives, Boston, MA

Tees	Par	Yards	Slope	USGA
Blue	70	6394	123	72.7
White	70	5935	118	69.0
Red	71	5205	113	69.3

DIRECTIONS: TAKE MASS PIKE TO EXIT 3. GO RIGHT ON ROUTE 10-202 TO ROUTE 20 WEST. TEKOA IS TWO MILES DOWN ON THE RIGHT.

Semi-private. Public play by reservation. 18 holes. Open April 1 to November 30. Rental gas and pullcarts and clubs. Putting green. Chipping practice area. Shower and lockers. Pro shop opens 7:30 AM. weekdays and 7 AM weekends and holidays. Public play by reservation on weekends. Teaching pro. Grill and bar.

Below left: The par three, 155 yard hole number three is a straight shot to the green with a large pond to the left. Don't hook it here, please.

From the day of its founding, Westfield was the westernmost town in the Massachusetts Colony. During the late 19th century, it changed from an agricultural center to a major manufacturing hub, which it remains to this day. It is 85 miles from Albany, 99 miles from Boston and only 134 miles from New York City. Those who choose to fly in can do so via Barnes Municipal Airport, the third largest commercial airport in New England.

The town has an outstanding array of natural resources, includeing abundant rivers and streams, fertile farmland and scenic rolling hills. Famed Stanley Park is one of New England's most outstanding attractions, covering 180 acres of painstakingly tended land containing a 96 foot carillon, arboretum, floral gardens, fountains, a dining pavilion, Japanese garden with tea house, and summer concerts. The town is surrounded by first class camping sites in state forests and has four golf courses: East Mountain, Shaker Farms, Blandford and Tekoa.

Tekoa is at the foothills to the Berkshires and winds its way along the Westfield River down to the Connecticut River just above Agawam, providing stunning views along the way. In the fall, the trees are dressed in brilliant golds, and in the spring, when the river runs full, there is no more dramatic sight. Tall pines line the fairways, and the greens are larger than on many Ross courses. Water comes into play on five holes. On weekends and holidays, the course is open from 5:30 AM 'til dusk. Of the nine holes Ross designed, those remaining are: two, three, four, 14 and 15. If you like golf in the Berkshires, you'll savor Tekoa Country Club—a well-kept secret among its regulars.

Nearby attractions include: Tanglewood, Berkshire Music Festival, the Clark Art Institute (with 30 original Renoirs) in Williamstown, the National Basketball Hall of Fame in Springfield, Old Sturbridge Village and its Auto Museum.

Above: The 397 yard second hole is a par four for the men, five for the ladies. A stream runs to the right with a bunker beside it. A big bunker yawns to the left of the good-sized green.

Tees	Par	Yards	Slope	USGA
Blue	70	6002	118	69.6
White	70	5655	116	68.2
Red	74	5115	116	71.0

Above: The 335 yard 15th is a par four, with a sharp dogleg left, a bunker on the left at the curve, two bunkers in front of the green, and one behind for good measure. A gorgeous hole.

Photos by Bob Labbance

112

WACHUSETT COUNTRY CLUB

1927

187 PROSPECT STREET, WEST BOYLESTON, MA 01583
(508) 835-2264   FAX (508) 835-4911
WEBSITE: WWW.WACHUSETTCOUNTRYCLUB.COM

DIRECTIONS: FROM ROUTE 140 EAST, TURN LEFT ONTO ROUTE 12. MAKE FIRST RIGHT ONTO FRANKLIN STREET, TURN LEFT ON PROSPECT STREET. CLUB IS AT TOP OF HILL.

Semi-private. 18 holes. Pro shop opens 7 AM. Open April 1 to December 1. Rental gas, electric and pullcarts and clubs. Driving range. Putting green. Chipping and sand practice areas. Teaching pro on staff. Restaurant. Snack bar. Facilities for weddings, corporate outings, private and golf outings for 50 to 300.

Below: Late fall afternnoon shadows charm golfers at Wachusett Country Club

Located about five miles east of Worcester and just 45 minutes west of Boston, this bent grass Worcester County course is typical of Ross' designs in New England. It is situated on flat terrain, with wide open, tree-lined fairways and water hazards on five holes.

Significant improvement have been made in the past three years, and today the course plays in peak condition. It has been rated the "Ninth Best Public Course in Massachusetts" by *Golf Digest Magazine,* and was voted "Best Public Golf Course in Central Massachusetts" by the MGA.

In the early 1900s, the West Boyleston land selected by the Wachusett Country Club members was prime farm acreage belonging to the Frost family. What obviously appealed to these golfers were the breathtaking views, encompassing the majestic Mount Wachusett and the Meropolitan Reservoir.

With a talented architect, a great view and a fine layout of rolling hills, sudden valleys and a winding brook, it had to be a winner. Right? Wrong! The Great Depression put Wachusett on the ropes, as it did so many other fine private courses in America. Hard times befell Worcester and environs, and in 1939, creditors seized the course. Joseph Marrone, a successful entrepreneur from Worcester, came to its rescue, took control of the deteriorating business and began what was to be a real turnaround story. It is now a fourth generation family business.

After a good round of golf here, the player has great food options in the fine restaurant. In good weather, the golfer, filled with satisfaction after a great round, can relax on the 3,500 square foot deck that overlooks the first three holes and features a great view of the reservoir.

Above: A great Massachusetts course that has stood the test of time attests to the enduring qualities of the Donald Ross genius.

Left: Just the right weather for a round of golf— picture postcard perfection.

Tees	Par	Yards	Slope	USGA
Mens	72	6608	124	71.7
Ladies	73	6216	120	70.0

Above: Ross grew up on the water in Scotland, but didn't like too much of it on his courses. At Wachusett Country Club, it only comes into play on holes two and five, both par fives.

Photos by Bob Labbance

DIRECTIONS: *FROM ROUTE 95, TURN OFF AT HATHAWAY ROAD EXIT TO ENTRANCE.*

Public. 18 holes. When renovations are completed, the club will again be open to the public year round. Rental carts and clubs. Driving range.

Below: The number 15 hole, seen from the tee, a Ross original. Avoid that mean rough on the right. This hole will remain a par four of 345 yards from the blues, 325 from the reds.

This course, formerly Whaling City Country Club and New Bedford Municipal Golf Course, has been closed for a complete renovation, and is scheduled to open in spring, 2001. There will be a clubhouse, pro shop, locker rooms with showers, a lounge and restaurant. The restoration is under the management of Johnson Turf and Golf Management, Inc. of Weston, Massachusetts.

The careful reconstruction has been complicated by the fact that the course never had an adequate irrigation system in place. Doug Johnson is overseeing a complete new irrigation system installation. Tees are being renovated and fairways converted to bent grass with bunker restoration and new cart paths.

The new plans take into account stringent requirements of the Environmental Protection Agency. Fairways will remain unchanged for the most part, and all green locations will not be disturbed. Some bunkers will be totally rebuilt, and various cart paths will be modified. When Johnson first saw the course and played it, he must have scratched his head and asked himself, "How could a course have gotten in such bad shape?" But all that will soon be changed, and New Bedford is expected to become one of the finer courses to play in New England.

Although the original Ross plans for this course have been lost over the years, the careful restoration is being guided by old photographs and the recollections of old-timers who have played the course for years. The spirit of Donald Ross may be smiling right now as he watches everyone struggling long and hard here in New Bedford to put his creation back together again.

At one time, there was talk of using this precious land for a gambling casino. The local, and extremely vociferous, golfers must have been louder and more passionate about their sport than the slot players, because the city fathers opted to improve the course rather than see it become Trump City North. When finished, this will be a prime asset for this venerable city—a real shot in the arm for its growing renewal.

The course was built as a nine holer in 1920 by Donald Ross; a back nine was added in 1947, and in 1970 the course was modified to accommodate highway construction.

The goal of the current work is to restore the course to Ross's original layout. Holes 15 to 18 are his for certain, and 12, 13 and 14 are very likely as he built them. The remainder are in the "Ross mode" and retain his well-known characteristics.

Below: The newly created par four, number six hole. It features this raised, large green that will play roughly 370 yards from the blues and 326 from the reds.

About New Bedford

Arriving in New Bedford, one is greeted by the famous Bela Pratt Whaleman's Memorial, which pays tribute to the brave men who dared to challenge the world's oceans in search of nature's largest creatures. The large bronze and granite statue depicts a harpooner poised at the bow of a whaleboat with the profound inscription, *A Dead Whale or a Stove Boat,* testimony to the courage needed to crew aboard a whaler.

When dedicated in 1913, Captain George O. Baker, the oldest living whaling master, unveiled the statue. Historic New Bedford, with its cobblestone streets, is literally drenched in whaling history. The city's New Bedford Art Museum, housed in the former Vault Building, is a must for any visitor interested in the history of this colorful New England coastal town. President Clinton signed into law in 1996, an act creating the *New Bedford National Historic District,* a 13 block, 20 acre area that includes the Schooner *Ernestina,* Waterfront Park, the Rotch-Jones-Duff House and Garden Museum, the Warfinger Building and the Bourne Counting House. Here one finds fine examples of Greek Revival architecture, restored buildings, restaurants, the Whaling Museum, the Seamen's Bethel, the Rodman Candlewicks and the U.S. Custom House.

Tees	Par	Yards	Slope	USGA
Blue	72	6250	120	70.1
Red	74	5908	111	70.1

117

DIRECTIONS: FROM BOSTON TAKE HIGHWAY 93 SOUTH, EXIT COLUMBIA ROAD TO BLUE HILL AVE.

*Public. 18 holes. Pro shop opens at 5:30
AM. Open year round. Rental gas and pull-
carts and clubs. Putting green. Chipping area.
Pro on staff. Snack bar.*

The par four sixth tee taken in August when the wild flowers are in full blossom

Early to embrace the sport of golf, Dorchester is a city of many "firsts." It was the first town to support a public school by taxation, and was the site of the first town meeting, the first water and powder mills in this country, and even the site of the first supermarket.

Here in this still bucolic setting, one finds the second oldest golf course in America, originally called the Franklin Park Golf Course. When we began this book, we could find no written evidence to show that Ross did the actual design work here. We'd discovered a small reference to the course in the February 6, 1922 minutes of the City Council of Boston that reads: "A new layout for the Franklin Park links has been made by Mr. Duncan Ross. Part of it will be necessary to get an additional $5,000 to install a water supply, and to buy and lay sods for the new greens."

We thought this was a clerical error, and that "Duncan" was really "Donald," since no prominent course architect we've asked, nor has any golf authority we've contacted, ever heard of a Duncan Ross.

In an article by Alan Banks in *American Parks,* April 1993, he wrote, "City Engineer John J. Murphy reports that the work of the Samuel Tomsellow firm on the links was

The $3.4 million clubhouse, built in 1998, features a pro shop, comfortable lounge with fireplace and snack bar, state-of-the-art locker rooms and a 200 seat function facility.

done satisfactory and to specification—but whose specifications?   One of the more popular rumors that has been written as fact is that it was designed by Donald Ross, the great Scottish-American golf course architect.   Interestingly enough, the park commission *was* in contact with him during this period in regards to designing a course at the Grew Property near Stoney Brook."

Paul Harber, *Boston Globe* sports writer, recently wrote: "Many people erroneously believe that Donald Ross laid it out. He didn't." We disagree with Mr Harber. We believed it is reasonable to assume that Boston's park officials would have selected a famous golf architect to design a course at its "crown jewel" park and not entrust the assignment to an unknown by the name of *Duncan* Ross. (Khris Januzik, the Tuft's archivist in Pinehurst, has told us that Ross has often been misnamed as Douglas, Duncan—you name it.. And of course, Frederick Law Olmsted, who built the park, and his son knew of the outstanding work Donald Ross had done at Pinehurst, the town they themselves had designed for its founder, James Tufts.

Ross had won the Massachusetts Open twice and was well known and highly regarded here. He maintained offices in nearby Rhode Island and in Massachusetts. Ross would later go on to design two more courses for Boston: Ponkapoag and George Wright, and in the fine book, *Golf Has Never Failed Me,* edited by Ron Whitten, Architectural Editor of *Golf Digest*, Ross is credited with the design of this course. So our theory was that he was responsible for all three we list in Boston.

Then, a week before publication date, Alan Banks called. He'd found the evidence! It's in an April 19, 1922 *Golf Illustrated* article that reports the "extension of the municipal course (at Franklin Park) to 18 holes, under the superintendency of Donald J. Ross." Three cheers and a big hosanna for Alan Banks!

charge 12.5 cents per round by selling his services. It is believed that the track for this course corresponds with routing shown in a 1914 map. The nine holes were altered in 1901 along with the addition of six holes at a cost of $400. When Willie died in 1900, his wife ran the course for a year, and then the city took over. By 1910, play had grown to 47 golfers annually. It was closed Saturday afternoons, Sundays and public holidays. In 1923, the "no fee" rule ended, and a fee of $10 a year was charged, or one dollar a round. The course was then upgraded to a championship, 18-holes with $3,000 spent on the expansion.

Golf legend Bobby Jones used land just off the 12th hole as a practice area. It was here that he honed his game while at Harvard, and went on to win the Grand Slam of Amateur Golf. He called the 12th the most challenging par four in the region.

In the twenties, the course was improved by Ross, but after the Depression and the war, it was allowed to deteriorate. The City of Boston had financial problems, and golf courses were a low priority item. In the '80s, it began its renaissance. Federal funds were secured, and Phil Wogan, Jr. was hired to rebuild the tees and greens under the aegis of Bill Flynn's management company.

Photo by Beth Dunn

Above the sixth tee stands a monument to Henry David Thoreau.

History

In 1890 on this site, which had been the home of Ralph Waldo Emerson, Willie Campbell, the famous golf pro at the Country Club in Brookline, created a nine-hole course here with empty tomato cans serving as holes. He was hired by Boston when he was fired by Brookline due to his favoring public-play golf. Willie was allowed to

Tees	Par	Yards	Slope	USGA
Blue	70	6009	120	69.8
White	70	5622	113	68.6
Red	72	5040	109	69.3

Franklin Park
and Frederick Law Olmsted

Franklin Park was a creation of Frederick Law Olmsted, the man who designed Boston's public parks, New York's Central Park and the Village of Pinehurst, now called "the golf capitol of the world." He considered Franklin Park his finest creation, but ironically, he hated golf and golfers because they caused disturbances in parks he thought were better suited to providing peace and quiet to city dwellers. Most importantly, he found that golfers in Franklin Park tended to "disturb the sheep" in the park's Country Meadow. His son wrote in 1905, "The introduction of golf playing is an unwise sacrifice of the pleasure and comfort of the many in the quiet enjoyment of the park ... not only are the attractive and harmless sheep driven out ... what is worse, the nerves of the visitor are further irritated by the anxiety as to being hit by the hard and swiftly driven balls." Olmsted had designed Franklin Park to be a *Rus in Urbe*, a total escape from the city while still within its boundaries. In time, alas, he would see the sheep give way to golfers.

Within six years of the date Olmsted submitted his plans for the park, George Wright of baseball fame had written to the city fathers, asking for permission to play golf in Franklin Park. He wrote that he would not draw a crowd nor "cause noise or injure shrubbery," and would guarantee that "if granted the privilege all will be well." Wright got his permission, and later he would donate land for the George Wright Golf Course in Boston, also designed by Ross.

On December 10, 1890, Wright played the first game of golf here on Sargent's field. He created six fairways that criss-crossed, and the holes were square. Twigs were topped with pieces of ripped flannel for the flags. *The Boston Herald* of December 11, 1890 reports that Wright had predicted there was "too much walking and hill climbing for the game to go over."

The 17th—the tee is directly in front of the creek, and the shot must pass through the chute to reach the green, which is elevated and very canted.

Today, the bent grass course is operated by the Sterling Golf Management Group, which has improved the property, while the city of Boston has provided an impressive clubhouse, which was erected in 1998. It features a fully stocked pro shop and a comfortable lounge with fireplace for those cool fall evenings after a brisk round. Corporate functions may be held here.

In this pleasant, Suffolk County, inner city environment, the public can play a top-rated course within minutes from downtown Boston. The course is noted for its especially wide fairways, which are unusual on a city course. Land is gently rolling and fairways are lined with mature oaks and firs. A pond may give problems on four holes. The signature hole is number 12, a 407 yard par four that plays up hill all the way. Another sign that Ross was here: sand bunkers and those ever-present mounds coming into play on most holes.

JOE KIRKWOOD WAS A ROSS FAVORITE

Joe Kirkwood was born in Australia in 1897 and was known as golf's premiere trick shot artist. He became famous in this country by winning the North-South Open (now the Texas Open), the Canadian Open and the Lossie Smith Open in Ireland. He finished in the top three in the British Open. Through thousands of exhibitions, he became a household word to generations of golfers. His son reports that his first exhibition was at Bethlehem Country Club, the Donald Ross-designed course in Bethlehem, New Hampshire, where several hundred came to see him play and perform. After the show Walter Hagen (the "Haig") suggested that the hat be passed, and over $200 was raised, opening Joe's eyes to the opportunity for new riches. He realized he could earn more money putting on golf exhibitions than in competing for small uncertain purses. And so, when new Ross courses opened, Joe was often on hand as a golf headliner.

Joe was soon noted for his unique ability to make a golf ball do his bidding, and he was a master at it, but he felt that his greatest achievement was spreading the game of golf around the world. He not only won many of the world's most coveted golfing championships, but also played exhibitions in cities, jungles, and deserts—from one side of the globe to the other. He played with Bing Crosby (a good friend), and was always cheered at Christmas to get a card from "Der Bingle," who never forgot his golfing buddies.

In his heyday, Joe and fellow professional Walter Hagen partnered on a circuit that took them to hundreds of golf courses and galleries throughout the world. Joe had 26 holes-in-one to his golfing credit, including one played off the face of a man's watch during an exhibition in Cedar Rapids, Iowa, and another earned while Grantland Rice's news cameraman filmed the event. He even shot two holes-in-one in one single round of play. He taught the Queen of England, the Emperor of Japan, Dwight Eisenhower, Richard Nixon and Jack Kennedy the game. He could hit a low shot, high shot, two balls with one club, and curve the ball to the right or left. He could also wrap a club with a lead shaft around his neck.

He'd grown up on a sheep ranch, living an active life, and was physically blessed with strong, awesomely large hands and wrists. Lowell Thomas called him the "most powerful man I ever knew. He could hit a seven iron farther than most man can hit with a driver. He did more to popularize the game than any man who ever lived." He was inducted into the Golf Hall of Fame in '69, and died in his beloved Vermont in 1970. In the world of golf he is in a class by himself.

Photo courtesy Ron Kirkwood. To read more about Joe, find his book, Links of Life, *published in 1973.*

(FORMERLY TOYTOWN TAVERN GOLF CLUB)
172 ASH STREET, WINCHENDON, MA 01475
(978) 297-9897   FAX: (978) 297-0911

DIRECTIONS: FROM BOSTON TAKE RTE. 2 WEST TO RTE. 140 NORTH TO RTE. 12 NORTH THREE MILES TO COURSE ON LEFT. 65 MILES FROM BOSTON, 35 FROM WORCESTER AND 20 FROM KEENE, NH.

Semi-private (privately owned/open to the public). 18 holes. Open May 1 to November 30. Rental gas and pullcarts and clubs. Swimming pool. Tennis. Pro shop opens 7 AM. Tee times may be made up to five days in advance. Putting and chipping practice areas. Teaching pro. Snack bar. Cross country ski trails. Basketball, soccer and lacrosse fields.

Below: The number five pin and fairway taken from behind green. Mount Monadnock in Jaffrey, NH is in the distance. This par four plays 385 yards, the number one stroke hole—dogleg to the right.

Ross to come to America to teach golf at Oakley Country Club, a pioneer course. When the course closed for the winter, Ross set up the first indoor golf school in Boston. He devised the original driving nets, and soon had a great many avid students.

One of them introduced him to James W. Tufts, the New England soda fountain manufacturer. Five years before, Tufts had established a village in a a town that would become Pinehurst. Tufts preferred croquet, but he had introduced the novelty game of golf for this guests and engaged Ross for the next winter. Donald Ross arrived in Pinehurst in the fall of 1900 and set to work to polish the very primitive 18 holes that Tufts and George C. Dutton had built in the sand. This old course lay on land that is now covered by Pinehurst No. 1.

Ross was fated to have his home in

Donald Ross created many wonderful courses in the State of Massachusetts. A great deal of his work was done in the environs of Worcester and Springfield, where he designed outstanding private courses as well as courses open to public play like Ellinwood, Petersham and Winchendon.

The connection with the state began when Harvard professor Robert Wilson visited Dornoch, Scotland and after playing a few rounds, approached Donald Ross. He invited

Pinehurst, but managed to combine his private and professional life there with an active course design career that brought him back to his beloved Massachusetts time and again. It would be 26 years from Pinehurst to Winchendon.

Winchendon is a short, narrow course with small greens (with many breaks) and hilly fairways that are basically untouched from the day Ross redesigned them in 1926. The bunkers on holes ten and 11 and tee sizes have been modified over the decades. It requires an accurate short game, and local knowledge helps the golfer overcome the often tricky lies.

The course features bent grass greens with narrow native grass fairways and rough. There are no homes on the fairways, allowing for magnificent views of the mountains and thousands of trees of many varieties.

One of the most striking views in New England golf may be the scene at the number one hole looking down from the 15th tee. Playing this course when the leaves change color is especially picturesque. The vivid reds, golds and oranges of the fall foliage are everywhere on this heavily wooded, yet open-fairwayed course.

Here is a course where Ross maximized the topography, keeping all its very best features. As little earth as possible was moved, and like many Ross courses, it looks far easier than it is. Ross lovers will love Winchendon very much, indeed.

Winchendon School

The course is on the property of the Winchendon School, which was founded in 1926 as the Wassookeag School in Dexter, Maine. It then moved to Rhode Island as the Hatch School, and came to its present 236 acre location in 1961.

This college preparatory boarding and day school enrolls boys and girls in grades eight through 12 and a postgraduate year. It has a long history of success with students

Above: Autumn view from the seventh green looking back over hilly fairway to the tee over the hill in the distance—a par four, 368 yards. A stream crosses the seventh and eighth fairways.

who have not previously reached their potential. Small class size, emphasis on moral, spiritual, physical and mental growth in an environment of caring and supportive faculty has shown results.

The student body is kept to 180 students, who attend from 17 foreign countries and join Americans from 27 states. It has a nationally recognized basketball program that has produced players for the NBA as well as many ranked college and university teams.

Tees	Par	Yards	Slope	USGA
White	70	5427	114	65.7
Red	72	5030	116	68.5

Michigan

Elk Rapids Golf Club

Rackham Golf Course

Rogell Golf Course

Shadow Ridge Public Golf Course

Warren Valley Golf Club,
East and West Courses

ELK RAPIDS GOLF CLUB

1923

724 Ames Street, PO Box 485, Elk Rapids, MI 49629
(231) 264-8891

DIRECTIONS: FROM HIGHWAY 31, TURN EAST ONTO AMES STREET. DRIVE 1.5 MILES AND TURN RIGHT INTO COURSE DRIVEWAY.

Semi-private. Nine holes. Plays 18. Open April 15 to October 15. Rental gas and pullcarts and clubs. On Wednesdays the course is closed to the public until 6 PM. All other days it is open. Pro shop opens 7 AM. Practice fairway and putting greens.

Above: The clubhouse in wintertime—no golf today!

The *Elk Rapids Progress* newspaper of October, 1922 reported that J.B. McGovern, representing Donald Ross, was in town to select land for a municipal golf course. Here is what McGovern reported to the golf course committee: "After having examined two parcels of land within the corporate limits of Elk Rapids, and also having looked over some land within the township limits, I am convinced that the Gumpert farm is the most suitable for a country club and nine-hole golf course. It is quite convenient to the village of Elk Rapids, a thing that must be considered in a resort proposition as you have.

"The waterfront property is suitable for building lots, can be tapped by the water mains, and it has the advantage of electricity. While the topography is in a sense very flat, I am sure that a nine-hole course built according to the plans will be a pleasure to play on."

The newspaper calls Ross and McGovern "golf course engineers," and adds, "any club fortu-nate enough to secure their services in selecting and laying out a course can feel assured that they have the best men in their line in the United States. If we tell a golf player that we have a Donald Ross course, nothing more need be said, as all golf players know that these courses have a national reputation."

The town raised $9,000 in a bond issue, which covered the purchase price of the property and the development of the course; the land alone cost only $6,750.

Almost two years later, July 3, 1924, the newspaper reported, "Golf Course Opens Tuesday." All businesses in Elk Rapids were closed on

Tees	Par	Yards	Slope	USGA
Blue	72	6132	111	67.8
White	72	5978	111	67.8
Red	72	5288	111	68.4

126

Beautiful Elk Rapids Lake and Golf Club photographed from overhead

Opening Day, July 15th, from noon until 5 PM. A Community picnic was held at the grove on the course. In 1988, the town celebrated the course's 75th anniversary. People from all over northwest Michigan attended.

Chick Herbert, who was the pro at the Ag Ga Ming Golf Club, gave free lessons to Elk Rapids members and also played the course. (Ag Ga Ming is located 15 miles north.) Chick won the 1939 amateur at Augusta, and in 1954 won the PGA 36th at the Keller Golf Club in St. Paul, Minnesota.

Today, the club has 200 members and a waiting list of another 335. Fortunately, holes one, two, three, five, seven and nine remain the same today as when originally designed by Ross.

One of the boundaries of the course is Elk Lake (one of the finest in the north), which comes into play on three holes. The course is well maintained, with the grounds crew constantly seeking ways to make improvements.

Of the nine holes, there are five blind approach shots created by large knolls and dips in the fairways. Conversely, this is a pleasant course to walk since the terrain is fairly level.

A brass plaque commemorating the contributions of Donald Ross in the design of the course is prominently and proudly displayed on a stone monument in front of the clubhouse.

RACKHAM GOLF COURSE

10100 West Ten Mile Road, Huntington Woods, MI 48070
(248)543-4040   Fax:(248)542-0814
E-mail: corporateservices@americangolf.com

Directions: From I-696 east, take Coolidge exit. Course is on left.

Public. 18 holes. Open year round. Rental gas and pullcarts and clubs. Pro shop opens 6 AM. Practice putting and chipping areas. Clubhouse. Snack bar. Junior programs. Tee times up to seven days in advance.

Below: Flowers in bright profusion spell out "R" at the entrance to the clubhouse.

Photos on this page courtesy of Mrs. John M. Sirhal

Rackham is located just west of the Detroit Zoo. In its long history, the more than 130 acre course has hosted The 4 Tops, Smokey Robinson, The Spinners and boxing World Heavyweight Champion, Joe Louis.

Louis loved golf and played regularly at Rackham, the scene of many Joe Louis Golf Tournaments. He worked hard to give black professional golfers the opportunity to play, and it was largely through his efforts that the "Caucasian Only" clause was lifted from the PGA.

Louis knew his rules of golf, too. He was playing a game of $2,000 Nassau ($2,000 on each nine, $2,000 on the round and a $5,000 wager on their medal scores). On one hole Louis' opponent was trapped, and the latter walked in the trap to play his shot, accidentally dropping his club. He picked up the club and played the shot, reporting a score of five for the hole. "No, I'm sorry, you had a seven on that hole," Louis announced. "There is a two stoke penalty for picking up your club before playing the shot." And he was absolutely right. As it turned out, Louis won the $5,000 by one stroke.

Louis for years would bet on a golfer named Teddy Rhodes, a protégé of his who shot a 70 in the first round of the 1948 U.S. Open at Los Angeles.

All holes on the back nine, and holes three through nine on the front are unchanged from when Donald Ross designed them here. The City of Detroit's Men's Amateur Champi-

The 530 yard, par five number one hole—not a typical Ross opener. He liked to start off easy, but this is the number three handicap. As these golfers teed off, the course was in mint condition.

onship tournament has been held at Rackham. The course is managed by American Golf and American Golf Country Clubs, which operates more than 300 courses nationwide, including Rouge Park, Palmer Park, Chandler Park, The Woodlands and Hilltop in the area.

The course and its fine brick clubhouse were donated to the City of Detroit by Mr. Horace H. Rackham in 1925. The clubhouse cost over $200,000 in 1925 dollars. A great believer in the benefits of outdoor sports, Rackham donated $500,000 so Detroit could have a course that would contribute to the health of its citizens.

Rackham, an attorney, was one of the first investors in Henry Ford's company, in which he subsequently became a director. He gambled $5,000 on the success of the new "horseless carriage," and, as they say, "the rest is history."

He was a director of the private Detroit Golf Club and loved the game, feeling strongly that it should be available to everyone, rich and poor alike. Rackham was a strict marker of the caddies' cards, indicating the performances of the boys, only rarely giving an "excellent."

When the course opened, he drove the first ball. It traveled about 200 yards straight down the fairway, a good drive. He was far from a scratch golfer, playing a creditable game, usually in the 90s. When he died in 1933, the course was closed for an hour in his memory.

When Rackham died, he left bequests to only five non-family members. Two such beneficiaries were Alec Ross ($30,000) and Charlie Kelly, who was Alec's assistant pro at Brae Burn Golf Club, West Newton, Massachusetts ($5,000). Alec had held that post 12

years before coming to the Detroit Golf Club at Rackham's invitation. At Brae Burn, Alec had won the National Open in 1907. Rackham played the game three or four times a week in Detroit, and often played with his good friends, Alec Ross and Charlie Kelly.

Several years ago, William T. Merriweather, Jr., who had caddied for Horace Rackham at The Detroit Golf Club when Merriweather was 12 years old, gave his recollections of the great man. He said that Rackham was a stickler for etiquette on the course. "We had

Below: Horace Rackham, circa 1914, with golfing companions, G.A. Magoon, A.S. Higgins and Herman Ellis, shot at Pinehurst, North Carolina. Alec Ross gave him his first lesson there when Rackham was 55 years of age. Very retiring and shy, Rackham said he found much in common with Ross, particularly their interest in good music and fine books.

H H RACKHAM   G A MAGOON   A S HIGGINS   HERMAN ELLIS

Tees	Par	Yards	Slope	USGA
Blue	71	6555	118	71.1
White	71	6253	115	69.8
Red	72	5413	115	70.7

to walk a certain way, dress a certain way, carry clubs a certain way. We'd carry extra balls in our pocket so that, if we couldn't find it on the grounds, we'd have one. They never knew whether it was the ball they'd hit or one from our pockets. We were paid a nickel a hole, and people could play all day for 25 cents."

Merriweather, who learned to play the game while caddying for auto industry big shots and famous people like poet Edgar A. Guest, a friend of Rackham's, continued: "We didn't have our own clubs and sometimes a member would let us use his club and if we had a good stroke he'd say, 'Here, caddie, take a dollar and buy a club.'

"It (Rackham) was peculiar and only a few people could play it. Sometimes peo-ple would come to play and the manager would give them their money back and tell them to go over to Palmer Park."

Today some parts of the old course look as if they had seen better times. A prominent Michigan golf course architect has advised that, although the course is very well attended by the public, it isn't adequately supported by the city.

Neal Shine, publisher of the *Detroit Free Press,* wrote poignantly not too long ago on *Remembering Rackham.* "Memories of those crisp, sunny mornings at Rackham, the grass of the fairways, brushed with dew, still linger fondly. I don't say much about it to my east side friends. I'm afraid they wouldn't understand."

Below: Joe Louis playing his favorite game—the Rackham clubhouse is in the background. Donald Ross didn't favor betting on golf or any other sport. Unfortunately Louis never heeded that advice and died broke.

Detroit Free Press *file photo*

130

THE ROYAL & ANCIENT GOLF CLUB OF SAINT ANDREWS CONNECTION

Photograph: The Old Course by Bill Roberton, Dalgety Bay Courtesy – St. Andrews Links Trust

After an early stint as a local carpenter's trainee in Dornoch, Scotland, Donald Ross moved on to apprentice to the master club maker and golf professional, Old Tom Morris of Saint Andrews in 1893. And, like they say, "the rest is history!"

Old Tom was in his 72nd year when Donald Ross arrived. Morris had been the winner of the British Open in 1861, 1862, 1864 at Prestwick, Ayrshire and won his fourth title there in 1867 after he'd become the pro at St. Andrews. Seven years before Donald went to work at St. Andrews, he had observed Old Tom when Morris had remodeled some of the holes at Royal Dornoch, creating the famous plateau greens that are still being played there to this very day. Once he had polished his skills at St. Andrews, Donald Ross returned to his beloved Dornoch in 1895 as pro and greenkeeper.

Five years later he crossed the Atlantic to become the pro at Oakley Club outside of Boston, and then moved on to Pinehurst and course architectural fame.

Now one may contact St. Andrews via the internet at www.standrews.org.uk and at www.linksnet.co.uk. E-mail address: linkstrust@standrews.org.uk. Since Ross' day the famous "Home of Golf" has changed dramatically to include six courses, a 44 bay practice center and two welcoming club houses open to everyone, attracting thousands of pilgrims from around the globe each year. What a difference a hundred-plus years make!

Here is what they have to say about Donald Ross at Saint Andrews today:

"It is gratifying to think that in some small way St. Andrews had an influence on the young Donald Ross that later conditioned his thinking about the best way to design golf courses for golfers to play. That he went on to design many of the finest courses in the USA and consequently had a major influence on golf course architects everywhere is a tribute to the stature of the man.

It does appear that the time he spent here in St. Andrews was when he really came to understand all aspects of the game, which was to be his consuming passion - just as it was in St. Andrews."

- Peter Mason
St. Andrews Links Trust
15 August 2000

ROGELL GOLF COURSE

18601 Berg Road, Detroit, MI 48219
(313) 578-8006   Fax (313) 578-8010 E-mail: ctowne@rec.ci.detroit.mi.us

Directions: From Seven Mile Road, go south on Berg, which is between Telegraph and Lahser Roads.

Photos by Angela Hipps

Public. 18 holes. A municipal course that is part of the Detroit Recreational Department. Open year round. Pro shop opens 7 AM. Rental gas and pullcarts and clubs. Putting green. Snack bar.

Above: An early August morning dew—shot from behind the fifth green looking to the fifth tee. Number five is a par three, 108 yard, "piece of cake."

This is one of the most venerable courses in the State of Michigan, having opened in 1912. It was originally the nine-hole Phoenix Country Club; Ross designed it into its present 18-hole format in 1921.

At a later date, the course became a public facility named Redford after that section of the city. In 1946, Detroit purchased the course, and it has been open to the public ever since. Rogell is the founding club for the Golf Association of Michigan and Michigan Professional Golfers Association, and has been the site for Detroit Newspapers' annual Hole-in-one tournament for the past 63 years.

Of the original Donald Ross holes six through 18 are the same today as when he designed them over 75 years ago. Unfortunately, the Rouge River runs right through it, causing severe water problems from day one. One prominent Michigan golf architect describes it as being "in a state of neglect, suffering over time from frequent floods. Many Ross bunkers have been removed. Not much effort is being put forth by the city, but the course is popular and gets lots of play."

Ironically, there is unusually beautiful rolling terrain here. When Ross designed it, there were about twice as many trees lining the fairways as there are now. A good score calls for staying on the fairways because, even with many of the trees gone, the course demands

carefully placed shots. As one older member, Sam Schwartz of Detroit, is quoted in an article in the *Detroit News* written by Robert Jones, "If you hit them straight, you'll be right." (Schwartz was 90 when he gave the advice, and had been playing the course since 1917, so he should know.)

Ross often expressed the opinion that the ideal course should start with a relatively easy hole, but for some reason, he didn't follow his own credo at Rogell. Hole number one, a par four, plays short, only 339 yards, but a tee shot into the middle of the fairway leaves a tricky and often tough 150 yard shot to a very small green. Like many a Ross green, hitting on isn't the problem; staying on the surface and not rolling off makes the difference.

The second hole looks easy at first, but Ross placed three bunkers, including two right near the green, on this short par five hole (467 yards), so be careful.

A player's first birdie opportunity happens on the very short par three number five—

only 108 yards off the tee. But the player has to go over the creek here, and that can be intimidating to the less skilled golfer. On the back nine the Rouge River runs through four of the last holes—and is known to catch an errant ball or two. The finishing hole looks like it should be a breeze and usually is (16 handicap), at only 166 yards—a par three near the clubhouse. It's a relatively short course, but can be fun to play and calls for skill when least expected.

Billy Rogell

The name of Billy Rogell (right), who played shortstop for the Detroit Tigers from 1930 to 1939, is revered in Detroit. It was this famous team that won the World Series in 1935. A few years ago, Rogell was interviewed by Joe Falls of the Detroit News. At the time, Billy was one of only four survivors of the '35 championship. The others were pitcher Chief Hogsett, catcher Ray Hayworth and pitcher Eldon Auker. Elson was the only one under 90.

Billy told Falls that his idol was Babe Ruth. He said, "We used the same tunnel and the other team had to go through our dugout to get to the other dugout. The Babe always came out before all the other Yankees—I don't know why he did this—and he'd stop and talk to us. He'd sit right down on our bench like it was the most natural thing in the world to do, and he'd chat with us for a long time. We just sat there and listened, loving every minute of it. He used to call me 'little guy.' That's because I was shorter than our other infielders—Hank Greensburg at first, Charlie Gehringer at second and Marvin Owen at third. He'd walk across the field to his dugout—everyone in the stadium stood up and applauded. He would wave his cap at them, and the applause got even louder. We loved the Babe. There was no one else like him in baseball. There still isn't."

Rogell told how when the Babe batted, the Tigers' infield would shift, leaving the entire left side open for him. Rogell said to him one day, "Babe, why don't you tap the ball to left so you'd never make an out?" Ruth replied, "Hey, little man, they don't come out to see me hit singles and doubles. They want home runs!"

Billy Rogell served 38 years on the Detroit City Council. He was never a little man. After all, how many 'little men' have a golf course named after them?

Above: Comin' home—on the short (166 yards) par three, 18th tee toward the green and the clubhouse

Above: Shortstop Billy Rogell of the Detroit Tigers

Photo from National Baseball Hall of Fame Library, Cooperstown, N.Y.

Tees	Par	Yards	Slope	USGA
Blue	70	6075	129	70.2
White	70	5828	125	69.2
Red	70	4985	117	68.3

1191 Kelsey Highway, Ionia, MI 48846
(616) 527-1180   E-mail: shadow-ridge-gc@yahoo.com

DIRECTIONS: FROM GRAND RAPIDS, GO EAST ON I-96. TAKE M-66 EXIT AND GO LEFT TO THE BLINKER. TURN RIGHT AT GRAND RIVER AVE. GO TWO MILES AND TURN LEFT ON KELSEY RD. ENTRANCE IS SIX MILES ON THE LEFT.

The par three number six hole plays 152 off the men's tees—133 off the ladies' —trees and two bunkers may give problems here.

Public.. Nine holes. Plays to 18. Open April 1 to October 1. Rental gas carts, pull-carts and clubs. Pool. Pro shop. Snack bar. Putting green. Teaching pro.

Ionia, located in the very heart of Lower Michigan, is between Grand Rapids, Battle Creek and Lansing. The town has many historic buildings. Twice yearly they are opened for a tour and a year-round self-guided "Volksmarch" walking or cycling tour. Each August the town is host to the largest Free Fair in the world. South of town is the 140 acre Sessions Lake, with fishing, sailing and swimming in addition to 20 miles of hiking and equestrian trails along the Grand River.

For visiting golfers, the authors recommend the Union Hill Inn on Union Street, a fine B&B in a wonderful Italianate mansion, decorated with antebellum furnishings.

Golfers who play the course say that Shadow Ridge offers three of the toughest par threes you'll ever find on an old course. All nine holes are the same today as when Donald Ross laid them out; straightforward golf is played here.

Originally Shadow Ridge was known as the Ionia Country Club and was built for well-to-do Michigan businessmen to play. Today, of course, it is open to all.

League play and outings are welcome. Ther are no homes to distract the golfer's view of this small gem. Sometimes smaller is better, as the town is able to keep it in great condition. Shadow Ridge was built when Ross was at his creative peak. Indeed, when he was working

on the famed South Course at Oakland Hills Country Club in Bloomfield Hills, he was also creating Ionia.

Jim Simons, course pro, has identified hole number six as the signature hole. He says, "There is a very narrow teeing area, trees and water right, bunkers and heather on the left. Anything hit pin high or longer is usually not a par because of greens that slope from back to front. When the green is mowed to normal height, the ball will seldom hold."

The number two hole, a 240 yard par three, offers the golfer a bowl-shaped green. Jim says, "Just hit it long and straight and you've got your par—if the pin is in the center of the green."

The numbers four and seven greens sit on a bluff 15 yards apart. If the wind is blowing, look out. Number five is a wonderful Ross lay-up hole; the fairway narrows from 260 yards to 290 yards, and if you hit it too far, the trees will block your next shot, so placement here is everything. Numbers three and nine are both reachable par fives and give up some birdies, but can also take many hostages along the way if the golfer is not very accurate.

Recently, golf history buffs participated in a televised *Hickory Shaft Tournament* here. If you like historic courses and real challenges, you will definitely enjoy Ross-style golf at Shadow Ridge.

Right: The number five hole needs a good drive. The fairway narrows around the green between rows of trees.

Michigan Kept Ross Busy

For 25 years (from 1911 to 1936), Donald Ross was active in the State of Michigan designing golf courses. He did city courses, suburban courses, rural courses and lake courses, and one is more beautiful than the next. He believed God gave him precious land to work with, and he performed his magic in Michigan as almost nowhere else in America.

Although a search of old records can often reveal different dates for Ross' work, the dates given here are our best estimates for his Michigan designs. Of these, only 90 holes are open to public play, and they are included in this book: Elk Rapids Golf Club in Elk Rapids (9 holes); Rackham Golf Course, Huntington Woods (18 holes); Rogell Golf Club, Detroit (18 holes); Shadow Ridge Golf Course, Ionia (9 holes); and Warren Valley Golf Club, Dearborn, East and West courses (36 holes).

His earliest efforts here were private courses at the Muskegon Country Club (18 holes), designed in 1911 and the Detroit Golf Club (36 holes, 2 remodeled) done in 1916. Two of the courses are no longer in existence: Fred Wardell Estate Golf Club, 9 holes (1920) and Brightmoor Country Club in Dearborn, 18 holes (1925).

Other private courses were: Barton Hills Country Club, Ann Arbor (18 holes), 1920; Bloomfield Hills (18 holes), 1936; Dearborn Country Club (18 holes), 1923; Franklin Hills Country Club (18 holes), 1926; Grosse Ile Golf and Country Club (18 holes), 1919; The Highlands Golf Club in Grand Rapids (9 holes remodeled in 1922, 9 holes added in 1927); Kent Country Club, Grand Rapids, (9 holes remodeled, 9 holes added), 1921; Monroe Golf and Country Club (18 holes), 1919; the famed Oakland Hills Country Club, Birmingham (North Course 18 holes), 1921; (South Course 18 holes), 1923; St. Clair Golf Club (18 holes), 1919; Western Golf and Country Club, Redford (18 holes), 1926.

A tribute to the way Ross' great courses stand the test of time is the fact that the private Oakland Hills Country Club in Birmingham, Michigan was selected as the site for the U.S. Open Tournament in 1924, 1937, 1951, 1961, 1985 and 1996.

Tees	Par	Yards	Slope	USGA
Blue	70	5978	123	70.3
Red	70	4700	122	70.8

135

WARREN VALLEY GOLF CLUB EAST AND WEST COURSES   1922

26116 W. WARREN STREET, DEARBORN, MI 48127
(313) 561-1040   FAX: (313) 561-1733

DIRECTIONS: FROM DETROIT AIRPORT, TAKE MERRIAM AVE. NORTH TO W. WARREN STREET. TURN RIGHT AND THE COURSE IS 3 MILES ON THE LEFT.

Public. Two 18 holes courses. Open March 20 to October 31. Rental gas and pullcarts and clubs. Putting green. Teaching pro. Restaurant and grill. Snack bar. Banquet facilities. New clubhouse (1994).

Below: Patty Berg, Pat Devany from Grosse Ile and Bobby Dawson from San Francisco at the seventh tee on the West Course—August 23, 1950

Above: The impressive clubhouse at Warren Valley

These two venerable courses get significant play, upwards of 80,000 a year. Unlike many 36-hole facilities that were built in two distinct phases, Warren Valley was conceived right from the start as a property that would present to the public two contiguous 18-hole courses. Managed by Wayne County officials, over the years the facility has not been given the kind of careful, loving attention it deserves, and today it is in improved playing condition.

There are two major problems here: unusually heavy golfer traffic and a flood plain location. The impact upon the course of so many players within Michigan's short (seven months) playing season puts tremendous pressure on both management and the course itself. And, as more junior players become enamoured of the game, this problem is expected to be exacerbated over time.

On the upside, a new, two-story clubhouse that overlooks course and river was opened in 1994, and over $300,000 worth of new equipment has been purchased to improve the condition of the course. And County Executive Ed McNamara, a golfer, is committed to making it a great course again. Writer Jack Berry says, "Warren Valley is only going to get better as the maintenance takes hold."

Both courses are dominated by one persistent physical factor, the Rouge River, that courses through the relatively flat land. On the East Course, it affects four holes, with a large pond located between the first and tenth tees and the third fairway.

On the West Course, it meanders more, affecting holes five, six, ten, 11, 12, 14 and 15. Both courses are reasonably similar in size; the West blue tees play only 63 yards shorter than those on the East, but it is deemed the tougher course to master at Warren Valley.

There are far fewer bunkers than one would expect to find on a Ross course, and this may reflect various modifications made over the years. Many public courses have eliminated fairway bunkers and reduced the count of bunkers near greens to cut costs and speed up play. Here only about half the greens are guarded by them. There are no sand bunkers on either courses' fairways, making par play more doable than on many similar sized Ross creations. But wait, we hear that's going to change. Plans call for restoring many of the removed bunkers—good news for Ross purists.

The West hole number 12 is a classic Ross model, playing short for a 139 yard drive over a flowing stream to a small green protected by two strategically placed sand bunkers.

Sports writer Ted Kulfan of the *Detroit News* calls holes 12 and 18 the best on the West Course, and likes number seven on the East.

Above: The 189 yard par three seventh hole on the West Course—the second easiest on the course

As he describes it, "water surrounds the front and right side of No. 7 green, making for an intimidating shot on the 147 yard hole."

On the demanding East, hole three is the number one handicap, and for the player starting his or her round, it can be daunting. It plays a long 521 yards off the blues. Fortunately no bunkers come into play on this dogleg to the right fairway, but the green can be difficult to hold. Because this is such a priceless recreational asset to the county, players hope to see increased public dollars and energies expended to improve Warren Valley in the near future.

According to the management, the only holes that are not original Ross designs on the West Course are: 2, 3, 4 and 17. On the East Course, all but 1, 2, 14, 15, 17 and 18 are exactly as Ross laid them out almost 80 years ago.

East Course

Tees	Par	Yards	Slope	USGA
Blue	72	6189	114	69.1
White	72	5920	110	67.7
Red	72	5298	113	70.0

West Course

Tees	Par	Yards	Slope	USGA
Blue	71	6126	115	68.5
White	71	5827	113	67.6
Red	71	5158	114	69.2

Above: The 375 yard par four fourth hole—a sharp dogleg right to a well bunkered green

Some of Warren Valley's cadre of 300 registered caddies, July 26, 1947—the good old days!

History

Warren Valley has had an up-and-down history, one not too different from many private courses built just before the Great Depression. Its story starts when John Nollar sold 192 acres along the Rouge River to Roy Montgomery and Bill Connellan for The Hawthorne Valley Golf Club. A half million dollars were invested in the creation of Hawthorne's two 18-hole courses, designed by Donald Ross.

Three years leter, the club opened another course on Merriman Road, the present New Hawthorne Valley Golf Course. This went broke in 1931, and the land reverted to Nollar, who leased it to Montgomery and renamed it the Warren Valley Golf Club. In 1944, the Nollar estate was paid $150,000 in compensation for the loss of the land, and the land went to the Wayne County Road Commission.

During the war, golf continued to be played

here, the USO held turnkey dinners at the club, and an ice skating rinks was built. In 1948, new fairways were constructed to replace two old ones that were disrupted by the construction of Hines Drive. In the '50s, a driving range was added, and in 1957, the land was traded to the Wallaceville School District for school use.

In 1984, the Road Commission was abolished, and the park operation was set up as a separate department within public services. In 1985, despite union resistance, Eric Reickel, who headed the department, instituted employment standards to the job description of the golf course manager's position that required the individual to have a degree in golf course or turf management. Once this was done, play increased 62%, and the course started to earn a profit for the first time in its long history.

138

New Hampshire

Bethlehem Country Club

Carter Country Club

Kingswood Golf Club

Maplewood Country Club & Hotel

The Mount Washington Course
At Mount Washington Hotel & Resort

Panorama Golf Course at the Balsams

Tory Pines Resort

BETHLEHEM COUNTRY CLUB

1910

1901 MAIN STREET, BETHLEHEM, NH 03574
(603) 869-5745 FAX: (603) 869-5830 E-MAIL: WTNPGA@THEGOLFCOURSE.COM

DIRECTIONS: FROM I-93 NORTH, GET OFF AT EXIT 40 AND GO EAST ON RTE. 302 FOR 2.5 MILES.

Public. 18 holes. Open May 1 to October 31. Pro shop opens at 7 AM. Rental gas and pullcarts and clubs. Putting green and chipping area. Teaching professional. Club repair. Snack bar. Tee time reservations available daily.

Below: Glorious oak and maple leaves in the White Mountains— Autumn comes to Bethlehem, New Hampshire

By the 1870s, over 30 hotels and guest houses were operating in Bethlehem as the area developed into an active summer resort community for New Hampshire's carriage trade. An article in the *White Mountain Echo* notes that local citizens had decided to acquire land for a public park that would include a golfing facility. It mentions the hiring of a Mr. William Lilywhite, who had been in charge of golf links in Florida for the East Coast System of Hotels. He recommended that a 75 acre tract of land owned by E.P. Brown be bought, and so it was. The group became known as the Bethlehem Park Association, with Fred White, a leading businessman, as its first president.

In his excellent book, *The Centennial History of the Bethlehem Country Club*, golf writer and photographer Bob Labbance quotes *The Echo* as follows: "An inspiring element on these links is the beautiful views obtained from them, encompassing the Northern, Presidential and Franconia Ranges of mountains."

As work proceeded, a clubhouse was built to accommodate the new nine-hole course, which "covered nearly a mile and a half, making a full game cover nearly three miles"

The first greenkeeper and professional

Above: In 1968, under professional Fred Ghioto, a junior program, starting with ten children, was instituted to provide summer recreation for local kids. Today, eager boys and girls participate, learning how to play and observe the rules under the guidance of professional Wayne Natti.

140

was Walter Baker, who had learned his craft in London at the Bredgorth Club. The course opened on July 22, 1898. Golfers had their choice of payment: green fees were $5 for the full summer season, $3 a month, $1 a week or 25 cents a day. Golf bags cost from $1 to $4.

In 1910, Donald Ross was called in to remodel the first nine and add nine more. A new clubhouse was built and formally opened in 1912, the old one hauled away to become a home for a family in Vermont.

Today, 12 of the holes are exactly as when Ross created them. Numbers five, seven, eight, ten, 12 and 13 have been modified, but the flavor of the grand old course is still vintage Ross. The fairways are quite narrow, and the greens are acknowledged to be among the finest putting surfaces in the area.

In its heyday, the course attracted many of the greats of golf, including: Harry Vardon, Francis Ouimet, Ted Ray, Jack McDermott and Walter Hagen. Later, Gene Sarazen, Tom McNamara and Walter Travis

played regularly. After the war, the name changed to the Bethlehem Golf and Tennis Club as four clay tennis courts were added. Evidently, tennis didn't produce any aces, and where they stood is now the parking area. In 1920, Wayne Stiles designed a nine-hole addition, but for some unrecorded reason, it was never built; the plans, however, remain.

The morning of September 2, 1922, two club members beat Walter Hagen, the British Open champ and Joe Kirkwood, the Australian champ, three up and one to go, but in the afternoon the champs had their way and beat Harry Cowie and Jack Fotheringham by seven and six. In 1916, Kirkwood returned to shoot a 69. In 1971, the first time Bob Murphy played a round, he fired a 64, setting the course record.

The Depression and war were hard on the facility, and in 1949 the Town of Bethlehem bought the course. Today, this, the highest elevation golf course in New England, is in great shape, and its junior program now has about 150 youngsters learning the game. Recent tournament play includes New Hampshire PGA Pro-Junior, the New Hampshire Golf Association Fourball, and the NHIAA Class M-5 High School Golf Championship.

Above: "Whaddya know, we all made it over the bunker."

Tees	Par	Yards	Slope	USGA
Blue	70	5808	114	68.2
White	70	5619	114	68.2
Green	70	5008	98	63.0
Gold	70	4470	102	64.8

The 16 handicap, 263 yard, par four 14th hole—dense, tall evergreens line the left side of fairways 16 and 17

Photos by Bob Labbance

DONALD ROSS—A VISION OF AMERICA

Young Donald Ross was probably slated by birth to be a hard-working stone mason as so many in his family before him, but fate moved him in other directions. Like all Highland Scots, he knew of the Promised Land beyond the sea, and that it offered the daring great fortunes. This was attested to by hundreds of Scots he knew in his early lifetime who had relatives in the States. And, being from Dornoch, he had heard many times the tale of the Scottish orphan, Andrew Carnegie, and the tremendous achievements he'd made by rendering coke and iron into steel and then into millions.

So when an invitation to come to America was given him, he was eager to leave his homeland and see just what he could achieve on the other side of the Atlantic. He'd had a dream for many years that it might be possible to convert what he had learned about golf into his fortune once he gained a reputation in the United States.

Late in his years, he was asked to speak about those early days. He said that when he was a lad, he had read about American businessmen and that they were "absorbed in making money." He added, "I knew the day would come when the American businessman would want some game to play, and I knew that game would be golf...I knew there'd be a great future in it. I came to grow up with a game in which I had complete confidence."

His gamble paid off. In his day, he was without question the premiere golf course designer in America and perhaps the world. He never for-got his Scottish roots nor strayed far from the lessons of his youth when Old Tom Morris and the other grand men of golf in Dornoch and Saint Andrews passed on to a boy named Donald the secrets of the game, as they understood how it should be played.

He became a pillar of the Village Chapel in Pinehurst, a church he helped found. To the religious Ross, closeness to the "Kirk" was important. Today, players on the Pinehurst courses can hear the carillon from that church peal on the hour, and four times a day listen to patriotic pieces and holy songs of praise being rung. It is a custom at the Chapel in Pinehurst on the first Sunday in December for kilted Scotsmen from North Carolina, accompanied by pipers, to converge for a "Kirking of the Tartans." Donald surely would have enjoyed the show.

He lived modestly and invested in conservative blue chip stocks, his only concession to showiness seeming to be his preference for large Packard motor cars. When he died, his estate in today's money would probably be around $5 million. It surely beat breaking rocks back in the old country.

CARTER GOLF CLUB

257 MECHANIC STREET, LEBANON, NH 03766
(603) 448-4483

1922

DIRECTIONS: FROM I-89 TAKE EXIT 19 WEST. CARTER IS ON THE RIGHT.

Semi-private. Nine holes play to 18. Open from April 1 to November 1. Open 6 AM seven days a week. Rental electric and pullcarts and clubs. Putting green. Chipping practice area. Complete pro shop. Restaurant and snack bar. PGA professional on staff.

It looks like any small Cape Cod home, but it is the comfortable clubhouse and pro shop at Carter Golf Club, where the public is always welcome.

Lebanon has the distinction of being called "One of the 100 Best Small Towns in America" by author Norman Crampton, with a number three ranking. The community is characterized by ridge lines, surrounding the bottomlands of the Mascoma and Connecticut Rivers. It is 60 miles from Concord, 120 miles from Boston and 120 miles from Burlington, Vermont. Elevations reach 1336 feet above sea level. One reason the fairways and greens are so emerald green in color is the fact that the area gets 35 inches of rain and 76 inches of snow each year. Highs in July rarely top 81 degrees and lows 51—perfect for golf. Although the course was redesigned by Howard De Goosh in 1995, holes one, four, six and eight are just as Ross designated.

The hilly setting here is spectacular, and could well illustrate what Ross said when he designed the Oakland Hills course in 1917: "The Lord must have intended this property for a golf course."

Carter looks deceptively easy to play, but the golfer soon discovers that he or she is faced with a hilly challenge with very small greens that can be hard to hold. It is a classic Ross layout, demanding strategic thinking and careful assessment before taking a swing and attempting shot making.

Four is the number one handicap hole.

Tees	Par	Yards	Slope	USGA
Blue	72	5600	116	68.1
White	72	5450	114	66.1
Red	72	5130	127	71.7

Although Ross liked to limit his water holes to no more than three per 18-hole course, he laid Carter out so that water, including two good-sized ponds, comes into play on four holes.

The longest hole is number three, a wide open, 485 yard par five, requiring a tee shot up a slight dogleg to the left. A second long iron shot may find the good-sized green awaiting.

To the jaded golfer, who has experienced the modern manicured courses designed in the past thirty years, with their different-textured grasses, railroad-tie bulkheads, dramatic water hazards and deadly large waste areas, a course that provides the simple flavor of early Ross with little disturbing the original terrain is a great joy. This is one of those special courses, a wonderful change of pace from some of the showier creations of recent years.

Lebanon was founded in 1761. For years it was a major textile producing center, but hi-tech industries have replaced the early factories.

The famed Dartmouth-Hitchcock Medical Center is located here, and the town is the home of some of the most technologically advanced technology companies in the world. Dartmouth College, the Amos Tuck School of Business Administration and Thayer School of Engineering are close by.

Golfers can reach the place easily on either interstate 91 or 89, and US Air flies into Lebanon Municipal Airport from New York and Philadelphia, carrying about 125 passengers daily. Business travelers: bring along the clubs and play a around at Carter. You'll be glad you gave it a try!

When not on the course, the area is rich with interesting side trips. Popular tourist attractions include: the Monshire Museum of Science, the Enfield Shaker Museum and Dana Robes Wood Craftsmen, Ruggles Mine, Enfield Historical Society Museum, Quechee Village and Quechee Gorge.

In autumn, the trees on the far mountain glow pink and red in the distance.

On Ross' Older Courses

"(His) bunkering tended to be profuse. He slowly began to realize in later designs that undulations, swales and grass bunkers called for more types of shots. He began framing greens with bunkers. Green size was determined by the amount of traffic a given course expected. Most were small. He managed to reduce the edge held by those who could putt well and play sand wedges well. Water was an unfair penalty. If it could be used naturally in a course, it would be part of the routing, but only to challenge the expert player. Otherwise water was a pretty backdrop."—*Richard Tufts, friend and associate of Donald Ross*

KINGSWOOD GOLF CLUB

24 KINGSWOOD ROAD, BOX 687, WOLFEBORO, NH 03894
(603) 569-3569 E-MAIL: KGC@WORLDPATH.NET

DIRECTIONS: FROM I-95 NORTH, TAKE ROUTE 16 (SPAULDING TURNPIKE) TO ROUTE 11 TO ALTON TRAFFIC CIRCLE. TAKE ROUTE 28 NORTH TOWARD WOLFEBORO. COURSE IS FIRST LEFT PAST HIGH SCHOOL.

Semi-private. 18 holes. Pro shop opens 6:30 AM. Open May 1 to October 30. Rental electric and pullcarts and clubs. Driving range. Putting green. Chipping and sand practice areas. Teaching pro. Restaurant. Clubhouse/lounge.

Wolfeboro is one of the most popular vacation spots in New England, located on glorious Lake Winnipesaukee. It has boating and fishing without match anywhere, and the Yum Yum Shop in town is where the loyalists, who come back year after year, generation after generation, gather.

For the golfers among these serious vacationers, Kingswood Golf Club, formerly Kingswood Country Club, offers great golf on a vintage Ross course that is in fine condition.

The club began as a purely social organization for summer residents. Fifteen citizens incorporated on August 16, 1907 for the purpose of "social recreation and general improvement of the Lake Winnipesaukee region." On July 10, 1915, as war raged in Europe, a nine- hole course officially opened.

Frank Butler, who stayed with the club for 49 years, was the original grounds superintendent and club administrator. In 1926, Ross was hired to add the back nine holes. His original sketches are in the possession of the club.

During the Great Depression the club nearly died, but persistence among those determined Yankees kept it going. In those days, the club operated a caddy system. The "A" caddies were paid 75 cents for 18 holes, while the "B" caddies received 50 cents. Each had to give the caddy master 10 cents. Many in time became members and even club champions, and today there are many third generation family members. With over 600 regular players, there is an active junior program, which is providing future members and excellent golfers.

Located on moderately hilly land that rolls gently, abutting 875 feet on Crescent Lake, Kingswood is the kind of bent grass course that

Above: The spectacular new hole number nine, a 375 yard par four, the number three handicap at Kingswood. A dogleg right, it features a good-sized green.

Photos and information from Tom Clark of Ault, Clark & Associates, Ltd.

146

can require the player to dig deep into his bag of tricks, because there is bound to be a water shot that comes into play, which will take all the skill one has. There is a pond or stream to be found on holes one, three, four, eight, nine, 14 and 15, so bring the retriever and carry a couple of "water" balls.

Although Tom Clark redesigned the course in 1990, the golfer will be pleased to learn that many of the holes remain largely unchanged from the day Ross designed them. One, two, three, six, seven, ten, 11 and 18 still carry the Ross signature. According to Tom, "The course was re-routed in order to provide a new clubhouse location, so only half a dozen holes remain intact." There are no homes on the course, so the player has an excellent opportunity to soak in all the natural beauty of this Wolfeboro property with no visual distractions.

Above: A true mountain course. Before carts were invented, this must have been a fun walk!

Right: This is the way golf was played at Kingswood in the early '20s, pre-Ross. Players are shown on the second green. Fairway grass was deep, and greens were large, flat and square-shaped. There were no golf carts, but caddies were plentiful and inexpensive. The golfers wore plus fours, jackets and ties, and walked the course.

Photo thanks to Club member Bill Sweeny

Tees	Par	Yards	Slope	USGA
Blue	72	6360	125	70.9
White	72	5860	122	68.6
Red	72	5300	130	73.1

DIRECTIONS: FROM I-93 NORTH, TAKE EXIT 40 TO RTE. 302 EAST. GO TEN MILES TO COURSE.

Resort. Semi-private. 18 holes. Pro shop opens 7 AM. Open May 15 to October 12. Rental gas and pullcarts and clubs. Grass driving range. Putting and chipping practice areas. Historic clubhouse restaurant. Lounge. Swimming pool. Tennis courts.

Below: Welcome to Maplewood—in the heart of the White Mountains.

Photo by Bob Labbance

The key word here is *scenery,* with views from the course of the towering Presidential Mountain Range. The golfer will be awed at the rugged granite peaks of Mount Jackson, Monroe, Jefferson, Adams, Madison, with Washington (6,288 feet) eminent above them all, as they march in solemn cadence. Particularly spectacular is the leafy wonderland of the fall, with its brilliant rainbow colors.

We can imagine Donald Ross, breathing the crisp, clear air as he arrived in this, the most mountainous of the New England states, to remodel nine and create nine new holes. The towering pines complemented his milieu, as he must have looked over the terrain, with its rolling hills and rocky streams.

At the turn of the century, this property was known as the Maplewood Casino & Country Club. It was a sparkling hub of activity, with the so-called "cream of society" from New York and Boston arriving each season for the annual Grand Ball and Cotillion.

Today, the spectacular, 34,000 square foot clubhouse, which was built in 1888, has been fully restored with historic accuracy, including a Grand Ballroom The hotel offers an atmosphere reflecting its rich heritage and a wealth of activity that will satisfy almost every interest. During golfing season, the area lends itself to great hiking, or simply taking walks along quiet country roads in a small settlement that is so sparsely populated (fewer than 800) that you are likely to meet more cows and horses than people.

Local automobile trips are also recommended. If the visitor drives south out of Franconia Notch and intersects State 112, which becomes the Kancamagus Highway, it is to discover one of New England's most scenic sections.

In the winter, there is some of the best skiing in America at nearby Cannon Mountain, Bretton Woods, Loon Mountain and Attitash, within minutes of the resort.

The resort claims that life is "simpler here...the pace is slower, the air is clearer, and the views are spectacular." It got that right.

Maplewood offers a special treat to the golfer who likes a course that is forgiving. There are tall, mature pines along the open fairways, but one seldom loses a ball on the sides that serve as dividing buffers to two fairways.

A great hole is number 16—one of the few holes in New England to play over 650 yaards off the blues. It's the number two handicap and is a par six—a rare bird indeed.

Is it rugged here? Well, here's what the scorecard says, "...a ball may be dropped within a club's length, without penalty (A) ball near rock or fairway, (B) ball driven from fifth or sixth tee into boulders in fairway (C) ball driven from tee on number 9 into ditch on right." Get the picture?

Above: Casino and pro shop
Below: Hole number two, a par four 399 off the men's and 279 off the ladies', is the authors' favorite. The number one handicap, it is broadly laid out, and only slightly doglegged to the left. The green—small and not easy to master.

Photo by R.B. Croteau

Tees	Par	Yards	Slope	USGA
Mens	72	6001	109	67.4
Ladies	71	5013	113	68.8

149

THE MOUNT WASHINGTON COURSE

AT MOUNT WASHINGTON HOTEL & RESORT
ROUTE 302, BRETTON WOODS, NH 03575
(603) 278-GOLF(4653)   FAX:(603) 278-8828
E-MAIL: GOLF@MTWASHINGTON.COM   WEBSITE: WWW.MTWASHINGTON.COM

DIRECTIONS: FROM I-93 NORTH, GO NORTH ON EXIT 35 AND THEN TO ROUTE 3 TOWARD TWIN MOUNTAIN. AT THE LIGHT, GO RIGHT ON RTE. 302 EAST FOR SIX MILES. COURSE IS ON LEFT.

Resort. 27 holes. (Mount Washington course—18 holes: Mount Pleasant course—nine holes*). Open May 15 to October 15. Gas and pullcart rental. Pro shop. Putting green. Chipping and sand practice areas. Teaching pro. Golf packages. Restaurants. Snack bar. Driving range.

Below: Reflections—the resort hotel gleams in the background as it presides over the venerable golf course and lake.

This magnificent course (one of two at this site) is an integral part of what has been called New Hampshire's last grand hotel resort. This architectural marvel with its 900 foot, wrap-around porch holding court over indoor and outdoor swimming pools, tennis courts, 200 guest rooms and suites, dining rooms, hiking and skiing trails, is all surrounded by the 18,000 acre White Mountain National Forest at the base of 6,288 foot Mount Washington, the highest peak in the Northeast.

Also part of the resort is the newly restored Bretton Arms, a vintage New England country inn that was originally built in 1896. The Inn is within walking distance of The Grand Hotel, and offers luxurious rooms and suites. In addition, there is a contemporary motor lodge facing the Grand Hotel. Visitors might want to include a trip on the Mt. Washington Cog Railroad.

Although Donald Ross designed over 300 courses, Mount Washington is one of those he

Above: Sometimes it's difficult to concentrate on your driving here on the third hole with the distraction of the magnificent mountain scenery.

personally supervised. "A thrill to play," according to David Gould in *America's Greatest Golf Resorts,* the course starts with a fairly flat front nine before challenging the golfer with a steeper and more demanding terrain on the back nine.

It has hosted four New Hampshire Opens, and well- known players include: Thomas Edison, Babe Ruth, Ken Venturi and Bobby Jones. Some past pros were: Lawson Little (two-time U.S. and British Amateur champion, who won the 1940 U.S. Open in a playoff against Gene Sarazen), Bill Melhorn and 1965 PGA Champion Dave Marr.

The par five, sixth hole is balm to the eyes and a challenge to the soul of the golfer, as the Ammonoosuc River babbles behind the tee and along the left side of the fairway, and the green sits nestled amid tall tress. The driving area is wide open, but the approach shot to the bunker-protected green must be given the utmost concentration.

The tenth, which is the number two handicap, is 549 yards from the blues to a small, forward-canted green at the top of a steep rise. You pick up your wedge and confidently arc a pretty shot at the flag, that was placed near the front on this day. But wait—if you don't hit it far enough, your ball will roll off the green and back down the hill. Of course, if you hit to the back of the green, you face a sharply downhill putt that all but disappears from view. Sound familiar, Ross fans?

The signature hole is number 14, a 235 yard, par three, requiring a tee shot down a narrow fairway that is tightly tree lined on the right to a very small green.

Variety is the keynote. Contrast the 511 yard 11th—situated within a chute of trees that face the bright white, red roofed hotel in the distance, with the par four 17th, with its backdrop of tall evergreens framing the green.

It's a limited season for golfers at Mount Washington, but the playing weather is ideal, with very few unbearably hot days, and in the late fall, as the days grow shorter, alpenglow may turn the snow-dusted Presidential Range to precious gold.

Tees	Par	Yards	Slope	USGA
Blue	71	6638	118	70.6
White	71	6154	113	68.0
Red	71	5336	116	69.7

151

Left: Putting on the third green—a 446 yard, par four beauty—the number one handicap hole on the Mount Washington course.

A Little History

John Sebastian Cabot first sighted the 6,288-foot peak of Mount Washington while exploring the New England coast in 1497. The first white man to climb Mount Washington in 1542, one Darby Field, supposedly went to his death claiming that the worthless quartz crystals he brought back were proof of great wealth hidden on the mountain.

In 1763, Royal Governor Benning Wentworth made the Upper Coös Land Grant, and settlers started looking for a shorter route to the coast than the three-week-long river trip to Portland.

In 1771, Timothy Nash found an old Indian trail penetrating the mountain barrier. With the promise of a Royal Land Grant, he fought his way through the rough terrain, and was awarded 2,184 acres for his trouble in the center of what is now the town of Bretton Woods. Unfortunately it was sold soon thereafter, and was added to the grant made in 1771 by Governor Wentworth to 83 men at The Tilton Tavern in Portsmouth. The 25,000 acre parcel was called "Bretton Woods" after Wentworth's ancestral home in England.

In 1792, Abel Crawford and his son each built an inn in the area, and entertained William Oakes, Daniel Webster, Ralph Waldo Emerson, and Nathaniel Hawthorne. In 1902, Ethan Allen Crawford III supervised the opening of The Mount Washington Hotel. Railroad construction defied the hazards of the Notch, and eventually as many as 57 trains a day brought carloads of people to visit the resort, rivaling Newport, Saratoga and Bar Harbor.

Railroad tycoon Joseph Stickney spared no expense in building the hotel. Innovative heating and plumbing systems were installed, along with a private phone system. The hotel attracted the fashionable and the rich, renting more rooms at $20 a day than other hotels offering the going rate of $5.

The Depression brought serious setbacks, but in 1944, the U.S. government used the hotel for an international gathering of financiers from 44 countries, and the building was completely restored to greet the arriving dignitaries of the now famous Bretton Woods International Monetary Conference.

In 1975 the Mount Washington Hotel was listed in the *National Register of Historic Places*, and 6,400 acres of woodlands were sold to the government for inclusion in the White Mountain National Forest. In 1986, it received National Historic Landmark designation.

*The architects for the nine-hole Mount Pleasant course, established in 1989, were Cornish & Silva. It is set up to play 18 holes of 6,430 yards from the blues with a 70 par. Blue Rating is 68.6, and slope is 124.

THE PANORAMA GOLF COURSE

AT THE BALSAMS GRAND RESORT HOTEL

1912

ROUTE 26, DIXVILLE NOTCH, NH 03576
(603) 255-3400   FAX: (603) 255-4221   E-MAIL: THEBALSAMS@AOL.COM
WEBSITE: WWW.THEBALSAMS.COM

DIRECTIONS: FROM BOSTON I-93 NORTH, TAKE EXIT 35 TO U.S. RTE. 3 NORTH TO COLEBROOK, TURN RIGHT ON RTE. 26 E TO RESORT ENTRANCE.

Resort. 18 holes. Open mId-May to mid-October. Starting times available within 72 hours. Pro shop. Putting green. Practice range. Chipping and sand practice areas. Teaching pro. Golf school. Restaurant. Swimming pool. Tennis courts. Golf packages.

The clubhouse from the 17th green

The 14th green at sundown

The mountainside setting of The Panorama Golf Course is among the most magnificent of the Ross legacy. Built high on the western side of Keazer Mountain, golfers may be momentarily diverted from their game by views of the Connecticut River Valley of northern New Hampshire, Mount Monadnock in Vermont and the rolling hills of the Province of Quebec in Canada.

Not for the faint of heart, there is no part of the game, from placement of a tee shot to the reading of a putt, that doesn't require consideration for the mountainside. A first-time player will swear that his putt breaks uphill until he learns to adjust to the slope. Small-to-medium size greens are hard to hit and hold, but the signature grass-walled bunkers serve as definition and perspective aids more than threatening hazards. This is a course that has been unspoiled by modern design or the desire for glitz. It is a must on the list of golf purists, almost entirely intact from Ross' 1912 design, and critics agree that it is among the top golf resorts in the northeastern U.S.

It has been named to *Golf Magazine's* list of Silver Medal Resorts and is rated the third

The ninth green and clubhouse

most difficult course in the state by the New Hampshire Golf Association. *Golf Digest* has rated it number one for 1999-00.

Some of the famous golfers who have played The Panorama are: President Warren G. Harding, Babe Ruth, Ben Hogan, trick shot artist Joe Kirkwood, Bob Cousy of the Boston Celtics, New England Patriots John Hannah, Paul Stookey of Peter, Paul and Mary, and U.S. Supreme Court Judge Charles Evans Hughes— a mixed bag with one common thread—they all loved golf.

The course has hosted the 1977 New Hampshire Amateur Championship, the Jim Berry Memorial, Daniel Webster Classic and the North Country Amateur Championship. Three-day Centennial Golf School programs are held in May and June.

In describing this course in *The Atlantic Monthly,* Robert Cullen said, "Many of Ross' best holes offer similarly measured allocations of risk and reward." Yes, the golfer has to take some chances with the myriad bunkers and tricky greens, but oh, that wonderful feeling when one makes that par!

The Balsams Grand Resort Hotel is a magnificent 15,000 acre private estate, welcoming resort guests with an all-inclusive American plan. During the summer, in addition to 27 holes of golf, it provides tennis, swimming in a heated pool and a private lake, boating and fishing, walking trails, mountain climbing and biking, a natural history program with guided tours, live entertainment, lectures and a renowned cuisine. In the winter, the resort offers a full range of snow sports.

It opened as a 25-room inn called the Dix House just after the Civil War. Named after a patriot of the American Revolution, Colonel Timothy Dix, it was taken over by his partner Daniel Webster after Dix died in battle. In the late 19th Century, the White Mountains developed into a popular summer resort, and in 1895, the Dix House was purchased by a wealthy Philadelphia inventor, Henry S. Hale, who renamed it The Balsams. He steadily expanded, and by 1918, an addition effectively doubled the overnight capacity to 400 guests. Since 1866, the resort has had only six owners.

The lower course fairway

Larger than Manhattan Island, The Balsams Resort covers more than 25 square miles and varies more than 2,000 feet in altitude!

Tees	Par	Yards	Slope	USGA
Gold	72	6804	130	72.8
Blue	72	6097	122	69.1
Silver	72	5069	115	67.8

Above: Across the tenth fairway to the pro shop and the clubhouse
Below: The ninth green and western horizon

TORY PINES RESORT

1929

740 2ND NEW HAMPSHIRE TURNPIKE NORTH, RTE 47, FRANCESTOWN, NH 03043
(603) 588-2923 FAX: (603) 588-2275 WEBSITE: WWW.TORYPINESRESORT.COM

DIRECTIONS: RTE. 101 FROM MANCHESTER WEST TO RTE. 114. TURN TOWARD RTE. 47 NORTH TO COURSE ON RIGHT.

Semi-private/resort. 18 holes. Open April 1 to November 1. Rental gas and pullcarts and clubs. Grass driving range. Putting green. Chipping and sand practice areas. Teaching pro. Pro shop opens 7 AM. Tee times may be made up to five days in advance. The Gibson Tavern (built in 1799) and sports bar. Tennis courts. Billiard room. Swimming pool. Conference facilities.

Below: The par three finishing hole plays 183 off the blue tees (170 from the whites) to an hourglass-shaped green with a large bunker on the right.

Donald Ross designed the first nine, and Tory Pines is listed in various Ross anthologies, but unfortunately his course was to become a dairy farm, and wasn't rebuilt until the '70s. The routings are now almost totally different. Ross' original plans were lost, as so often happened to Ross courses, so they were not available to guide Tory Pines' reconstruction. Maybe one day his plans will surface, and the course will once again be played as he envisioned it. However, according to course superintendent Robb Horne, who has spoken to old-time members with long memories, the first and second fairways remain intact, but tee boxes and greens are lost. Only hole seven remains as Ross laid it out over 70 years ago: tees, fairway and green.

According to pro Scott Shields, the narrow course requires careful course management to score well. It has been recently renovated, and is in excellent condition. Its popularity is attested to by the fact that between 30 and 35 tournaments are held annually. Many golfers come to appreciate the spectacular views of Mount Monadnock, which is the second most climbed mountain the world. The

hiker may be breathless from the 3,265 foot climb to the summit, or from the magnificent views.

Unfortunately, due to many changes of management over the years, historical records of the golf course and resort are not available, but the community is most interesting. Of course, if the plans of Ross ever do surface, count on them to be relied upon again here.

Francestown, established in 1784, is a rural charmer located in a sector of lower New Hampshire noted for its friendly natives, beautiful scenery and many tourist attractions, including the Currier Gallery of Art, the Manchester Institute of Arts and Sciences, The Cathedral of the Pines, great mountains to hike, clear streams and lakes to fish. It is situated near the towns of Manchester, Nashua, Keene and the state capital in Concord, with its Historical Society Library and Museum, the Pierce Manse, and the Concord Arts and Crafts Center. The white town hall serves as a public meeting hall and community center. Here plays produced by the Francestown Community theatre and monthly Contra Dances are held. The Little Red School building, where the ancestors of present-day residents studied, still stands. The George Homes Bixby Memorial Library offers the user a fine collection of 15,000 books or about ten books for every man, woman and child in town.

The Tory Pines Resort has 32 condominiums for rent, and many golf packages are offered. The Dennis Meyer Golf School is on the property and offers two-, three- and four-day programs.

History

Today, Francestown is small and secluded, but at one time it was a thriving center of commerce. When the Second New Hampshire Turnpike thrust its way through the center of town in 1800, it became a major artery for traffic heading west into Vermont, the northern part of the state and Canada, reshaping it into a commercial center and prominent toll road stagecoach stop.

The Gibson Tavern flourished, and soapstone, discovered in 1792, contributed to growing affluence as it was quarried in great quantity. The Francestown Academy, founded in 1801, imparted a cultured ethos to the town, and its pupils numbered governors, congressmen, U.S. senators, and Franklin Pierce, fourth president of the United States.

The arrival of toll-free roads and rail transportation caused the town to decline, and when railroads bypassed the town, its ambitious entrepreneurs moved away, and

farming again took over. Then, in the 1930s, Bostonians rediscovered the town, restoring its priceless old houses and preserving them with great care and attention to historic detail, so that today it looks just as it once did centuries ago.

In 1927, Donald Ross designed a nine-hole golf course on the site known then as Mt. Crotched Country Club. These nine holes on the mountain are the present-day front nine at Tory Pines. Mt. Crotched Country Club remained popular through the 1930s, but with the advent of World War II and gasoline rationing, tourism declind sharply, and farming once again took over the land. The club closed its doors in 1941 and reverted to pastureland, operating under the name of Tavern Farm operated by the Prince family.

In April of 1977, the property passed into the hands of a golf professional and his wife, who toiled to clear the hayfields and find the Ross fairways of the past. It was at that time that the back nine holes were developed, cross

Above: The Clubhouse Tavern as it looks today—a haven for golfers and wedding receptions, too.

Tees	Par	Yards	Slope	USGA
Blue	71	6111	138	70.7
White	71	5530	133	68.0
Red	71	4604	121	68.4

157

country trails were blazed, and an 18-hole course reopened in the fall of 1979.

The course was sold in the '80s, and residences were constructed along the adjacent hillside. The old Gibson Tavern was remodeled and a pro shop added in 1987. The remodeling basically destroyed all historical detail such as rare fireplace mantles, panel molding and exceptional Moses Eaton sten-

ciling in the tavern.

Tory Pines is included as a good example of the importance of preserving course architectural plans. Here they were lost, with 17 of Ross' 18 holes sadly lost with them. But the good news: Francestown is a rare find—well worth a visit and a round of golf.

Above: Just a few clouds drift by holes nine and four. Nine is the second most difficult hole on the front nine, a par four (422 yards from the blues), with the most severe dog-leg on the entire course. Number four hole is the longest on the front (504 yards), a par five and the number one handicap.
Below: The starting hole, over water with bunkers on each side of the fairway, and a long bunker fronting the green. An 11 handicap, par four, it plays 370 from the blues. Keep it straight.

Historic information courtesy of Veda O'Neil, Historical Rooms
All Tory Pines photos by Arthur Boufford

New Jersey

Seaview Marriott Resort, Bay Course

SEAVIEW MARRIOTT RESORT BAY COURSE   1915

MEMBER OF HISTORIC HOTELS OF AMERICA
HOST TO SHOPRITE LPGA CLASSIC EACH JUNE, MAINTAINING ONE OF THE HIGHEST PURSES ON THE TOUR
401 SOUTH NEW YORK ROAD, ABSECON, NJ 08201
(609)652-1800   FAX: (609) 652-2307
WEBSITE: WWW.MARRIOTTHOTELS.COM/AIYNJ/

DIRECTIONS: FROM NORTH, TAKE GARDEN STATE PARKWAY, EXIT 48, GO SOUTH 7 MILES ON RTE. 9. FROM WEST, TAKE ATLANTIC CITY EXP., EXIT 12, TURN LEFT ON 575 FOR 3.8 MILES, TURN RIGHT ON JIMMIE LEEDS RD. GO EAST 5.9 MILES.

Resort. Two 18 hole courses. Open year round, with a forecaddie program between May 1 and Nov. 1 to accompany each foursome. Rental carts, clubs and shoes. Tee times may be made by calling pro shop or on the internet at www.seaviewgolf.com. First class dining. Elizabeth Arden Red Door Spa. Outdoor and indoor swimming pools. All weather tennis courts. Jogging and nature trails. Complete pro shop. Putting green. Chipping and sand practice areas. Teaching pro. Grass driving range. 300 guest rooms and 270 proposed two-bedroom units. The Faldo Golf Institute by Marriott, a state-of-the-art facility to accommodate golfers of all levels.

S eaview Marriott Resort, on 670 pine acres across the bay from Atlantic City, is a world-class facility with superior accommodations, beautiful surrounding woodlands and distinguished service. The hotel is rated by Zagat's as one of the best in the area, and *Golf Digest* gives it four-stars in its Places to Play guide. Its reputation for excellence over the past 88 years includes two 18-hole championship courses, the Pines and the Bay, each with its own historic significance.

Donald Ross was called in to design the Bay Course in 1915. The Pines Course was designed by Flynn and Toomey in 1932 after being laid out by Hugh Wilson. (When lists of the 100 great U.S. courses are made, Ross is usually credited with 23 of them and Flynn and Toomey with 19.)

The history (or myth) of Seaview is that industrialist Clarence H. Geist, in January of 1914, grew impatient while waiting to tee off at

Top: The Seaview Marriott Resort in all its glory
Bottom: The spectacular 419 yard, par four number ten hole—a two handicap

The par four, 434 yard second hole—the number one handicap here at Seaview

the Atlantic City Country Club. Maurice Risley, Seaview's co-founder, was quoted as saying, "Mr. Geist, if I had as much money as you, I'd build my own golf course." And he did.

Presidents Harding and Eisenhower played here, and the 1942 PGA Tournament was won by Sam Snead on Ross' Bay Course. Snead beat Jim Turnesa, who had beaten Ben Hogan. Snead shot a 60 foot chip into the hole on the 35th hole to win.

This course was fully restored in 1997-8 to its original Ross Design, with 13 bunkers being added. On hole one, the sand bunker stretches 140 yards (longest on the course.) Holes four and five have bunkers of 130 yards each, and trees were cut down to allow the famous shore breezes to come into play.

The course is defined by short, bushy pines along its fairways and, although it is wide open, precision is needed to score well. There are great bay views, yet water comes into play on only one hole, the par three number seven.

Nestled on Reeds Bay, overlooking the Atlantic Ocean, the Bay Course offers undulating greens well protected by bunkers in the links style. It is a perfect blend of on-shore breezes and the

natural terrain inherent to southern New Jersey in all but the severest winter weather.

When Donald Ross set foot on the seaside plot of farmland over 85 years ago, his major thrust was to incorporate the gentle rolling farmland and seaside views into a golf course that would be admired for many years to come. He dotted the landscape with chocolate drop mounds, cross bunkers, sand mounds and of course his often vexing small greens. Some of the deeper pot bunkers and high-faced bunkers require great dexterity and concentration in order to keep scores low.

Visitors will see the original Ross architectural designs for the course proudly displayed inside the clubhouse, just outside the Gallery Room. Few of the more than 300 courses he designed have their original plans.

Tees	Par	Yards	Slope	USGA
Blue	71	6247	122	70.7
White	71	6011	120	69.5
Red	71	5017	114	68.4

161

Above: The ninth hole at Seaview, a 415 yard par four
Below: The shortest hole on the famed New Jersey course—the 115 yard, par three 13th

New York

Chautauqua Golf Club, The Lake Course

Mark Twain Golf Club

Rip Van Winkle Country Club

The Sagamore Resort & Golf Club

Thendara Golf Club

Tupper Lake Country Club

CHAUTAUQUA GOLF CLUB THE LAKE COURSE   1923

ROUTE 394, PO BOX 28, CHAUTAUQUA, NY 14722
(716) 357-6211   FAX: (716) 357-6318   E-MAIL: SMGOLF@CECOMET.NET
WEBSITE: WWW.CHAUT-INST.COM

DIRECTIONS: FROM NY THRUWAY (I-90), TAKE 394 SOUTH DIRECTLY TO CHAUTAUQUA.
FROM PENNSYLVANIA, TAKE 474 NORTH OR 89 NORTH TO 394 NORTH.

Public. The Chautauqua Institution Golf Club operates the famed Lake Course; 18 holes designed by Donald Ross and the newer Hill Course built in 1989, designed by Xen Hessenplug. Open April 15 to October 15. Rental power and pull carts. Driving range. Snack bar. No alcoholic beverages. Complete pro shop. PGA instruction.

Right: July 21, 1896—A golf club was organized in the Department of Physical Culture. Here they are playing from the tee box using a sand tee.

The Chautauqua Golf Club was founded in 1896, when local golf enthusiasts laid out a "links" course on stunning property located at Lake Chautauqua. The first nine-hole course opened in 1914. It was remodeled and expanded to 18 holes by Donald Ross in 1923, formally opening in 1924. Today on this Mecca for golfers are two of the finest courses in North America, offering the picturesque beauty of the Lake Course and the naturalistic views from the famed Hill Course.

Both courses have hosted exhibitions by some of the world's leading players and continue to be played by dignitaries visiting the famed Chautauqua Institution. It is one of only two 36-hole courses between Cleveland, Ohio and Rochester, New York.

Famous players who have played here include: Walter Hagen, Ben Hogan, Sam Snead, Gene Sarazen, Porky Oliver and Horton Smith. It was recently played by President Bill Clinton, Johnny Mathis and Willie Nelson.

There are still 17 holes of the 36 that carry the signature of Donald Ross. They are holes one through 13, in addition to 17 and 18 on the Lake Course and holes one and 18 on the Hill Course.

Ross was a frugal Scot, and didn't like to see players hitting expensive balls into water. His rule of thumb: no more than three water holes on any course. At Chautauqua today, one finds seven out of 36 holes are water holes.

Each year Chautauqua's finely groomed fairways and lush greens host an annual Pro-Am tournament with both a men's and women's division. This is the site of the Western New York Professional Golfer's Association Senior's Championship.

164

Top: About 1916. Note the size of the
caddy—and the bag he's carrying.

Bottom: A golf exhibition in the '30s. From
left: Al Sharpe, president of the club; Horton
Smith; Johnny Farrell; Jack Cawsey, club professional; Gene Sarazen is to the right of
seated Judge Lewis of San Antonio, Texas
and behind him, Dr. Arthur Bestor, president
of Chautauqua Institution.

Tees	Par	Yards	Slope	USGA
Blue	72	6449	112	70.2
White	72	6148	109	69.0
Red	72	5423	112	70.2

From left: Suzanne and Thurston Reid, members; Dinah Shore, the singer and promoter of ladies' golf, and Stan Marshaus, golf professional at Chautauqua since 1974

About the Institution

In 1999, the Chautauqua Institution celebrated its 125th anniversary. It was established as a national forum for open discussion of public issues, international relations, literature and science. Approximately 100 lecturers appear at Chautauqua during a season, which runs for nine weeks in the summer.

It is a place where some of the leading thinkers of our time come to share the concerns and issues of the real world. Here an abundance of music, dance and the visual arts find their own forms of expression. It is Chautauqua's extraordinary mix that draws over 142,000 people each summer to its 750 acre site in southwestern New York State.

Over 8,000 students enroll annually in the summer schools, which offer courses in art, music, dance, theater, writing skills and a wide variety of special interests. The Chautauqua orchestra performs thrice weekly with leading soloists in the 5,000 seat amphitheater.

"Golf would have made little progress if the early architects had not been wise enough to give us courses that are beautiful and restful to the eye, offer a fair but not difficult test and can be maintained at a reasonable cost.

"Donald was a man of considerable ability and would have made a success in any profession. Fortunately for us he chose golf. His policy regarding golf architecture can best be described by a quotation often used: 'Golf should be a pleasure, not a penance.' His interpretation of the word pleasure was very broad, implying not only a fair course which presented problems and challenges to all types of golfers in all departments of the game, but which was also as natural as possible. To obtain these effects, many of his courses were both designed and built by him under contract using a construction engineer who was a member of staff.

"Many of Donald's friends, including myself, urged him to write his autobiography. This did not interest him and one got the impression that he felt he had failed if his courses did not speak for him more eloquently than he could himself."—Richard Tufts, President Pinehurst, Inc. and close friend of Donald Ross

From Donald Ross of Pinehurst and Royal Dornoch *by Donald Grant, MA, FRGS, Sutherland Press, Golspie, Scotland 1973*

MARK TWAIN GOLF COURSE

2275 CORNING ROAD, ELMIRA, NY 14903
(607) 737-5770   FAX: (607) 737-5772

DIRECTIONS: FROM RTE. #328 IN ELMIRA, TAKE RTE. 14 NORTH FOR 2.5 MILES. COURSE IS ON LEFT.

*Public. City-owned municipal. 18 holes.
Daily fee. Open April 1 to December 15.
Pro shop opens 6:30 AM. Snack bar.
Rental gas and pullcarts. Putting and chipping practice areas. Teaching pro. Snack bar.*

Although readers of Mark Twain's works are likely to associate him with the Mississippi River towns or his final home in Hartford, Connecticut, the fact is that, for some of his most productive writing years, he lived in Elmira, New York.

In 1874, Twain's sister-in-law, Susan Crane, built an octagonal study for him at her Quarry Farm residence in the hills above the town. Twain and his family routinely spent their summers there. He described it this way, "It has a peaked roof, sits perched in complete isolation on top of an elevation that commands leagues of valley and city and retreating ranges of distant blue hills...a cozy nest with just room in it for a sofa and a table...and when storms sweep down the remote valley and the lightning flashes above the hills beyond, and the rain beats upon the roof over my head, imagine the luxury of it." It was here he worked on *The Adventures of Tom Sawyer, The Adventures of Huckleberry Finn* and *A Connecticut Yankee in King Arthur's Court,* among others. The building is now part of the campus of Elmira College, which houses the Cen-ter for Mark Twain Studies. Twain loved Elmira, and Elmira honored him by naming its golf course after him.

When you walk the course of Mark Twain, you can almost feel the presence of Ross, even though he created it over sixty years ago. Whether you play Royal Dornoch, Pinehurst Number Two or Mark Twain, the Ross vision of the way the game should be played is as evident today as it was then.

Located between Pennsylvania's Appalachians and the Finger Lakes of New York in Chemung County, Mark Twain follows Ross' basic design principle of establishing a green with slightly raised surface three or four feet above the level of the fairway. He'd then fashion subtle undulations and gradations to make it

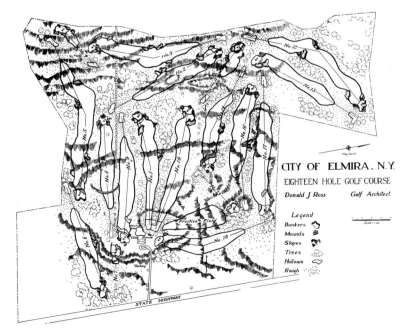

Original Donald Ross Plans

as daunting as possible. This meant that the slightly erring shot would tend to roll off rather than hold on the fringe, thus creating a particularly delicate chipping challenge. It is possible that the character of the 14th at Royal Dornoch, the course of Ross' youth, inspired some of the greens here.

Over the years, the best testimony to the quality of the Mark Twain course lies in the names of the golf greats who have played the course: Jack Nicklaus, Arnold Palmer, Gary Player, Lee Trevino, Lanny Wadkins, Doug Sanders, Bruce Devlin, Laura Baugh and Tony Jacklin.

Fortunately for the player who is a Ross fan, the operators of Mark Twain have left all the original holes undisturbed. There are no homes on the course to block the natural views, and with the excellent irrigation, the fairways are usually found soft and plush. *Golfweek's America's Best Courses* rates this venue as 25th in the nation out of all municipal courses. Other Ross courses on that prestigious list are George Wright in Boston and Mill Creek Park, South Course in Youngstown, Ohio.

The genesis for the course's creation was a meeting in January of 1937 in Ross' Rhode Island office with Elmira golfer, H. Tryon, and Elmira's city engineer, Thomas Supple. They reviewed ideas for a course in Elmira and the costs to make it happen. An estimate was rushed to the New York State Division of the WPA. Within 30 days, the course was approved, and construction started in the summer. By late 1939, the second nine holes were finished, and it opened as an 18-hole course.

Ross visited the course during August second and third of 1939 to inspect the work, and to consult on maintenance and upkeep. His letter to Ralph Klebes, city manager, states, "The course as a whole is fully up to my expectations. It is a grand one and given two more years of careful maintenance it will stand out as one of the finest courses owned by any city in America."

In the 1939 budget of $7,176 for the course's operation, these figures are reported:
Golf Pro and Manager– 7 months salary @ $100 per month—$700
Greenskeeper—8 months salary @ $130 per month—$1040
Water and seed, sand and fertilizer—$800

3 laborers (7 months of 22 days)—$1848
Maintenance of equipment—$925

The special Ross formula here for fairway grass was: 40% Kentucky Blue Grass, 40% Blue Tag Colonial Bent and 20% Red Top, with fairways seeded at 150 pounds per acre. He specified, "The rough, which will be 30 feet wide bordering both sides of each fairway, will be seeded at a rate of 75 pounds per acre. Tees similar rate as fairways." He added: "100 pounds of bone meal be applied to the greens before the planting of Bent Stolons" and the fertilizer formula was to be 6-10-2 and applied at the rate of 400 pounds per acre shortly before seeding. Putting greens were planted with Washington Strain Best Stolons—the greens would average 6,000 square feet each.

The city of Elmira has 27 city parks, two pools, playgrounds and ball fields, but Mark Twain continues to be given special attention, and it shows. Several bunkers have been carefully replaced following Ross' original drawings, and in 1995, the 14th hole was modified, restoring a small pond directly in front of the green, which can be seen in the original drawings.

The course averages almost 45,000 rounds of play annually with plans afoot for a much more ambitious junior golf program. In an article about this course, golf writer Matthew C. Jones in June of 1997 wrote, "Elmira's Mark Twain Golf Course remains a testament to the genius of its designer and represents golf in its purest and most traditional form."

What would Mr. Twain make of all this interest in the game of golf? Were he alive, he'd most likely find it all amusing, seeing grown men and women avidly pursuing a little white ball and then seeking desperately to deliver it into a small hole in the ground.

Tees	Par	Yards	Slope	USGA
Blue	72	6829	123	73.6
White	72	6323	117	70.1
Red	76	5571	121	72.3

169

RIP VAN WINKLE COUNTRY CLUB

BOX 190, PALENVILLE, NY 12463
(518) 678-9779

1919

DIRECTIONS: FROM NY THRUWAY SOUTH TAKE EXIT 20 TO RTE. 32. GO RIGHT SEVEN MILES TO INTERSECTION OF 32 AND 32A. GO LEFT ONTO 32A TO LIGHT IN PALENVILLE.

Semi-private. 9 holes, plays to 18. Open April 1 to December 1. Rental carts. Driving range. Putting green. Clubhouse has full service bar. Lunch is available Wednesday through Sunday.

Below: Rip Van Winkle is gorgeous in the fall.

ing to stay and rehabilitate the then sleeping golf course. Ray was resident pro for many years, sometimes calling from his tractor to novice golfers, "Head down, follow through!"

The picturesque course is situated at the foot of Palenville's North Mountain. This is where Washington Irving's Rip Van Winkle took his 20-year nap, with majestic views of North Mountain, rising abruptly

This tree-lined course, at a 900-foot elevation, was formally opened in 1920 and was operated by members until 1942, when it was closed during wartime. It was purchased in 1949 by the late Raymond Smith and his wife Patricia and soon reopened. The Smiths were New York City residents who had built a summer home a few miles west of the village of Catskill and fallen in love with the place, decid-

Now we know what they mean by "golf nuts."

1,500 feet from the very western edge of the links.

Perched on the summit is the famous Mountain House, summer haven of presidents and millionaires from pre-Civil War days until it faded out of fashion in the '30s. The turntable site, where one changed cars from the Catskill Mountain Railroad to the spectacular straight-up-the-mountain Otis Railroad (for Mountain House passengers) is now Rip Van Winkle's sixth green. Many players come here from the Catskill-Saugerties-Kingston area.

Holes three and 18 remain exactly as Ross designed them. Others have been slightly modified over the years, but the course maintains a venerable Ross "look." The fairways are wide, and out-of-bounds markers are liberal. The topography is basically flat for the area. The fairways and greens are in very good shape, with a new irrigation system, and it is not easy to hit a ball out of bounds.

For the golfer who can drive straight, this course is set up just right, with all the holes placed so the pin is in line with the tee. The most challenging hole on the course is the 131 yard par three third hole. It is surrounded by four sand bunkers, so if you don't have a high drive, you're likely to find yourself in sand. The green has difficult undulations, breaking in three directions. Your ball may find water on four, five, seven, eight and nine. The large pond on eight is particularly daunting.

The course sponsors the Raymond J. Smith Memorial ProAm Tournament each year. Today, John L. Smith, grandson of Ray Smith and Ferris graduate is the PGA professional.

In the early days of golf, clubs gave holes nicknames. That was the custom here. The imaginative names are: Old Rip, Village Tavern, Young Rip, Dame Van Winkle, The Glen, Dog Wolf, Bowling Green, The Dwarf, Hudson's Crew, Nine Pins, Schnapps, Last Drink, Long Sleep, Thunder Lightning, Rip's Awakening, Long Beard, Rusty Gun and Journey Home. The names still appear on the scorecard, keeping the tradition alive.

Brave souls

Tees	Par	Yards	Slope	USGA
Blue	36	3005	115	68.5
Red	36	2698	118	70.1

171

THE SAGAMORE RESORT & GOLF CLUB 1928

FEDERAL HILL ROAD, BOLTON LANDING, NY 12814
(518) 644-9400 FAX: (518) 743-6389 WEBSITE: WWW.THESAGAMORE.COM
RESERVATIONS: 1-800-358-3585

DIRECTIONS: TAKE I-87 (ADIRONDACK NORTHWAY) TO EXIT 22. TURN LEFT TO 9-N. GO EIGHT MILES TO LIGHT. TURN LEFT ON HORICAN AVENUE. GO RIGHT ON FEDERAL HILL ROAD TO TOP OF HILL.

A four-diamond resort. 18 holes. Full club-house operation and pro shop. Open April 25 through November 10. Rental carts and clubs. Driving range. Putting green. The Club Grill is an ideal spot to relax after a round.

Right: An elevated green with one of the most impressive sand bunkers in the Adirondacks

The Sagamore has been awarded *Golf Magazine's* Silver Medal, which distinguishes it as one of the best golf resorts in America. *Golf Digest* ranks the course fifth in New York State and one of the top 500 in the nation. It's a course where almost all the golf greats have played at least once, including Tom Kite, Mark O'Meara, Gary McCord, Walter Hagen, Ted Kroll, Ben Hogan, Gene Sarazen and Craig Wood. It has been the home of many great tournaments, and hosted the Northeast PGA Championship in 1987 and the USGA Senior Open Qualifying Northeast Section from 1996 to 2000.

Unlike most Ross courses, and to its great credit, every hole at The Sagamore remains exactly as Ross designed it and supervised its construction. In 1985 it was fully restored to its earlier glory using Ross' original blueprints.

Here the player faces holes that are routed naturally through an upland meadow and the magnificent Adirondack woods. It is a memorable challenge, and in the fall its colors are spectacular.

This is one of the authors' favorite resorts in the country. Situated on its own 72 acre island on Lake George, it faces this glacial body of water of fabulous beauty and tranquility. The landmark main hotel is kept in mint condition, and there are seven adjacent lodges, some with their own fireplaces and balconies.

The Veranda Lounge, overlooking the lake, offers afternoon tea, creative appetizers, cocktails or late evening coffee and piano music. There is a world-class spa with sauna, whirlpool, indoor pool and massage—great after a round of golf. A large tennis operation, croquet, water

Hole number one—a straightaway medium par four with the best view on the course. Accuracy is needed off tee with O.B. right and heavy trees left. The approach shot plays half a club longer than it appears, or a full club if the wind is in your face.

skiing and sailing offer recreation and relaxation.

The golfer finds "hogback" contours rising and falling with the Adirondack terrain. White birches enliven the evergreen forests, and ancient heather, brought from Scotland by Ross, highlight the course.

The course sits on a ridge two and one half miles from the hotel and provides views of Lake George and the mountains. Hitting the greens here in regulation is not an automatic two-putt—not by a long shot.

Water can come into play on holes three, five, six, 13 and 16. The number one handicap is number seven, playing 425 off the blues. It takes a tee shot to the right center of the fairway, which will put the player in the most level position for a long uphill approach shot. Take one club more than you think, and keep your second shot left of center of the green, avoiding the large green-side bunker on the right front. A birdie here is a rare bird; a par is considered top-notch playing.

Above: Autumn in the Adirondack woods

Above right: The Sagamore's signature hole—a long par four requiring a very accurate tee shot. Water on the right (blind from the tee) and heavy pine woods left. The approach shot is over water and uphill, so take an extra club to reach this Ross masterpiece.

Tees	Par	Yards	Slope	USGA
Blue	70	6890	130	72.9
White	70	6410	128	71.5
Red	70	5211	122	73.0

History

The Sagamore Hotel has had a rich and colorful history as a luxurious resort on Lake George since its opening in 1883. In the late 1800s, the southern Adirondacks became renowned for their scenic beauty and recreational pleasures. The Sagamore's grandeur attracted the rich and famous of the day. Business tycoons began building mansions along the west side of the lake, known as Millionaire's Row.

The first hotel was one of the poshest in America, but it soon burned down. In 1894, a new hotel opened with Edison incandescent electric lights, telegraph, telephone, private baths and a steam elevator, tennis courts and a small golf course. In 1914, this edifice also burned down.

In that year, 188 acres were purchased on Federal Hill in Bolton Landing, a few miles from where the Sagamore Hotel had stood, for a golf course. Between 1919 and 1926, six of the eight national golf tournaments had been held on Donald Ross-designed courses around the country. That caught the attention of the Sagamore management, and they hired Ross to create a course here.

A new hotel opened on July 1, 1930, with the resort fully restored. In the '40s, the Brandt family of New York acquired the property. In 1981, Norman Wolgin, a Philadelphia real estate developer, bought the property from the Brandts. A $75 million restoration was begun, and a renewed Sagamore Hotel reopened in 1985. All 240 lodge accommodations were totally redone in 1998.

The enclave includes seven Adirondack-style lodges on the edge of the lake; The Hermitage, a former carriage house that has been converted into an all-suite, historic executive retreat; Conference Center; tennis and racquetball courts, health and fitness center, and six restaurants. It is a landmark, listed in the *National Register of Historic Places*.

Left: As you play through rolling mountainside terrain, you'll discover that each hole of this 6,950 yard course was designed by a master to be enjoyed by golfers of every ability.

174

White birches and dark shadows frame a classic Ross green.

THENDARA GOLF CLUB

FIFTH AVENUE, BOX 153, THENDARA, NY 13472
(315) 369-3136   FAX: (315) 369-6686

DIRECTIONS: FROM UTICA, GO NORTH ON ROUTE 12. FROM ALDER CREEK EXIT, TAKE ROUTE 28 WEST. COURSE IS ON WEST SIDE OF TOWN OF OLD FORGE.

Semi-private. 18 holes. Open May 1 to October 11. Rental gas and pullcarts and clubs. Walking allowed. Driving range. Putting green. Chipping and sand practice areas. Teaching pro. Pro shop opens 7 AM. Restaurant and patio. Lockers. Guests may phone two days in advance for tee times and Thursday for Saturday and Sunday.

Right: The Thendara scorecard features an original painting of the course in the autumn.

If you like mountain courses, you'll love Thendara, located ten miles north of Utica in the rugged Adirondacks on the Moose River. The Indian word, Thendara, means "edge of the woods," and when the fall foliage is at its peak, being at the edge is an exceptionally beautiful experience. Large rocks jut out along the forest-lined fairways filled with nature's brightest colors, and black bear, deer and fox are often seen by sharp-eyed golfers.

In the early part of the 20th century, with the development of rail travel, the Adirondacks became accessible to tourists. Many wealthy families visited the area, and large resort hotels and private great camps allowed these people to enjoy the beauty and serenity of the mountains and lakes.

In 1921, five businessmen decided the time was ripe for a golf course in Thendara and formed the Western Adirondack Corporation to build and operate a nine-hole course. Donald Ross was hired as the designer, and the course opened in the spring of 1922. It remained a nine-hole course until after the war, when Russell Bailey was hired to design the remaining nine holes. He carved them out of the wilderness

Wild turkeys crossing the third fairway

along the Moose River.

Many famous golfers have challenged the mountain geography here, including: Arnold Palmer, Tony Lema, Doug Sanders, Gary Player, Julius Boros, Jack Nicklaus, Bruce Devlin, Sam Snead, Frank Beard, Billy Casper, Tony Jacklin, Lee Trevino, Chi Chi Rodriguez, Lee Elder, Bob Murphy, Marlene Hagge, Betsy Cullen and Shelley Hamlin. Dave Marr holds the course record of 63. The New York State Golf Association held its Senior Women's Tournament here in 1984 and 1998.

The general layout of the course remains today as it was in the '20s. Holes one, two, eight and nine are played as designed by Ross; holes three to seven are played in a different order and reverse direction, the greens and tees being opposite from his design.

The ninth hole on the 179 acre course is its signature. It is one of the toughest on the course, with a plateau green and steeply pitched approach apron. Even though it is only a par three, it is hard to master and has caused many a golfer to shake his head in disbelief at this treacherous green.

The seventh is difficult, too—a real putting challenge with two large mounds and a valley between. The 11th is particularly scenic, as the rushing water of the Moose River delights the eyes and ears.

To the first-time player, the front nine looks benign, with its wide open fairways, large greens, not too many tress, no water hazards and few but strategically placed bunkers. The greens, which have been slightly enlarged with poa annua, are true but quick. However, when it comes to tally up the score, the golfer realizes the genius of Donald Ross. It is fair, but very challenging of one's golfing ability, with-

out gimmicks or tricks. It is simply the golfer against the course, and in most instances, the course wins!

Sports writer Brian Siplo, writing for *New York Golf,* describes the greens at Thendara in these words: "unquestionably, the best architectural feature at Thendara is the greens. If the land selected for the course was level by mountain standards, Mr. Ross reversed this anomaly on the putting surfaces. Every green has slopes to vex the finest practitioners of the 'game within the game' should their approach stray too far from the hole."

Above: The par five, 438 yard fourth hole features five strategically placed bunkers, two guarding the small, raised green. It plays straight, but narrow.

Tees	Par	Yards	Slope	USGA
Blue	72	6426	123	70.9
White	72	6195	121	69.8
Red	73	5755	123	73.2

TUPPER LAKE COUNTRY CLUB
1936
COUNTRY CLUB ROAD, BOX 899 (OFF ROUTE 30), TUPPER LAKE, NY 12986
(518) 359-3701   FAX: (518) 359-3701   E-MAIL: TLCC@CAPITAL.NET

DIRECTIONS: ROUTE 30 SOUTH OUT OF TUPPER LAKE. GO THREE MILES. TAKE LEFT ONTO COUNTRY CLUB ROAD.

Semi-private. 18 holes. Open May 1 to October 31. Rental carts and clubs. Driving range. Pro on site. The Clubhouse Restaurant and Lounge opens 11 AM, dinner starting at 5 PM. Closed Thursdays in June.

Below: Unspoiled rugged mountain beauty and breathtaking vistas are the theme here.

Donald Ross sculpted this fabulous upstate New York course at the base of Mt. Morris in 1936 at a time when money was short, and very few courses were being built. His munificent fee for the task: a whopping $750—just $42 a hole—quite a bargain!

The lush, rolling fairways with small greens are available for play only six months of the year because of the climate, however this classic 6,254 yard Adirondack course provides the nature-loving golfer with some of the finest fall foliage vistas of any course in America. Mid-September to mid-October is gorgeous here, with the deep blue of the lake, the emerald shades of grass and the fall leaf coloration. This mountain course is fun, but requires careful shotmaking to finish with a respectable score. Late afternoon shadows from the adjacent trees can make finding the ball a real task. Although it is on a lake, there are no holes with water hazards to vex the player, but Ross has strategically placed enough bunkers, of both grass and sand, to get the attention of long iron hitters.

It has a typical northern short season, but is great to play and attracts top golfers; Wayne Levi, Lee Elder, Doug Ford and Charlie Sifford all played in the Tupper Lake Open.

During the summer, Tupper Lake is a splendid place to take the family for a wide variety of recreational facilities in addition to some first-rate golf.

July 4th weekend is especially challenging to the serious athlete, with over 500 entrants competing in the famous Tinman Triathlon Contest. Men and women ages 15 to 70 begin with a 1.2 mile swim around a reverse V-shaped course. (The average water temperature in the fresh water lake is usually 65 to 75 degrees.)

This is followed by a 56 mile bike leg (supported by seven aid stations, lots of water to drink, power drinks and plenty of bananas). It all ends with a grueling 13.1 mile loop course run, where water and oranges are offered the intrepid runners.

Makes a round of golf seem tame, doesn't it?

HOW ROSS WORKED

Between 1913 and 1948, Ross created an estimated 25 courses in the Empire State. Four closed, and only six are available to public play. Most of these were built without the master being on the scene. He just couldn't be in two places at once, and when the courses were being constructed at their peak rate during the '20s (the Golden Age of golf course creation in America), he was often working on eight to ten plans simultaneously.

He had a terrific crew of construction supervisors, however. Walter B. Hatch, James B. McGovern, James Harrison, Henry Hughes and Walter Johnston carried out his instructions and saw to it that plans were followed meticulously. Because they were on the scene, and often Ross was not, there was a tremendous amount of delegation of authority by Ross to his trusted lieutenants. As a result, sometimes work had to be redone because Ross would examine a photo of the finished bunker, tee box or green and make last minute changes.

At this time in his career, the work was of the very highest order of course architecture, and the results were self evident. The irony was that one great course completed would stimulate demand from pleased players for yet another for their hometown—and so it went until the market bubble burst.

Above: Boulders, uneven terrain and plenty of aged trees...lots of roll here. Holes six, seven and 10 are excellent examples of Ross-designed doglegs, which he felt were a delightful addition to any course, giving pleasure to all classes of players.

"What has set the Ross stamp on courses was his meticulous detail, notably in green siting and contour and the intriguing amalgam of beauty, strategy and subtlety; and it is eloquent of his creative flair that, notwithstanding the match of ideas and many changes in the game, three major championships were played as recently as 1968 on courses designed by Ross forty years ago."

Frank Moran, President, Association of Golf Writers
Edinburgh, 1973
From *Donald Ross of Pinehurst and Royal Dornoch*

Tees	Par	Yards	Slope	USGA
Blue	71	6254	121	69.7
White	70	6003	126	70.8
Red	72	5389	113	67.9

179

North Carolina

Asheboro Municipal Golf Course

Buncombe County Municipal Golf Course

The Grove Park Inn Resort Golf Course

Lenoir Golf Course

Linville Golf Club

Mid Pines Inn & Golf Club

Monroe Country Club

Mooresville Golf Course

Pinehurst Resort & Country Club

Pine Needles Lodge & Golf Club

Richmond Pines Country Club

Southern Pines Golf Club

Stryker Golf Course

Wilmington Municipal Golf Course

DIRECTIONS: TAKE HGWY. 64 TO PARK ST. EXIT AND TURN RIGHT. IT IS A SHORT DISTANCE TO COURSE.

Public. Owned by the City of Asheboro. Nine holes set up to play 18. Open year round. Clubhouse opens at 8:30 AM. Snack bar. Gas and pullcart rentals. Putting green. Chipping practice area. Teaching pro. Fivesomes allowed.

Donald Ross built golf courses at 42 venues in North Carolina. The only state to receive more of his creative attention is Massachusetts.

We are very pleased to bring this course to your attention. It seems that Asheboro slipped through the cracks of history, and has never been listed in the authoritative books as a Ross course. Then a few years ago, municipal workers discovered Ross' original plans. They are shown on the next page. It was thought that they might have been fakes, but research through old town newspaper articles turned up an article published on April 4, 1937, headlined, *"Asheboro Municipal Golf Course Formally Opened to the Public."* It reads, "The citizens convinced WPA officials to contribute $30,000 worth of labor and materials while interested individuals put up $5,000 in cash." It goes on to identify clearly the course architect as Donald Ross. The reporter says Ross was, "an expert in such work who worked at a very nominal figure." He wrote of the course "it lies beautifully, offering almost a golfer's paradise."

The original 65 acres were McCadden land, and were leased by the Golf Commission for 15 years. A later lease allowed the land to be acquired for $7,500 or only $115 an acre. Not a bad deal! In 1935 and '36, when it was built, Asheboro and the Blair Park Course in High Point were the only facilities in the area, and Asheboro the only one between Greensboro and Pinehurst. In future years, it may have inspired others to follow.

Note that, on his architectural drawing, Ross has indicated to the right of the south directional arrow, "To Pinehurst." The original plans by Ross remain proudly in the possession of the City of Asheboro. The Randolph County

The number eight hole from the ninth fairway—remind you of Pinehurst?

course has undergone very little change, with the exception of the addition of many trees along the fairways. Martin Roesink and Billy Jo Patton have tried their hands at besting Asheboro, and Lanny Watkins played here as an amateur.

Asheboro's course was built on fairly hilly ground, so the player will often find uneven lies. The Donald Ross-designed greens are deceptively fast and the to-be-anticipated narrow fairways are surrounded by mature oaks and pines. The golfer will find water hazards coming into play on holes three, four and eight, and myriad sand and grass bunkers to trap the errant ball. The course may be played as nine or 18, using an additional set of men's tees. It's a "user friendly" course, and pullcarts work well here.

A Special Note about Asheboro

If you are visiting Asheboro, keep in mind that you won't want to leave town without paying a visit to the nation's largest walk-through animal habitat, the North Carolina Zoological Park, located nearby, appropriately on Zoo Parkway. Here you'll see sea lions, polar bears, gorillas, baboons, rhinoceros, giraffes, zebras, bison, alligators, river otters, elephants and elk, many almost within touching distance as they stroll about their natural habitats. (None of the beasts are as fierce as a determined golfer who has just missed a one-foot putt!) There are over 1,100 animals and 30,000 plants to see—a great way to top off your visit to this attractive town.

Above: The "boys" socializing at the clubhouse. Asheboro is a place where longtime friends gather regularly to play and to "critique" other players. Everyone we met extended genuine southern hospitality to us and made us feel most welcome.

Left: The par four, 385 yard eighth hole is dramatic. On this one, the golfer plays up over water to the green. Love grass can snare the ball if your drive is far to the right.

Tees	Par	Yards	Slope	USGA
Blue	70	6148	123	68.9
Red/White	70	5520	119	66.0
Ladies' Yellow	70	4982	116	67.8

BUNCOMBE COUNTY GOLF COURSE

226 FAIRWAY DRIVE, ASHEVILLE, NC 28805
(828) 298-1867   FAX: (828) 298-4259

DIRECTIONS: FROM ROUTE I-40 TAKE EXIT 53B TO I-240, TAKE EXIT 8 AND TURN NORTH ON FAIRVIEW ROAD. FOLLOW TO HWY 81 AND TURN LEFT. GO ONE BLOCK AND TURN RIGHT ONTO FAIRWAY DRIVE.

Public. Operated by the Buncombe County Recreational Services. 18 holes. Tee times available weekends and holidays. Pro shop opens 7:30 AM. Open year round. Rental gas or pullcarts and clubs. Putting green. Chipping and sand practice areas. Driving range five minutes from course. Snack bar.

The Buncombe County course has bent grass greens and Bermuda fairways and tees. It was formerly called the Asheville Municipal Golf Course, and before that, Happy Valley Golf Course.

Ross must have been partial to Asheville and its natives because he built four courses in this one North Carolina location within seven years. They are: The Biltmore Forest Country Club, The Grove Park Inn, The Asheville Country Club (originally known as the Lake View Park golf course) and the Buncombe County Course.

Buncombe is located about five miles from downtown and about the same distance from the Grove Park Inn. If you visit the Inn to play golf, you should not leave town without playing the Buncombe course. It is now in excellent condition, thanks to improvements made by the County Recreation golf course staff.

The front nine holes, located off NC Highway 81, play on reasonably flat terrain for a course located in the famed Blue Ridge Mountains. But the back nine, located near US 70, are typical mountain holes. The back is heavily wooded off the fairways. The number two handicap hole is the par three 15, playing 212 off the blues.

Ross didn't do the golfer any favors at Buncombe. The greens are consistently small, requiring accuracy on the approaches, and the fairways are narrow with a few very demanding doglegs. The front nine only has three doglegs to contend with, but the back nine challenges the player with four to master. Water is not a problem here.

Keith Jarrett, sports writer with the *Citizens Times Graphic,* has called the par three, 15th

The 333 yard, dogleg right, par four hole number 16

hole "a prime example of the work of famed architect Donald Ross." It is particularly difficult, in part, because of the almost overgrown trees lining both sides of the fairway. It almost looks like an alley of green to the golfer teeing off. When Ross designed the hole over 50 years ago, it was wide open. Now the trees are mature and hard to master. The result: a straight, high, long uphill drive in order to hit an inverted green that is saucer-shaped. As Jarrett describes it, "Ross left room for a run-on shot to the green, allowing a good bounce or low runner to be rewarded by a green hit in regulation." This green has recently been enlarged, providing a more generous landing field.

One of the nice features at Buncombe is its emphasis on junior golf. The Blue Ridge Mountains Junior Golf Association encourages young men and women 11 to 17 to learn the game. Founded in 1997, it is an ever-expanding program with qualifying events, awards and banquets.

History

There was big news in Asheville on May 21, 1927. For the grand opening of Buncombe County Golf Course, Joe Kirkwood, the celebrated trick shot artist, played in a match with Ray Cole, the course's pro, together with Frank Clark and George Ayton, Asheville Biltmore Forest Country Club pros. The original plan had been to match Kirkwood with Walter Hagen, Bobby Jones and Watts Gunn, a member of the Walker cup team. Jones and Gunn were both having final exams at their schools, and Hagen was away.

In those days, building lots in Beverly Hills on the course went for $1,500. The realtor's slogan: Seclusion without isolation.

Above: Par three 188 yard hole number eight with the Blue Ridge Mountains in the background.

Tees	Par	Yards	Slope	USGA
Blue	72	6480	122	71.1
White	72	5914	116	69.0
Red	72	4744	115	67.2

THE GROVE PARK INN RESORT GOLF COURSE   1924

290 MACON AVENUE, ASHEVILLE, NC 28804
(800) 438-5800 (TEE TIMES AND ROOMS)   FAX: (828) 252-0357 (GOLF)
E-MAIL: DRAIFORD@GROVEPARKINN.COM

DIRECTIONS: FROM I-40 TAKE HGWY. 240 EAST TO EXIT 5, CHARLOTTE ST. GO NORTH 1.5 MILES
TO EDWIN PLACE. TURN LEFT AND GO 2 MILES TO COUNTRY CLUB RD.

Resort. 18 holes. Open year round. Club-house. Locker rooms. Rental gas carts and clubs. Golf clinics. Swing analysis classes and playing lessons. PGA pros on staff. Putting green. Chipping and sand practice areas. Pro shop opens at 7 AM. Snack bar.

Right: "Constructed of enormous boulders, weathered stone and oak woodwork, The Grove Park Inn continues to stand watch over Asheville, a city of 65,000 people nestled in a 26-mile-wide valley carved into the Blue Ridge Mountains." — Bruce Johnson, Architectural Digest

Bobby Jones loved the Bermuda fairways and bent grass greens of this Buncombe County course, located at North Carolina's oldest resort. The golf wonder from Georgia described it in these terms, "As gentle as the south, and as difficult to conquer."

The Grove Park Inn, one of the region's oldest and most famous grand hotels, was built in 1913 overlooking Asheville's skyline and the Blue Ridge mountains. Its architecture is unique, with the historic Main Inn constructed of native granite boulders quarried from nearby mountainsides. On the *National Register of Historic Places* and a member of *Historic Hotels of America,* the Inn houses the world's largest collection of arts & crafts antiques under its red-tiled roof. The Inn is famous for its splendid views, old world charm, massive fireplaces and a long tradi-

tion of exceptional service and hospitality.

Allan Gurganus, in *Travel and Leisure,* wrote: "If the spirit of F. Scott and Zelda Fitzgerald's complex glamour can be felt anywhere in Asheville today, it still swirls around the lobby of the Grove Park Inn."

Amenities at the 510-room resort include a century-old, Donald Ross-designed golf course, indoor and outdoor tennis, two pools, sports complex, shops, fine dining and children's programs. In the year 2000, the resort added a world-class, 40,000 square foot spa to its amenity list.

Ideal climate assures fine greens and healthy fairways.

Between 1933 and 1951, the course was on the PGA tour, playing host to all the golf greats of the era: Vardon, Jones, Hagen, Sarazen, Snead, Demaret, Nelson, Hogan, Forgol, Burke, Mangrum, Palmer and Nicklaus. Presidents Eisenhower and Bush were admirers of Grove Park, and at one time, Henry Ford, Harvey Firestone and Thomas A. Edison made an impressive threesome.

Today, the course design is essentially the same as that drawn up by Ross in 1924. At that time it was called The Asheville Country Club, which had been founded in 1899. Ross had beautiful land to work with here and did all he could to preserve the natural beauty of the course. The land has not been attacked and filled with artificial impediments as is so often the case with works by some modern golf architects. No, here Ross selected prime land and used the natural terrain that has stood the test of time. It remains one of the finest courses in America.

The authors remember that, when they played the course, uneven lies are very common on this hilly land. The fairways are narrow in the Ross style, and often sloped. Water comes into play on holes two, three, six and seven. It is a course with strategically positioned bunkers and subtle greens that demand accuracy and finesse. It is a great place for both the low handicap golfer and the average player.

A planned restoration of Donald Ross' design will mandate course closure from June to November, 2001.

Above: The Grove Park Inn Golf Course—circa 1920

Tees	Par	Yards	Slope	USGA
Gold	70	6501	126	71.1
Blue	70	5997	120	69.5
Teal	70	4644	111	68.6

187

Above: Brilliant flower colors could be a pleasant distraction, but the good-sized greens are a joy.
Below: Late afternoon shadows at Grove Park—pink skies—"blue" mountains—heaven on earth

Donald Ross—A Modest Man

Over his working lifetime, Ross was asked many times for interviews and to publish his biography. He invariably declined. A genuinely modest man, his position was that "my works are my best testimony."

He did, however, acquiesce to write in the *1926 Championship Program* at Pinehurst as follows. "I build courses that require abilities in a proportion that will not permit excellence in any one department of the game to largely offset deficiencies in another. Penalties must be provided to exact a toll for those who make mistakes, yet not so severe or of a nature that will prohibit a full recovery by the execution of an unusually well planned shot."

DONALD ROSS—THE EARLY YEARS

One year after the Tin Whistles organization was begun, it started a long-standing tradition of taking photographs of its members seated on the steps of the recently constructed clubhouse at the Pinehurst Golf Course. On this page we have reproduced a picture of a young Donald Ross that we do not believe has previously been published. It is from 1905 when Ross would have been 32 years old. Donald Ross is fourth from the left, top row; his brother Alec is second from the right, in the front row. High button shoes (no spikes) were the vogue. Many of the clubs were more than likely handmade by Donald for the players.

Donald Ross was born in a humble stonemason's house that still stands at number 3 Saint Gilbert Street in Dornoch, Scotland. He spent his happi-est years away from his beloved homeland in Pinehurst, in a house he'd designed and built, called fittingly, "Dornoch Cottage." It too, still stands. Summers were spent in Rhode Island.

Before coming to America, he was well-known in the British Isles, having competed in the British Open in 1910, finishing eighth. In his native Scotland he had apprenticed as clubmaker to Old Tom Morris at Saint Andrews and served as greenkeeper, professional and clubmaker back at Royal Dornoch. Although thought of as primarily a designer of golf courses, Ross was first and foremost known as a top-notch player of the game of golf. In the states he went on to enter the U.S. Open seven times, and finished in the top ten four times. He never lost his touch around a green or on the fairway and was still shooting his age on Pinehurst No. 3 when he was in his mid-sixties.

LENOIR GOLF CLUB
701 NORWOOD STREET, BOX 1201, LENOIR, NC 28645
(828) 754-5093   FAX: (828) 757-2109

DIRECTIONS: FROM HIGHWAY 321, TAKE EXIT FOR HIGHWAY 18. TURN LEFT TO COURSE

Semi-private. 18 holes. Open year round. Public play Monday through Friday. Rental gas carts. Restaurant and snack bar. Putting green. Chipping and sand practice areas. Pro on staff. Pro shop opens 8 AM.

Right: The meandering stream approaching the par five, number three hole. Several narrow cart bridges span the waterway.

The City of Lenoir is often called the furniture capital of the south. Broyhill, Kincaid, Bernhard and Fairfield Chair all have their corporate headquarters here. The golf club was chartered in 1926 to be a non-profit, non-equity organization by two furniture manufacturers, James Merritt and T.H. Broyhill. It remains today just as it was planned.

It has been rumored that Donald Ross was commissioned to create an 18-hole course at Lenoir, that he submitted those plans, but only nine were built. Sadly, if he did the plans for the second nine, they were never found.

In the late '50s and early '60s, nine holes were added to make an 18-hole course. These were designed by Pat Allison in a similar fashion to the original holes with traditional Ross features including small crowned greens and sloping runoff areas to challenge shot making around the greens.

The club was built on the outskirts of town in a flood plain. As the years have passed, highway construction and widening of roads have taken away parts of the originally designed course, but several holes of the original design are in the same location. Holes four, five, eight, ten and 18 fairways have not been affected, and the green complexes of four, five, ten, 16 and 18 are still original.

Two creeks that drain the town run through the course. The waterways have been incorporated into the design, forcing the golfer to go over water 14 times. All crossings come into play as you navigate around the course.

The creeks also caused an interesting addition to the course. In the late '40s, T.H. Broyhill, installed one and two foot high wooden barriers so balls would bounce back instead of rolling into the dreaded waterways. Several members have reminisced about the "thwack that would save their balls from untimely demise."

In the '60s, some of the wealthier members

built another golf course farther out of town. Many members left for the newer facility, and the club struggled. The membership was finally able to purchase the club in the early '80s, and it has prospered. Care is being taken to improve the course to ensure this Carolina jewel remains a top course for years to come.

Lenoir hosts the Caldwell County Amateur Tournament and other local club competitions on a regular basis.

Left: The fifth green with the elevated sixth tee box behind the golfer putting. Whoops...he left it short!

Left: Over the bridge, you get a peek at players on hole number ten. The photo is shot from the 11th green.

Lenoir—it's pronounced Len-ore

This is a course with a distinct personality. Starting out from the clubhouse, the going is flat. Before you know it, it's playing alongside a rushing stream situated within a deep bank. (Balls struck here are long forgotten.) Then the player begins an uphill climb and is soon playing an almost *mountain course*, to descend steeply to a lower, flatter valley. Wide ranges of topography, occurring with a short time frame, contribute to its interest.

Tees	Par	Yards	Slope	USGA
Blue	71	6372	125	71.3
White	71	5786	117	68.5
Red	71	4839	111	68.4

LINVILLE GOLF CLUB
83 ROSEBORO ROAD, LINVILLE, NC 28646
(828) 733-4363

DIRECTIONS: FROM I-40, TAKE HWY. 221 NORTH TO LINVILLE. COURSE IS AT TRAFFIC LIGHT.

Resort. 18 holes. Driving range. Open mid-May to late October. Rental carts and clubs. Pro shop opens 8 AM. Putting green, chipping and sand practice areas. Teaching pro. Restaurant and snack bar. Golf community.

Nelson MacRae, who had returned home to Linville a captain after service in the Army's new air corps during World War One, had been fascinated by golf all his life. Educated at MIT, his ambition was to make Linville a leading golf resort. With this in mind, he hired the Boston firm of Stearns and Brophy to build a hotel reminiscent of buildings in the Austrian Tyrol. Eseeola Lodge would have a covered terrace overlooking a swimming pool and an 18-hole golf course to be designed and constructed by "a golf architect of recognized ability, and will be one to attract golfers of the highest reputation," stated a promotional brochure. Donald Ross filled the bill.

Ross' plans called for 18 holes over 6,303 yards. As he had at Pinehurst, he followed the contour of the land. The course went south, forming a lopsided Y with one short arm following Grandmother Creek up a narrow valley and the longer arm ending a greater distance to Lake Kawana. Grandmother Creek meandered through the crux of the Y, its route crossing the course fourteen times. On two holes, number 13 and 15, the creek covered one flank of the fairway. The longest hole was number eight. Today it plays 532 yards; Ross designed the hole with a hard right turn about 290 yards off the tee. (Today the longest hole is the 560-yard number 13.) He had to cope with a valley that was soggy with water flowing from small springs that would appear in one spot one year and another the next.

A fire destroyed the hotel in 1940, a flood washed out roads, and a fungus infected 85 percent of the forests in the Great Smoky Mountains National Park. With these setbacks,

Above: The 427 yard, number two handicap 11th tee and fairway with Grandfather Mountain in the distance

in addition to the Second World War and the Depression, the resort was about to go under.

In 1944, the owner arranged with Richard Tufts, who had succeeded his father in Pinehurst, to manage the Lodge and golf course while the search for a buyer continued. Several wealthy men raised $160,000 to invest in a place with an uncertain future, but even under the Pinehurst management, the resort continued to lose money.

Tufts resigned in 1951, and management was assumed by John Pottle of Southern Pines on a temporary basis. At this point, the resort was $50,000 in debt, bookings were low, and many of the cottages were for sale. However, with astute management and aggressive promotion, the profit picture began a slow turnaround. Pottle was asked to stay on, with a permanent contract. The next setback was arson, destroying the clubhouse, but again, money was raised and Linville was rebuilt.

In 1955, golf was growing in popularity and Linville's course, which was open to anyone who paid $5, attracted golfers from all over. The course was chosen for a number of amateur tournaments, the hotel filled up, and the caliber of golf was excellent. Pottle's diligence and constant improvement showed results. Additional buildings were erected, a new swimming pool built, and the course was filled with players—only five years after it came close to bankruptcy.

Today, the Eseeola lodge maintains the elegance of its 1926 origins, with 24 rooms and suites featuring handmade quilts and authentic antiques. Its excellent cuisine and magnificent views of the Blue Ridge Mountains and tranquil trout streams combine to make it a very special place.

The golf course, too, remains true to the original Ross design, complete with the natural dips and bumps of the fairways, a subtle signature of the crude earth-moving equipment of the 1920s. The golfer can still feel the soft spots caused by the moving underground springs.

The 331 yard, par four, dogleg left hole number ten

The signature hole is number three, a 449-yard, par four, requiring a tee shot over the crest of a hill to a valley, then uphill approach shots over the creek twice to a small green.

Golf Digest has rated this as the 16th "Best in State" and also placed it 19th among the "Top 75 Affordable Golf Courses." In addition, *Golf Magazine* has ranked it 25th in the category of the "Top 100 Courses You Can Play in the U.S., and *Golfweek* named it 88th among "America's 100 Best Classical Courses."

Burt Dale, who joined as pro in 1968, said, "It's so unique. You can build a modern golf course, but you can't replace this. Donald Ross built it, and it still plays the same."

In 1979, Linville earned a listing on the National Register of Historic Places. What John Pottle had begun as a temporary engagement, and been extended to a three-year contract, became a lifetime career of rebuilding and growth of a national treasure.

Tees	Par	Yards	Slope	USGA
Blue	72	6780	135	72.7
White	72	6279	129	70.4
Red	72	5437	117	68.5
Ladies	72	5086	119	69.3

Above: Grandmother Creek running through the 449 yard, number one handicap number three fairway
Below: The 565 yard, par five, number four green with Lake Kawana and Grandfather Mountain in the background

View of the 331 yard, par four number ten alongside a flowing Grandmother Creek

Julian W. Morton (left), vice president of the Linville Improvement Company and father of photographer Hugh Morton, supervised the construction of the Linville Golf Course in keeping with the plans of Donald Ross. Hugh was about seven at the time, and remembers meeting Mr. Ross.

MID PINES INN & GOLF CLUB

1010 MIDLAND ROAD, SOUTHERN PINES, NC 28387
(910) 692-2114   FAX: (910) 692-4615 E-MAIL: INFO@ROSSRESORTS.COM

DIRECTIONS: TAKE MIDLAND ROAD EXIT FROM US 1. TURN RIGHT. THE COURSE IS 1/4 MILE UP ON YOUR LEFT.

Resort. 18 holes. Open year round. Tee times up to 255 days in advance. Carts, pullcarts and clubs for rental. Complete pro shop. Putting green. Chipping and sand practice areas. Teaching pro. Restaurant and snack bar. Grass driving range.

round as when it opened. As Donald Ross planned it, there is distinct variation in the holes at each tee. The 13th, at 230 yards from the blues, demands power, but placement is the name of the game on the shorter par fours like three and four. The 14th green challenges the golfer to stay below the hole, while 12 has been called a "strategic jewel," running 380 yards from right to left down the fairway.

To the right is all the driving room you need,

Mid Pines was first opened as a private club. It is now owned by the Peggy Kirk Bell family, which has also owned Pine Needles, located directly across Midland Road, since 1953. Both clubs have been awarded the Silver Medal by *Golf Magazine* in its biennial listings, since 1996. The magazine notes that the two Southern Pines resorts "reek of golf the way it ought to be." The Georgian-style inn, the dining room, pro shop and Cosgroves Lounge have all been recently renovated, and a veranda has been added, overlooking the 18th hole.

Of the seven Donald Ross courses in this area of Moore County called The Sandhills, Mid Pines is the only one with every hole in the same place and with the same order in the

Above left: The 18th—par four, 411 yards off the blues
Above: The 178 yard par three hole number two

but a horrific angle can set you up for a fall. The hourglass-shaped green is narrow as a triple-A shoe, and there's a long bunker filled with might seem to be ball magnets. So the question is, do you play it safe from the tee and hope for a magnificent approach or do you give it all you've got and hope to land on the green with your second? Your guess is as good as mine.

History

Pop and Maisie Cosgrove worked at Pinehurst Country Club as bartender and kitchen supervisor starting in 1939, but during World War II, the club was shut down and used as a base for military personnel.

In early 1944, Homeland Investment was ready to open Mid Pines, and the Cosgroves leased the property, acting as managers. The resort was in shambles, with holes in the walls, army beige paint covering the once ornate interior and brass fixtures, and feathers everywhere from what must have been a massive pillow fight.

Grass on the golf course had grown to hip height, and grape plants had to be pulled out with bulldozers. The Cosgroves and their children worked day and night, repairing, replastering, waiting tables, cleaning rooms and ironing uniforms. When Homeland Investment felt it was time to sell Mid Pines, the Cosgroves were offered first refusal. Needing cash out of Pine Needles, across the road, they sold to the Bells. In November, 1955, the Bells became full owners of Pine Needles.

If you admire an authentic Ross course, you'll have a great game here, and your bonus will be that the management keeps it in tip-top shape.

Above: The 174 yard par three 11th

The 13th—a 230 yard par three hole

Tees	Par	Yards	Slope	USGA
Blue	72	6515	127	71.3
White	72	6121	124	69.6
Red	72	4907	120	68.2

Number eight at Mid Pines—a play of light and shadows—par three, 179 yards from the blues, taken when the dogwoods are in full bloom. This is said to be the second easiest hole on the course.

ROSS AND THE CAROLINAS

Tom Fazio is quoted as saying about Ross, in the book, *Sandhills Classics— The Stories of Mid Pines and Pine Needles* by Lee Pace: "The quality and playability of his courses stand out in my mind. He was responsible, more than anyone else, for making golf course architecture a profession."

Because he was based in Pinehurst, it was only natural that Donald Ross would develop his architectural practice from the Sandhills. He produced just four courses in South Carolina, and three of them are featured in this book. Of these, only Camden Country Club, which he remodeled in 1939, was an 18-hole facility.

He made his mark, of course, in North Carolina, where he designed courses for 40 venues. Unfortunately, Carolina Pines Golf Club in Raleigh was destroyed, and James Barber Golf Club, although planned, was never built. Overhills Country Club in Vass was allowed to go back to nature, and the land is now owned by the U.S. Army, with some hope of a reincarnation some day.

Interestingly, one course, Waynesville, is listed in several Ross anthologies as his handiwork. Pete Jones recorded it as "S"— stroke fee only, and Ron Whitten includes it in his book, *Golf has Never Failed Me*. However, a call to the club convinced us that, although Ross visited the site, he was never commissioned to provide either routing or plans. That leaves 17 (counting the four Ross courses at Pinehurst) of the master's creations that the public can play in the State of North Carolina.

MONROE COUNTRY CLUB

HIGHWAY 601 SOUTH, PO BOX 69, MONROE, NC 28111
(704) 282-4661   FAX: (704) 225-0593

DIRECTIONS: ENTER TOWN ON I-74, WHICH RUNS INTO RTE 601 SOUTH. TAKE TO BOTTOM OF HILL IN CENTER OF TOWN. COURSE IS ON THE RIGHT.

Public. 18 holes. Open year round. Rental gas and pullcarts. Lighted driving range and putting green. Snack bar. Pro shop opens at 8 AM. Tee times are only reserved for weekends and must be made on the previous Thursday. Teaching pro. Ballroom for parties and weddings.

Welcome to Monroe Country Club. Crepe myrtles in full blossom divide fairways 15 and 16.

Monroe is in the center of the *Land of Jackson*, the home of Scotch-Irish settlers in Carolina backcountry called the "Waxhaws." This is the true middle of North Carolina; Union County is just southeast of Charlotte and a booming area of the state.

Here the Union County Community Arts Council offers several festivals each year in Stallings (June); Indian Trail, Waxhaw and Monroe (July); Wingate (Spring) and Weddington (Fall). The Blooming Arts Festival in May is held in downtown Monroe at Belk-Tonawanda Park. The Wycliffe Bible Translators and the Summer Institute of Linguistics operate from its JAARS (formerly called Jungle Aviation and Radio Service) facility. The Indian

Above: Pure Ross—a typical pushed-up green, well bunkered

Pow Wow in October is at Indian Trail. There are Civil War reenactments in July, and the clans gather at the Waxhaws Scottish Fair and Games in October.

The Andrew Jackson Memorial Museum, the largest presidential museum in the state, documents the events that took place in this region from 1650 to 1900, a time that shaped the course of a young nation and gave that nation many of her greatest sons, including William R. Davie, the first U.S. governor of North Carolina and our seventh president, Andrew Jackson. Art and antique galleries abound, and Monroe boasts a 40-piece orchestra and 35-member chorus.

Paid by WPA funds, Donald Ross designed nine holes at this Union Country course in 1936. These are now holes numbers ten to 18. In 1981, golf architect Tom Jackson put in what are now known as the course's front nine holes. There is water on several holes on the front nine, but none comes into play on the back nine. This course can be especially tough on the golfer who has trouble playing out of sand, because some of the bunkers are serious in both size and depth. Getting out and then holding the elevated greens can be quite tricky in many instances. The Carolinas Open was held here in the late '30s and early '40s.

The signature hole here is number 18, a 212 yard, par three, which calls for a demanding shot to an elevated green. When we visited the course on July 7th, the flowers showed off their vivid colors, in deep magentas and reds around the ballroom entrance, and impatiens were in great profusion. This popular course is carefully maintained and was in prime condition when the authors paid their visit. Monroe is well worth a special trip—quite a sight.

Tees	Par	Yards	Slope	USGA
Blue	72	6759	118	71.8
White	72	6310	116	69.9
Gold	72	5949	108	67.3
Red	73	4941	117	68.6

MOORESVILLE GOLF COURSE

1947

WEST WILSON AVENUE, BOX 878, MOORESVILLE, NC 28115
(704) 663-2539 FAX: (704) 799-0624 E-MAIL: CBRGOLF@CI.MOORESVILLE.NC.US
WEBSITE: WWW.CI.MOORESVILLE.NC.US

DIRECTIONS: FROM I-77 NORTH, TAKE EXIT 33, TAKE A RIGHT ON HWY. 21 NORTH. GO TWO MILES TO A RIGHT ON W. WILSON AVE. THE COURSE IS ON THE RIGHT.

Public. 18 holes. Open year round. Rental carts and clubs. Driving range. Pro shop opens at 8 AM. Putting green. Chipping and sand practice areas. Teaching pro. Snack bar.

This large, old dam is one of the colorful sights one experiences on this rustic Carolina country course. Seen through the opening—a golfer putting.

Mooresville began in 1855, when John Franklin Moore saw a need for a train depot and cotton-weighing station between Statesville and Charlotte. He bought 500 acres and invited interested parties to help him build the town, which was incorporated in 1873. Mooresville is now a thriving community of close to 20,000, directly on Lake Norman, with diverse water sports, shopping and entertainment.

In 1948, Donald Ross designed the front nine holes of today's Mooresville Golf Course. The back nine were designed by J. Porter Gibson in 1978. This was undoubtedly one of Ross' very last efforts at golf course creation. He never visited the site, but consulted closely with the builders of the course.

Previously known as the Moore Park Golf Club, it was originally built by Burlington Mills (now Burlington Industries) for the recreation of its employees. In 1976, the town leased the facilities from Burlington, intending to purchase the entire property, and in 1978 the town welcomed citizens and guests to its newly purchased golf course and recreational facility. The course was able to expand by the purchase of extra land from two local families.

The good news is that holes one, two, four, five, six, seven and eight remain the same today as when the course was opened back in 1948. The greens are small and quick, having been modified only slightly over the years so they still play pretty much the way Ross had in

Environmentalists rate Moorseville high. It's a natural setting for golfers, geese and ducks—all in impressive numbers. Above is the clubhouse vista with three large ponds and tall native grasses.

mind when he first drew the plans.

The property is attractively landscaped, with a long, tree-lined road leading to the clubhouse. An old dam and pond accent the view from the pro shop porch. Substantial mounds are seen on the first and third fairways, which are common Ross trademarks. (When removing stone during construction, he would pile it up and cover with dirt rather than haul it away—a frugal Scot's approach to course architecture.)

There is a very active golf program to teach the game to youngsters, and when visiting the course, we saw a good number of children playing in foursomes and also with their parents.

Visitors to this Piedmont community are as likely to be coming for the autos as the golf. The town offers a museum that's a must for auto buffs—The North Carolina Auto Racing Hall of Fame. Here they will find on display many rare racers in excellent condition. Also fun for visitors is the Lazy 5 Ranch, featuring more than 400 animals from around the world. One may do a car safari through the property and see South American llamas, water buffalo, American bison and rare African watusi.

In 1963, the Catawba River was dammed at Cowans Ford, creating the largest body of water in North Carolina. Lake Norman, a 32,510 acre lake that has a remarkable 520 mile shoreline, is the boater and trophy bass fisherman's dream. Caught here are catfish; shad; yellow perch; white, striped and largemouth bass, and black crappie. Here one finds fishing boats and all kinds of pleasure craft from the smallest canoe to yachts—even an old Mississippi paddle-wheeler. This is a marvelous place to take the family for a well-rounded vacation that can be topped off with some fabulous golfing experiences. We recommend a visit here. The folks are friendly, and the course is well-preserved and maintained with care.

Tees	Par	Yards	Slope	USGA
Blue	72	6603	126	72.4
White	72	6082	123	70.1
Red	72	4917	113	68.5

PINEHURST RESORT & COUNTRY CLUB

Carolina Vista, Village of Pinehurst, NC 28374
(910) 295-6811   Fax: (910) 295-8111   E-mail: contactus@clubcorp.com
Hotel reservations: (800) 487-4653

Directions: From Raleigh, take Rte. 1 south to Hwy. 15-501 south to resort. You can fly into nearby Moore County Airport.

Resort. Hotel guests and members of Pinehurst Resort. Eight championship courses with a ninth planned for opening in 2002. Guest packages available. All courses are 18 holes. Pro shops open 6:30 AM. Caddies are available. Reservations may be made by calling 800-487-4653 or 910-295-6811. Public play available year round with resort reservations or membership. Guests may reserve tee times up to a year in advance. 24 tennis courts. Outdoor swimming pool and fitness center. Croquet and lawn bowls. Choice of five accommodation venues: Carolina Hotel, Holly Inn, The Manor, Villas and Condominiums.

Below: The resort clubhouse and pro shop

This world-class resort was a gleam in the eye of Bostonian James W. Tufts in 1895, when he acquired 5,000 acres of fallow land in the Sandhills for an average of $1.25 an acre. In 1900, he brought Donald Ross to Pinehurst as its second golf professional, which included giving lessons, course maintenance, rules official and pro shop operation. Somewhere around 1903, Ross started to build courses, and his first full 18-hole design, Pinehurst Number Two, was completed in 1907.

Although some still think he built five courses, history tells us he updated No. 1, built 2, 3 and 4, built nine holes of 5 and a small, short employee course. All have been modified, renovated or removed. No. 4 was abandoned and later replaced by the new course by Fazio, No. 5 is credited now to Ellis Maples after Ross' nine were eliminated, and the employee course was simply abandoned. No. 6 was done by Tom and George Fazio, and Fairwoods on 7 is a Rees Jones creation. Although all are fun and challenging to play, the Ross purists will want to start on No. 2, the famous championship course that has few peers in all the world, where the U.S. Open was sited in 1999, and will be played again in 2005.

Our research shows the following record

of Ross' architectural work at Pinehurst over his entire career:

Course No. 1: remodeled nine holes with further remodeling in 1913, 1922, 1937, 1940 and 1946.

Course No. 2: nine holes built in 1901 and lengthened in 1903. Eighteen holes were completed in 1907, with remodeling in 1922, 1923, 1934, 1935 and 1946. Also, in 1935, sand greens were replaced with grass. In 1907, Ross proclaimed No. 2 "the fairest test of golf I have ever designed."

 Course No. 3: nine holes built in 1907, with nine holes added in 1910 and remodeling in 1936 and 1946.

Course No. 4: six holes built in 1912, three added in 1914 and nine more added in 1919, but all of Ross' efforts were abandoned in 1938.

Course No. 5: nine holes opened in 1928 and abandoned in 1935. The second nine were never built.

Donald Ross was as much an artist as an architect, and like many great artists, he believed in continuous modification and experimentation. To Ross a great course might evolve over time with improvements—some subtle, some significant. Because he was constantly designing and building courses all over America, he used Pinehurst as his experimental station. At Pinehurst he developed grass tees and

greens, and refined his bunker designs and specifications. He continually experimented with various grasses and irrigation techniques.

Of all his works, these courses were his lifetime favorites, with the possible exception of the heather and gorse-lined course of his beloved Dornoch in Scotland—his hometown course.

For the serious golfer, the beauty of the Pinehurst Resort operation is that its management is dedicated to maintaining it in a superior condition. That fact contributed to the USGA's decision to bring the U.S. Open to Pinehurst in

Above: The 13th hole on Course No. 2, 386 yards from the gold tees. The green is starkly elevated.
Left: The 613 yard par five hole number ten on Course No. 2. Tiger Woods and John Daly were hole high in two shots during the '99 U.S. Open.

Tees	Par	Yards	Slope	USGA
Gold	72	7252	138	75.9
Blue	72	6869	133	74.1
White	72	6337	129	71.5
Red	74	5825	130	74.6

1999, and to return in 2005. The North and South Men's Amateur Championship began here in 1901 and The North and South Women's Amateur in 1903. The PGA Championship was held in '36, The Ryder Cup in '51, U.S. Amateur in '62, World Golf Hall of Fame Classic/World Open in '73 to '82, the TOUR Championship in '91 and '92, the U.S. Senior Open in '94, the Club Pro championship (Pinehurst No. 8) in '97 and '98, and The U.S. Open in '99—won by the immortal Payne Stewart with a faultless 20 foot putt.

Today, the No. 2 course features Penn G-2 grass on the greens, Tifway 419 Bermuda on the tees (Zoysia on four, five and 12) and Tifway II Bermuda on the fairways. The rough has both Tifway II and common Bermuda grasses. These greens were totally rebuilt to USGA green construction guidelines, carefully referring to Ross' original designs. The greens are mowed once or twice each day. On its 196 acres, it presents 109 sand bunkers (52 fairway/57 greenside). On hole 16 there is a pond (10,200 sq. ft.). Holes three, eight, 11 and 12 offer native grass/sand areas planted with wiregrass and broomsedge. Lake Pinehurst provides water, using a Toro Site Pro (616 radio controlled heads) irrigation system.

Here, over the years, Ross devoted more time and attention to course No. 2 than any other. He lived nearby, in a home just off the course, and kept his small office there, When not in Pinehurst, he worked in Rhode Island and spent untold days travelling, mostly by rail, to course sites across the nation.

The authors live in Pinehurst and have an opportunity to play the courses at least once a week. Because carts are not allowed on No. 2 fairways, they prefer to play courses 1, 3, 5 and 6. They like the fact that, with the exception of 6, it is almost impossible to lose a ball on any of these courses unless it is deposited in a pond. That is because the fairways are generous in size, and when in a wooded area, the ball will usually be found lying below a longleaf pine tree, sitting up on the ubiquitous pinestraw.

The management of the courses has endeavored to protect the threatened red-cockaded woodpecker by maintaining existing cavity trees and by adding more to the property. They cooperate with the Audubon Society, whose members monitor the course for wildlife protection.

The dominant squirrel on No. 2 is the large fox squirrel. On the other courses, one finds the common gray squirrel. Large hawks and golden eagles will often be seen circling overhead. There are large colonies of bluebirds here, and on rare occasions, a fox may be seen

Hole number 15 on Course No. 2—206 yards—a long and difficult par three

The 224 yard (from the gold) hole number six—the most difficult par three in the '99 U.S. Open, with competitors averaging 3.4 strokes

scampering across a fairway.

Pinehurst was the first resort to offer 72 holes of golf. Yet even from the beginning, it was clear to visitors and players alike that No. 2 was something special, something to be admired and, yes, feared. It was a masterpiece of simplicity and beauty, yet possessed of terrible challenges, with the undulations, some subtle and some severe, par is difficult to achieve. To chip and hold here is often seemingly impossible. As Sam Snead said, after playing in a North-South Tournament here, "You've got to hit 'every shot' on old No. 2!" It's one course that demands very careful shot analysis and planning. Relaxed, easy play just doesn't do it.

The records at Pinehurst resort indicate that Ross never built an 18-hole course until No. 2 He evidently had modified some courses, built several holes of one course, but had not done a full course. Ross had created courses in Massachusetts before coming to Pinehurst. It was here that he really grew in his craft. Yet, busy as he was over the years, particularly in the '20s, he kept his position as professional, and later as golf course manager, at Pinehurst. It was his base of operations. Everything flowed from Pinehurst.

He was not the first full time golf course architect. John Dunn, the cousin of John Dunn Tucker, who built the second nine holes of No. 1, was a full time architect before Ross, and certainly one of the most prominent full time architects of his time. However, Donald Ross shed his "golf professional" title in 1910 to become a full time architect.

In 1996, Secretary of the Interior Bruce Babbit specified Pinehurst as a National Historic Landmark, one of 26 so named in the nation. The designation includes an area encompassing: the village, the Carolina Hotel (erected 1899 and opened in 1901) and resort clubhouse, golf courses No. 2, 4 and some holes on 1 and 5, most of the houses in the area built before 1948, Midland Road (the first four-lane road in the state), the Pinehurst Harness Track and the traffic circle, due to its serving as the entrance to Pinehurst and being consistent with the curving roads designed by famed architect, Frederick Law Olmsted.

Today, on the grounds of Pinehurst No. 2, just outside the members' clubhouse, is a handsome bronze statue of Ross and Richard Tufts, the grandson of the founder. They are cast, both looking out at the final hole. One would like to think that somewhere, they still are.

The par four, seventh hole—401 yards off the gold tees—the sharpest dogleg on Course No. 2

Hole nine—the shortest hole on the front nine of course No. 2. David Duval double-bogeyed here in the final round to fall out of contention in the '99 U.S. Open.

DIRECTIONS: TAKE MIDLAND ROAD EXIT FROM US 1. TURN RIGHT. THE COURSE IS 1/4 MILE UP ON YOUR RIGHT.

Resort. 18 holes. Open year round. Tee times up to 255 days in advance. Carts, pullcarts and clubs for rental. Complete pro shop. Putting green. Chipping and sand practice areas. Teaching pro. Restaurant and snack bar. Grass driving range.

A first class championship course with beauty to spare

An offspring of the Pinehurst Resort and Country Club founded by James W. Tufts in 1895, Pine Needles was created by Tufts' son, Leonard, as a resort just a few miles down the road from the world-famous resort. While the golf course and five-story hotel would be featured, it was one of the earliest golf-related home communities. Due to the depression of the '30s, the project went bankrupt and lay fallow for years. It was then purchased by George Dunlap, a partner in the Grosset & Dunlap publishing house, and was later sold to the Roman Catholic Diocese of Raleigh, which planned to use it as a hospital and rest home.

In 1953, a rising young golfer, Peggy Kirk and her new husband, Warren "Bullet" Bell, purchased the course with Frank and Maisie Cosgrove and Julius Boros. Two years later, the Bells bought out their partners.

The old hotel had become a hospital called St. Joseph of the Pines, and the Bells leased some small buildings on the property to house the visiting golfers. When the lease was up, Frank Houston of Occidental Life Insurance loaned the Bells the money to build the current clubhouse on what was then the first hole. Bullet had all the designs already planned. The first hole would be the site of the new clubhouse. Then each hole would be moved up one, the second to the first, and so on. Nothing else would be changed from Ross' design. (That is why the halfway house sits at the ninth tee.) With that seed money, the Bells built the four lodges that now stand to the right of the clubhouse.

The second hole and St. Joseph in the background

The Pine Needles golf course sits nestled in the sandy loam, pinestraw and wire grass, much as it did some seventy years ago. Finesse is the key word in the play, inspiring golfers to use all the clubs in the bag, making them think. On the eighth, for example, one must drive to the left side of the fairway. Conversely, if the flag is on the left side of the green on number twelve or eighteen, it is best to approach from the right. Just to mix things up, the sixth fairway has a crown in the landing area so the approach should be hit from the top of the crown, where there is a level lie, rather than hitting fifteen yards farther and having to cope with a downhill lie. With that in mind, the thinking golfer must use just the right club at the right time.

The par threes range from a tiny third hole of 134 yards downhill across a pond to the long fifth of 208 yards across a chasm.

Water hazards come into play on seven holes, and the most difficult stretch is said to be holes three through five.

The 6,708 yard, par 71 Pine Needles course has been ranked among *Golf Digest's* Best Public Courses in the State, with a four and one-half star rating; in *Golf Magazine's* the Top 100 You Can Play in the U.S. and *Golfweek's* America's 100 Best Classical Courses.

Peggy Kirk Bell

In addition to her many championships, Peggy Kirk Bell has been a world-famous golf teacher, having given lessons to actors, CEOs, governors and golf pros. She has won countless awards and penned dozens of instructional articles, the book, *A Woman's Way to Better Golf,* produced an instructional videotape, and taught thousands through her *Golfaris,* Learning Centers and private lessons.

Tees	Par	Yards	Slope	USGA
Gold	71	6708	131	72.2
Blue	72	6318	126	70.2
White	72	6003	124	68.6
Red	72	5039	118	68.4

Under her direction, many tournaments have been held here, including the 1996 U.S. Women's Open featuring 150 of the world's best players, with a purse of $1.2 million and $212,500 to the winner. The Women's Open returns in 2001.

Pine Needles is not only a premiere facility, but it is testimony to her vision. At the height of her professional career, this unique lady and sportswoman owned her own plane and flew from one tournament to another. She tells the story about the time when, in 1959, she was flying from Findlay, Ohio to Southern Pines, and a snow storm blew in. Visibility was so short that she had to fly low and follow a railroad track for navigation over Virginia. She said a prayer, "God, if you get me down safely, I promise I'll never fly again."

Eventually she spotted an open field, did a 180° turn and landed safely, making it home to her husband and two little girls. She kept her word, sold the plane and used the proceeds to build the swimming pool at Pine Needles. The golf world benefited when she gave up the dangers of solo flight for the perils of the competitive greens, where she was among the very best.

Moles and Voles Make the Rules

The score card at Pine Needles states the following : "A ball lying by or touching the hole or runway made by a burrowing animal may be lifted and dropped a club length away not nearer the hole without penalty."

Above: The 375 yard, par four eleventh

The 434 yard, par four sixth

FROM MODEST BEGINNINGS

1906

Alec Ross, front left, Donald second row second from the left—Pinehurst, '06 with Tin Whistle friends

As a Scot, Donald Ross brought to his craft of course design an instinctive conservatism and frugality, always making it a point to use the terrain provided to him to the fullest. He sought to maximize the environment of the land as he found it, and to disturb it as little as possible. His course philosophy was that "every hole must present a very different problem to the golfer. Each hole must be built so that it wastes none of the precious ground at my disposal and takes advantage of every possibility I can see."

This attitude almost assured his success because in the early years, golf budgets were very thin, and the architect who could produce a course for a low fee and low construction costs was often just the man to grab. If earth had to be moved, he kept it to a minimum. He was self-taught. He never had the luxury of Golf Course 101, or Grass 102; he invented as he went along. At his peak he had over 3,000 men working for him building courses. In his day he completed over 400 courses.

After a few years spent in the Boston area, Donald Ross was invited by James Tufts to help him improve a rustic golf course that had been created at his new resort in Pinehurst. After several years he was expanding his outlook and designing courses for other golf venues, while retaining his tie to Pinehurst and the Tufts family. It was a tie to last a lifetime.

Ross spent much of his professional life at Pinehurst, and the fact that it is today one of the premiere golf centers of the world is testimony to his genius.

Over the years these courses have received all kinds of accolades, but the truest honors are the tournaments that are played on them. In this book we list his courses selected by the USGA for its Opens. Writer Brad Klein has named his best Ross courses in this order: Pinehurst No. 2, Worcester, Wannamoisett, Plainfield, Oakland Hills, Essex, Interlachen, Inverness, Oak Hill, Salem, Franklin Hills, Holston Hills and Seminole. Ranking is a very subjective thing, but we find no fault with Klein's list. Note that only one of those courses, Pinehurst, is open to public play; the rest are all private.

Today the authors estimate there are well over 300 golf course in existence in the U.S. that Ross had a hand in designing. He did twelve fine courses in Canada that are still in operation. Only one is a public course, and unfortunately it has been redesigned in a way that has totally removed any trace of Ross' original work. He also did two grand courses in Cuba (The Country Club of Havana and the Havana Biltmore Golf Club) that no longer exist, but the talk there is that they will be reopened for play.

Photo courtesy The Tin Whistles

213

RICHMOND PINES COUNTRY CLUB

145 RICHMOND PINES DRIVE, BOX 1538
ROCKINGHAM, NC 28379
(910) 895-3279   FAX: (910) 997-2300

DIRECTIONS: FROM HWY 74 WEST, TAKE HWY 1 NORTH. COURSE IS JUST PAST THE HIGH SCHOOL.

Semi-private. 18 holes. Open year round. Rental carts and clubs. Driving range. Pro shop. Putting green. Chipping and sand practice areas. Teaching pro. Snack bar. Golf community with homes on the course.

A stream across the fairway presents a challenge on the par four, 393 yard 15th.

Richmond Pines Country Club was established in 1928 by 50 local members who invested $1,000 each to build the course and clubhouse and purchase the land. 125 acres were purchased for an unbelievable $7.50 an acre! Originally called the Rockingham Country Club, it started out as a nine-hole course, with P.H. Haskins as architect. The original contractor was land engineer, L.E. Dye. It took six months to build. Joe Wyatt was the first professional. He had worked for Stuart Maiden, an instructor of Bobby Jones in Atlanta. It opened to public play on January 22, 1931 for a greens fee of $1.00 a day. The first nine holes are presently holes number ten through eighteen.

That same year, as a favor to a member, Donald Ross walked the course and redesigned it. His method was to go over the original nine holes, draw sketches for each one, stake out bunkers and give detailed instructions for the reshaping of the greens and other general improvements.

This was at the peak of the depression, and Ross would accept no fee from the members, many of whom were his personal friends.

In later years, the members changed the name to Richmond Country Club, and then again to Richmond Pines Country Club. It remained a nine-hole course until 1963, when a totally new front nine was built. The course is typical of the Sandhills of North Carolina with slightly rolling terrain. Water comes into play on five of the back nine holes, and is lateral to the 17th fairway, but out of play. One of the nice aspects of the course is the fact that the cart paths are still sand, not concrete or blacktop. Hit onto it and, because you don't get a huge bounce, the ball need not be moved; just hit it from where it lies.

Today the Plantation Junior Tour site is here, as is the Eastern Junior Golf Association Tour and The Triangle Tour.

Richmond is a course that, like fine wine, has improved with age. The narrow fairways are lined with tall, mature pines that require the golfer to shoot straight or pay a price. The greens are not as pronounced as Pinehurst, to the north, but they still require a good eye and a deft stroke to make par. Ross described Richmond Pines as "one of best 'small courses' in the south." He was right then, and he'd be right today. It is a gem.

Above: Number six—This fifth handicap, par five hole is unusual in that the love grass may be found in the surrounding bunkers. It adds to the fun!

Above: Hole Number 13—One of the prettiest holes in the State of North Carolina. Par three, number 17 handicap. Quite a trick over water with a large waste bunker guarding the front and right side. Take your time and swing easy! Plays 154 off the blues, only 117 off the whites.

Tees	Par	Yards	Slope	USGA
Blue	72	6267	127	69.9
White	72	5833	120	67.9
Red	72	5051	113	65.0

SOUTHERN PINES GOLF CLUB

1923

280 Country Club Circle, Southern Pines, NC 28387
(910) 692-6551   Fax: (910) 692-589
Website: http://home.pinehurst.net/sp6c

Directions: From Pinehurst, take highway 501 heading south. At U.S. Highway one, turn right and proceed to Country Club Circle. Turn right into the club.

Semi-private. Owned and operated by he Southern Pines Elks Lodge. 27 holes. Open year round. Rental carts. Driving range and putting green. Pool. Restaurant/lounge. Banquet facilities. Meeting facilities for 600 people.

Above: Players leaving a slightly elevated green on the Azalea Course

As Geoffrey A. Foster, head pro describes it, "This is as 'Ross' as you can get it!" Because Ross had learned his trade to a large degree designing courses in Pinehurst, by the time he got to Southern Pines (contiguous to Pinehurst), he had developed a unique style and attitude about golf courses.

At Southern Pines he really put it all together to create a commanding presence of a golf course that best summed up what Ross believed in: beautiful wooded fairways, traditional Ross greens that are often hard to hold and always a challenge to reach, and views that are spectacular. This is North Carolina Sandhills golf at its very best.

This was originally operated as a winter

resort for wealthy northerners who liked to flee the nasty weather and trade it for that of Southern Pines. It was easy to travel down: just get on a train, light up a cigar in the smoking car and before you knew it, you were there. Because there was no air conditioning or course irrigation, summer play was something for the future.

After the early success of Pinehurst Golf Club in the '20s, Ross found himself managing an operation that was turning away golfers in droves—sometimes as many as 15,000 during the busy season of March, April and May. It was obvious that there was a market for golf, and adjacent Southern Pines was the next logical place to be developed after Pinehurst.

Five years after Ross created the original

Azalea and Bluebird courses, he was invited back to build the nine-hole Cardinal. And according to today's management, the 27 holes built by Ross are very much the way they were when he designed them. Any changes are subtle. New Crenshaw/L93 putting surfaces on Azalea and Bluebird and bent grass on Cardinal; lush Bermuda grass on all the fairways, and all sprinkler heads are marked to the center of the green. Concrete car paths and a double-row irrigation system have made this an ideal course for tournaments.

Tall longleaf pines set the mood at Southern Pines. At peak flowering season, thousand of azaleas bloom here.

9-Hole Cardinal I

Tees	Par	Yards	Slope	USGA
Blue	36	3137	118	69.6
White	36	2962	111	68.6
Red	36	2479	113	68.5

18-Hole Azalea and Bluebird

Tees	Par	Yards	Slope	
Blue	71	6268	123	70.1
White	71	6005	120	68.8
Red	74	5318	122	71.1

The 17th hole at Southern Pines Golf Club looking from the green to the tee

From the number nine green, looking up the sixth fairway

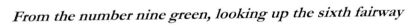

WHERE ROSS MADE HISTORY

This is what Pinehurst looked like when Donald Ross first arrived upon the scene. It was a segregated society, with black caddies and white players, and the matches were as much important local social events as exciting athletic happenings. The course was closed during the summertime—irrigation would come later. The greens were flattened areas on the course that were swept clean and oiled. The flags hung, not from standard length poles, but from long sticks of uncertain length, just as they had in Ross' native Scotland.

The famed North-South Tournament began here in 1903. The Civil War had been over less than forty years, and memories were still bitter. James Tufts thought a tournament matching players from both regions of the country would do much to alleviate hard feelings. The first competition took place just a short time before the Wright Brothers flew at Kitty Hawk. The first year, Donald Ross won the competition. As sports writer Herb Graffis pointed out several years ago, Ross probably hit one of his drives almost as long as Wilbur and Orville flew, since their longest flight was only 284 yards. The North-South golfing tradition continued until 1951 when Tommy Bolt won it.

In time Ross would create a driving range, to be affectionately known as "Maniac Hill," and it would be located not too far from where these players are standing.

In 1999, the U.S. Open was held on Ross' No. 2. Thousands came. There were more media people at the event than there had been players and spectators in Ross' time. Dozens of corporate tents lined the fields, filled with food and drink. (And this was sponsored by the same USGA that ousted Francis Ouimet for being too commercial!) What do you think the frugal Scot would have thought of such a splashy show?

219

STRYKER GOLF COURSE

Bragg Boulevard Building K-1219, Fort Bragg, NC 28307
(910) 497-1752 Fax: (910) 497-8318   E-mail: digbyg@bragg.army.mil

Directions: From I-95 south in Fayetteville, take Bragg Blvd west ten miles. Follow signs to course on left.

Military. 18 holes. Open year round. Rental electric or pullcart. Lighted driving range. Pro shop opens 6:30 AM. Restaurant. Snack bar. No homes on the course. In order to play Stryker, one must have proper I.D. and be active or retired military, or a government employee. Civilians may play as guests of military personnel.

Looking down the par four 18th

This fine Bermuda grass course gets plenty of play. Situated in the center of the world's largest military base and in the midst of a community filled with retired military personnel, it features a water hazard on hole 11, tall pines and the typical Ross greens. Recent improvements include a new clubhouse, driving range, putting green and an advanced irrigation system.

All the holes with the exception of the greens on numbers four and 12 remain the same today as when Ross built them 54 years ago. The greens on these two holes are scheduled to be rebuilt to conform with the original Ross plans, which are still in the possession of the club.

The course was named after PFC Stuart S. Stryker, who was posthumously awarded the Congressional Medal of Honor in 1945. PFC Stryker was killed in action near Wessel, Germany on March 24, 1945.

The course was host to the All Army Championships in the fifties. Interestingly, the front nine was an area with barracks on it for many years, and coal deposits from the stoves are still found on some of the holes.

The original plans called for 27 holes, but this was reduced to 18 by order of the general in charge.

The clubhouse, built in 1997, was paid for by Non-Appropriated Funds. (No tax dollars went towards the building.) As a matter of information, all military courses are self-supporting, and no tax dollars go for their operations.

Above: Figuring out the putt on the par three 17th

The clubhouse—built in 1997

A bit of trivia: What golf enthusiast and perhaps the greatest baseball player who ever lived, hit his first home run in professional baseball in the town of Fayetteville? You guessed it—Babe Ruth!

Tees	Par	Yards	Slope	USGA
Blue	72	6612	125	71.6
White	72	6310	121	70.1
Red	72	5233	116	70.1

WILMINGTON MUNICIPAL GOLF COURSE

311 SOUTH WALLACE AVENUE, WILMINGTON, NC 28409
(910) 791-0442   FAX: (910) 791-1312

DIRECTIONS: THE COURSE IS LOCATED ONE BLOCK EAST OF THE INTERSECTON OF COLLEGE RD. AND OLEANDER DRIVE.

Public. Owned by the City of Wilmington. 18 holes. Open year round. Rental gas and pullcarts and clubs. Pro shop opens at 6:30 AM. Locker room. Pro shop. Snack bar. Putting green. Pro on site.

The 405 yard, par four tenth green—three rugged bunkers front left—shades of St. Andrews

All 18 holes on Wilmington's 6,564 yard Bermuda grass course are the same as they were when Ross designed them, a precious rarity these days. The course was opened in 1926 to great local fanfare and carefully restored in 1998 with the help of the Donald Ross Society. Ross is quoted as saying, on opening day, "This course is much too difficult for a public course."

The course is nestled in the center of the City of Wilmington. All Wilmington Amateur Championships for men and women are traditionally held here, and the Coastal Junior Tour takes place every summer.

The course plays fairly wide open, with usually straight fairways, yet there are mature live oak and pine, some dripping with Spanish moss, that can cause a golfer to change strategy at the last minute to avoid serious trouble. Entrances to the greens are classic Ross: narrow, requiring a skilled pitch to avoid the pesky bunkers that can be foreboding in appearance.

The greens are slightly elevated, having subtle undulations, but they are not the turtlebacks one finds at Pinehurst. Here they are relatively flat—yet firm.

When Ross designed the course, the greens were composed of sand, and the size of the present greens follows the original layouts. The reconstruction of the course has resulted

Left: One of the authors standing on the 17th green—a typical Wilmington bunker in the foreground
Right: The elevated fourth tee to a raised dance floor—a downhill par three—184 yards from the blues
Below: From the 18th tee box toward the clubhouse—two mean-looking small bunkers on the right

fairway that extends to the right side of number five. A small ditch runs through fairways two and 12. The limited number of fairway bunkers are usually found about 100 to 125 yards away from the greens. Hole 18, a 430 yard par four from the blues, and a par five, 367 yards from the ladies' tee, is considered the signature hole here at Wilmington. It takes careful execution of uphill shots that very often will play into a strong wind.

The course rests on a 143 acre tract of land that was once considered the boondocks of Wilmington. Because it was so far from town, the city was able to acquire the Hugh McRae property for only $15,625.

For its first 28 years of existence, Wilmington was a segregated course. Finally, in 1954, the first African Americans to play the course were Dr. D.C. Roane and attorney Robert Bonel. Some whites quit the course at that time and set up a private course called Pine Valley Golf Club. However, within a few years, most white patrons returned, and Wilmington began to increase play from year to year, welcoming all golfers.

Muni is "walker friendly," and roughly 60 percent prefer to walk rather than ride. The price of a round of golf here is especially low, making this one of Eastern North Carolina' best golf bargains. Try it.

in many bunkers that had been destroyed to reappear, bringing it back to its original design. Before the modifications, only 35 of the original bunkers were in play; now 72 are in operation.

Muni, as it is called by the locals, allows both low and high handicap players to enjoy a fine round of golf. It is not too punishing, but trouble can develop quickly when concentration wanes. It's been said that you can never take Muni for granted.

There is a pond at the foot of the fourth

Tees	Par	Yards	Slope	USGA
Blue	71	6650	128	71.8
White	71	6267	123	70.6
Red	72	4978	119	69.0

OHIO

ELKS COUNTRY CLUB

GRANVILLE GOLF COURSE

MANAKIKI GOLF COURSE

MILL CREEK PARK GOLF COURSE

ELKS COUNTRY CLUB

19787A STATE ROUTE 73, McDERMOTT, OH 45652
(740) 259-6241 FAX: (740) 259-6513 E-MAIL: ELKSCC@CRAMNET.NET

DIRECTIONS: US 23 SOUTH INTO PORTSMOUTH. TAKE 73 WEST FOR FIVE MILES TO COURSE.

Semi-private. Members are BPOE 154 Elks Club members. The public can play on a daily fee basis. Open year round. Rental gas and pull-carts. Driving range. Putting green. Chipping and sand practice areas. Pro shop opens 7:30 AM. Pool. Restaurant. Snack bar.

Below: Plenty of strategically placed trees, and deep bunkers on both sides of the green, make this par four, 328 yard 15th hole most interesting.

Formerly Portsmouth Country Club, this classic 6,677 yard Scioto County Ross bent grass course has no homes on the property. It was built on semi-rolling terrain, featuring small greens with many large, mature trees along its narrow fairways.

The south central Ohio course was built near the Ohio River in 1923 and opened in 1924. During America's economic crisis, the course was sold in a sheriff's sale in 1937. It was renamed the Valley Country Club in 1939, and in 1941 became an Elks Club course.

It may be the only course in the nation to have a cemetery right on the land. Brigadier General William Lucas, Jr., who had served his nation during Jefferson's presidency, is buried here on land he had purchased from his brother Joseph in 1801.

Above: Two deeply sculptured bunkers to the right of the tenth green, in addition to an uphill lie, offer a fascinating challenge on this par four, 440 yard hole.

Ross was offered a choice of two pieces of adjacent land on which to build the Elks course. One was an ancient Indian burial site of Mound Builder native Americans of the Hopewell culture. The other parcel was of varied terrain with level stretches, deep swales and knobby high points. Donald Ross picked the latter site. Today it is a wonderful example of his architectural skills, and fortunately the historically important Indian site has been preserved.

From 1992 to 1995, this was the location of Hooter's T.C. Jordan tournament. It was here that a young Jack Nicklaus won the Ohio Jaycee Jr. Golf Tournament in 1955. His best round was a 66 the first time he'd seen the course, shooting 32 on the front side with two birdies and an eagle. Go, Jack!

There is only water on one hole, number four, a par three that plays a short 135 yards off the blues. It looks deceptively easy, but the golfer soon discovers that danger lurks here. It is all carry, off the tee, with a green that slopes severely back to front with a tricky lateral cutting through it. A shot left above the flag anywhere on this green will make the putter hold his or her breath. It is rated the 18 handicap hole, but that rating can be deceptive.

Hole ten is the signature hole—the toughest hole on the course. The view from the tee presents golfers with a downhill drive with the customary Ross room on the right. The left side of the left-turning fairway is protected by a stand of tall forty-year-old pines. If you land in the middle of the fairway on your drive, or land on the right side (the perfect location), your second shot, usually from an uneven lie, is up a severely steep hill to a knobby green only 26 yards deep. If you miss long and left, your ball will end up on the 11th tee. If you miss right, you are deep in the woods.

The straight-on 185 yard par three 17th requires a blast from the tee to a somewhat larger green, but golfers who still have not straightened out their slices by now will end up in the looming sand bunker to the right of the green. Those players who overclub will find themselves at the bottom of a very long grass bunker hiding behind the green.

After playing 17 holes here, the trip back to the clubhouse is quite special. The building looks magnificent from a distance, perched on the high ground, white against the emerald of the course and the two greens that rest before it—the practice green and the 18th's oval-shaped putting surface. This is the original 1920s-style clubhouse, having undergone several additions and renovations over the years. (The snack bar serves fine breakfasts and lunches.)

At 371 steadily uphill yards, number 18 is a terrific finishing touch to Ross' design. A large grass bunker is off to the right of the green, while shots missed left and long end up somewhere near the tenth tee.

Tees	Par	Yards	Slope	USGA
Blue	72	6677	116	70.7
White	72	6377	113	69.3
Red	74	5660	115	70.4

Above: The par three, 182 yard 17th hole offers the golfer a fine vista of the clubhouse.
Below: The par five, 473 yard 14th green is an exquisite play of sunlight and late day shadows.

Above: The par four, 328 yard 15th elevated and rolling green, looking back uphill toward the tee
Below: The par three, 135 yard fourth green overlooks a tranquil lake that can spell trouble. Here the ladies get a break; it plays only 108 from the reds.

GRANVILLE GOLF COURSE

555 Newark-Granville Road, PO Box 440, Granville, OH 43023
(740) 587-0843 Fax: (740) 587-2057   E-mail: pro@granvillegolf.com
Website: www.granvillegolf.com

Directions: From Port columbus Airport, take I-270 north to Hwy. 161 east. Take Granville/Lancaster exit and turn left. Go to light and go right on Broadway. Course is 6 blocks.

Public. Golf community with homes on course. 18 holes. Open mid-March to mid-November. Gas and pullcarts, and club rental. Pro shop. Putting green. Sand and chipping practice areas. Driving range. Pro on site. Restaurant. Snack bar. Beverage cart.

At the top of its hill, and before it continues to Donald Ross Village, Pinehurst Drive intersects with Donald Ross Circle, with the course spreading below.

The 396 yard par four fifth green viewed from the ninth tee

Few villages of approximately 5,000 can boast a golf course as outstanding as Granville, the literature of which states it is "a masterpiece created by the immortal Donald Ross." The fact that Ross, at the zenith of his remarkable career, ever came to Granville is a story in itself.

When John Sutphin Jones married Granville's most eligible debutante in 1885, he was an obscure young railroad conductor, who left town with his new bride soon after the wedding. By the time he returned a few years later, he was a nationally known coal, rail and financial tycoon. J. S. Jones was a familiar figure in the business and social life of New York, Chicago and Florida, where golf was already the rage, and when he returned to Granville, he decided that the town should have its own golf course.

It was a notion he held during World War I, a period when he was acquiring all the

The Ross classic, par four signature 18th

230

land available between his palatial home, Bryn Du, and Granville. When the farmland and wooded hills that are now the course were his, he was ready for Donald Ross. By that time, Ross was a big name, with a staff of 225 who had created 22 courses during that year. Jones offered a large fee, and more importantly, a latitude of operations. Ross was free to design the course as he pleased, as long as he gave J.S. a layout that "will challenge the very best golfers we have in the country, and still be a course that Granville golfers and guests at my hotel can play … and enjoy."

During planning and construction, Ross was a frequent guest at Bryn Du, less than a mile east of the course. He could walk to the job in fine weather, and when the day was raw, he rode in a chauffeured Pierce-Arrow or Cadillac. In 1925, both the course and the inn were completed, and Jones showed it off to his business and social friends, including the golfing greats of that era, Walter Hagen, Chick Young, Horton Smith and Gene Sarazen. The circumstances that brought Donald Ross to Granville forged a relationship with Royal Dornoch, and it was probably at Ross' suggestion that Jones found his first club professional, Alex Murray. The following year, Murray died suddenly, and the next pro, William Campbell, was also from Dornoch.

Over the years, under several different owners, the course suffered some tough times, with a stream, which courses through four holes, becoming eroded and weed-choked. In 1987, the course was purchased by William Wright, and the once-ugly banks have been terraced and retaining basins built to tame the sometimes rampaging stream. An upgraded care and maintenance program is steadily curing the ills induced by nearly ten years of neglect.

Today, as Ross designed it, the greens are small and the bent grass fairways narrow. The signature hole is number 18, a 370 yard par four featuring a tee box located approximately 150 feet above the fairway. Ross strayed from his usual dearth of water hazards by including ponds on five separate holes.

The current owners are nurturing this classic old course the way Ross himself would have liked it to be. If you enjoy old-time golf, the "old pro," Phil Stockdale will be there to welcome you.

Above: A fairly easy (number ten handicap) number 13— a 323 yard par four—dogleg right

Tees	Par	Yards	Slope	USGA
Black	71	6559	128	71.3
Blue	71	6210	125	69.7
White	71	5530	121	66.6
Red	71	5197	123	69.6

MANAKIKI GOLF COURSE

35501 Eddy Road, Willoughby Hills, OH 44094
(440) 942-2500   Fax: (440) 942-5071

DIRECTIONS: FROM AIRPORT I-71 NORTH TO DOWNTOWN CLEVELAND, PICK UP I-90 EAST. TAKE EXIT 189 (OHIO 91), TURN LEFT AND FOLLOW 3/4 MILE. TURN LEFT ONTO EDDY ROAD.

Public. 18 holes. One of six courses operated by the Cleveland Metroparks. Open March 15 to December 31. Gas and pullcart rental. Club rental. Pro shop opens 7 AM. Putting green. Chipping and sand practice areas. Teaching pro. Discounts for seniors (62 and older) and juniors. Restaurant. Snack bar. Ballroom and caterer.

Above: The par five hole 12 and par four hole 16 in all their fall glory

Manakiki was a million dollar club when it was laid out by Donald Ross in Willoughby Hills in the eastern suburbs of Cleveland. He was particularly proud of his achievement here, commenting: "In one respect Manakiki is unique. In almost every golf course, no matter how modern or how expensively constructed it may be, there usually are two or three of the holes that resemble each other. That is because the architect must do what he can with the topography he is presented. Ordinarily he can't help but make some of the holes similar in design. But not at Manikiki. Every hole is different. As you go around the course, you will never have the idea of sameness from any tee. That, I believe, is one of the most interesting features of this very splendid course."

The first recorded ball driven here was in 1929, when the club was known as the Willowick Country Club. The Indian name to which it was changed was one of which Ross approved, saying: "I like Indian names—they are so distinctive; they stay in the mind. Minikahda, for instance, carries a definite impression of a great golf course—no other name is like it; the same is true of Manakiki."

Over the years, thankfully, there has been great respect for Ross' creation, and most of the holes have been left exactly as he prescribed.

It opened to the public in 1963 and has recently hosted the Cleveland Amateur and the Nike Tour Qualifying. The clubhouse is large and imposing, and there are no homes lining the course to inhibit the magnificent views, with dramatic elevation changes before the golfer's eyes. The club has hosted the Carling Open, which was won by Cary Middlecoff in 1954.

The once private, exclusive retreat is now a very well-maintained public course. It is Ross all the way, with undulating terrain, plenty of difficult doglegs to master, sloping greens, and two holes that demand carefully executed shots over ball-tempting canyons.

Ross rarely looked for water opportunities on his courses, so Manakiki is unusual in that regard. Here there is plenty of water to challenge the player. It comes into play on six holes: at the lakes on three and 15, at the creek and lake in front of the blue tees on eight, and there is a persistent small creek to contend with on 12, 17 and 18. There are, in fact, lateral water hazards all over the course, so bring enough balls in your bag.

The eighth is a very difficult par four, said to be one of the toughest in Ohio, particularly since the tee box was returned to the original Ross position a few years ago, sitting back in the woods and forcing a drive across a nasty ravine. It is the number one handicap hole.

Here the theme is "Play ready golf." Management takes play time seriously. The USGA slogan is stressed: "In the interest of all, play without delay."

Manakiki was built on land that had been the 220 acre summer estate of Howard Hanna, a famous Cleveland industrialist. His farm had been called "Sleepy Hollow," and was donated by Jim and Fanny Brown to the park board, now Metroparks, which leased it for 99 years with the lease renewable every year. A thank-you note to the Browns, on a brass plaque, is mounted on a huge stone in front of the clubhouse.

Above: The 17th, a par four that looks like a five. When the fairway crests, it drops like a roller coaster, hits bottom and goes straight up to the green.

Left: The number two handicap tenth hole (430 yards from the blues) plays from an elevated green into a snake-like valley and then rises at the last 50 yards to a big green.

Tees	Par	Yards	Slope	USGA
Blue	72	6625	128	71.4
White	72	6189	126	70.1
Red	72	5390	121	72.8

DIRECTIONS: FROM CLEVELAND, TAKE RTE. 224 EAST. TAKE SECOND LEFT ONTO W. GOLF DRIVE FOR ONE MILE.

Public. Two 18-hole courses. Open March to December. Rental cars, carts and clubs. Practice putting greens, chipping green and sand bunker. Extensive golf instruction programs available. Field house, snack bar and pro shop.

At the Mill Creek Park Golf Course you will find almost everything that the golf enthusiast expects from championship courses. Unique to this area are two 18-hole courses, both designed by Donald Ross, that offer a diversity of playing experiences. Fairways are framed by thick groves of mature trees, numerous bunkers and meandering streams that test one's golfing skills, all amidst the beauty and splendor of a park setting.

Above: Getting ready for the big smash

The courses are operated by Mill Creek MetroParks. Plans to build the courses began in 1925 when park commissioners and Poland Country Club both announced plans for the construction of a golf course in the Mill Creek Valley. The two groups were surprised to find out they had selected the same 260 acre site owned by private individuals. The park board wanted to acquire the property since it was surrounded by the park.

The park board began eminent domain proceedings to prevent the private club from acquiring the land. This action was in response to the club's notices to members to subscribe $200 each toward the purchase of the land. Lawsuits were filed, but a long court case was avoided when the trustees of Poland Country Club decided to purchase another tract of land.

The park commissioners retained the services of Donald Ross, and the North Course opened for play on July 31,

234

1928. Laid out on gently rolling terrain, this course plays to a par 70 at 6,412 yards.

Frank Hughes served as superintendent of construction under Ross During the development of the North Course. Hughes later became park superintendent and assisted in the development of the third nine hole, which opened on July 4, 1932. The fourth nine opened on August 7, 1937. The South Course is designed on level land with narrow, tree-lined fairways. Par is also 70 and it plays to 6,511 yards. The South Course was recently rated the 26th "Best Municipal Course" by *Golfweek's* course raters. Most of the design integrity still remains at Mill Creek. Several greens have been softened and a few fairways raised. Restoration began in 1997 with the implementation of a master plan developed by course architect Brian Silva. A main goal of the plan is to restore the sand bunkers to their original shape and depth.

Above: The theme here: a park setting of well-irrigated, wide fairways, bordered by very tall, mature trees.
Below: Ladies' Golf Championship, 1946

	Tees	Par	Yards	Slope	USGA
South Course	Blue	70	6511	129	71.8
	White	70	6302	127	70.8
	Red	75	6102	118	74.9
North Course	Blue	70	6412	124	71.9
	White	70	6173	122	70.7
	Red	74	5889	117	74.4

Photo taken in 1919

DONALD ROSS & THE TIN WHISTLES

Donald Ross and his brother, Alec, were both honorary members of the Tin Whistles, a national golf organization, which had its beginnings in Pinehurst, North Carolina in 1904.

The authors now give you a bit of the club's history from its handbook. There are many conflicting accounts of its founding. They run all the way from one that a tin whistle was blown in the village street to call the players to the links to another that the whistle was blown at the spring, near the present twelfth hole on the No. 1 course, advising golfers that a corn concoction was being served.

However the consensus is that a group of New Yorkers were vacationing at the Holly Inn, dividing their time between the links and the little brown jug. They organized a tournament, the prizes being "two Scotch golf clubs," to be opened at the finish and dispensed, forthwith. The winners carried the "clubs" back to the Inn, beneath checkered vests, and with great pomp and ceremony, promptly consumed them. At this time, outsiders called them the Wow Wows.

During this Pinehurst visit, a copy of Alfred Henry Lewis' book, *The Boss,* appeared. It is a story of old Tammany and gave consider-

able space to a hoodlum gang known as the Tin Whistles. The name was given to them because they were summoned to their duty of breaking up polling places, which were unfriendly to Tammany Hall, by the blowing of a whistle.

For some reason, unknown, this appealed sufficiently to have golfers adopt the name, "The Tin Whistles" to their organization. The objectives were, "To promote a golfing fellowship at Pinehurst and to maintain there a neutral zone for a choice and chosen few from outside organizations to which it will be pleasant to return year by year."

It also stipulated that "It shall be the duty of each member to suppress the incipient conceit of any fellow member who thinks he is in line for the United North and South Amateur Championship." In recent years, the Constitution has been rewritten and more prosaic wording states, "It is formed for social purposes and to promote an interest in the game of golf at Pinehurst, N.C."

In stark contrast to its rather rowdy beginnings, the group has now established an ongoing educational and research foundation, providing college scholarships and grants for agronomy research at North Carolina State University.

Pennsylvania

Bedford Springs Golf Course

Buck Hill Golf Club, Blue & White Courses

Immergrün Golf Club

Pocono Manor Inn & Golf Resort, East Course

Tumblebrook Golf Course

2138 BUSINESS ROUTE 220, BOX 108, BEDFORD, PA 15522
(814) 623-8700   FAX: (814) 623-3948

DIRECTIONS: TAKE EXIT 11 OFF PENNSYLVANIA TURNPIKE, TURN RIGHT ON BUSINESS RTE. 220 SOUTH AND GO FOUR MILES TO COURSE.

Public. 18 holes. Open mid-March to mid-November. Gas, pullcart and club rental. Pro shop. Putting green. Sand and chipping practice areas. Driving range. Pro on site. Snack bar.

Below: The clubhouse beyond the par five, 575 yard 18th green

Largely agricultural Bedford County has a history of important events—from the French and Indian Wars to George Washington's visit during the Whiskey Rebellion. President James Buchanan used The Bedford Springs Hotel as his summer White House. The U.S. Supreme Court met here, the only time it met outside of Washington, and rumor has it that the Dred Scott decision was discussed on the front porch of the venerable hotel. Presidents Hayes, Garfield and Harrison stayed here, as did the famous Kentuckian, Henry Clay. And it was here that Buchanan received the first trans-Atlantic telegram from Queen Victoria.

From 1912 to 1947, the remarkable Donald Ross brought his magic to 31 golf courses in the State of Pennsylvania. He did his work here in the '20s, when he was at his creative peak. The Bedford Springs course is located at the site of the famous hotel that built its 19th century reputation on the curative powers of delicious spring waters on the property.

Hole number four is said to be the start of the prettiest holes on the course. This long par five can be reached in two from the whites, but it is a doubtful gamble from the blues. This is a tree-lined hole on both sides and nearly straight away, but at 563 yards, it is a handful. Par is an excellent score on this hole, and the great view is worth the price.

Hole number nine is Ross at his best. A par five, it is 494 yards and reachable in two, but a small ditch comes into play 170 yards from the green, and the nefarious Shober's Run will swallow shots straying too far to the right. This is another characteristically small green with plenty of Ross undulation to contend with. This hole surprisingly yields a fair number of birdies.

Bedford Springs is a long course—par 74. The back nine plays 3,548 yards with three par five holes that are 598, 575 and 575 yards each. Hole 16 is a long par three, playing 204 yards off the blue tees and 186 off the whites. It is the number one handicap hole. Called the Volcano, it is by far the toughest hole here. Indeed, it may be one of the hardest par threes that Ross ever created, demanding a powerful straight drive up hill.

A velvet-textured green sits atop a hill fronted by four good-sized bunkers and trees. Stray shots that do not land on the green trickle helplessly down front and side embankments, ending up either in the bunkers or beneath trees. The green has two levels and slopes from back to front. Here par is deemed a personal triumph.

The course ends with a difficult par five hole, a gently rolling three shot of 575 yards. A great driving hole, a tee shot down the left center would be the ticket. For your second shot off the fairway, you will likely encounter a lie below your feet. The pro's advice: aim left and hold on. If the ball leaks too far right, a very large oak comes into play for the approach shot to a small, billowy, well-bunkered green. Par is considered top-notch golf on this hole.

Above: The 563 yard, par five fourth hole
Below: The short, par three, 115 yard tenth, with two different looks, depending on which tee box you use. On the lower, the hole sits dramatically above. Short tee shots usually roll to the bottom of a steep embankment, nearly fifty feet below the green.

Tees	Par	Yards	Slope	USGA
Blue	74	7000	130	73.0
White	74	6603	127	72.3
Gold	74	6127	124	72.0
Red	74	5535	125	72.5

BUCK HILL GOLF CLUB

BLUE & WHITE COURSES

120 GOLF DRIVE, BUCK HILL FALLS, PA 18323
(570) 595-7730 FAX: (570) 595-9426 E-MAIL: BUCKHILLFALLSCO@NOLN.COM
WEBSITE: WWW.BUCKHILLFALLS.COM

DIRECTIONS: FROM RTE. I-80W, EXIT 44, LEFT ON RTE. 611 NORTH TO MT. POCONO. RIGHT AT LIGHT ONTO RTE. 940 EAST. GO 3.1 MILES TO RTE. 390 LEFT AND FOLLOW SIGNS 4.7 MILES.

Semi-private. Public play is very limited on summer weekends. The club has three nine-hole courses that are played in three nine-hole combinations. The red holes play to 2,850 yards at par 34; the whites to 3,180 at par 36; the blues to 3,060 at par 36. Ross designed the blue and white course holes only. Open April 15 to November 15. Gas carts and clubs. Driving range. 5000 sq. ft. putting green. Teaching pro. Pro shop opens 7:30 AM. Fairway Grill Restaurant. Olympic size pool. Ten Har-tru tennis courts. Lawn bowling. Trout streams.

Above: The number four green on the Blue Course

vinced other members of the Society of Friends that the incredible beauty they had witnessed would convert to an ideal summer settlement.

In 1901 an inn with 18 rooms and two cottages were built, 43 lots were sold, and it was on its way to becoming a popular retreat. It appealed to guests in winter as well as summer, and the first ski tow in Pennsylvania was operated here. Soon a larger inn with 40 rooms, a huge ballroom and

Located within 30 minutes of Stroudsburg, Buck Hill Golf Club is in the heart of a semi-private resort community. Samuel Griscom owned Buck Hill Falls in the late 1800s, and was able to persuade a group of prominent Philadelphia Quakers to explore the possibility of establishing a summer retreat.

Although it took three trains and a wagon trip to reach the property, the Quakers marveled at the sheer beauty of the place—a forest paradise of verdant trees, sparkling streams and the tumbling wonder of the three falls. They returned to Philadelphia and con-

The par three, 203-yard number nine green on the White Course

many public rooms was built. This served as a cultural center for years, with operas and musical concerts performed in the ballroom.

Today the Buck Hill Falls community is nestled in over 5,000 acres. In 1919 the Buck Hill Falls Company brought Donald Ross here to design and build what is today considered one of the finest examples of his work in America. Fourteen of the 18 holes on the white and blue courses are almost exactly as Ross originally designed them. Holes six and seven on the white course and holes five and six on the blue have been changed over the last 75 years.

The avid golfer will want to experience all 27 holes deep in the Pocono Mountains. It is, of course, a hilly property with plenty of deep woods and gradual rolling fairways. The greens and fairways are kept in excellent condition for peak play. The Poanica greens are known to be steep with subtle breaks and slope from front to back. The player must keep the ball on the lower part of the green or faces a difficult downhill putt that can go out of control. As Tom O'Malley, head pro, cautions, "Don't be above the hole!" Water from Buck Hill Creek can be a troublesome factor. Balls may find a wet fate on five holes.

Ross was a firm believer in democracy on the golf course. He said of the cost of play: "It need not be made greater than the purse that any man could afford." In his native Scotland, the shepherd and the king could easily play the same course. He was a strong advocate for public access to great courses, regretting the fact that to many, golf seemed the game of only the rich. Here in the Poconos, one finds a course fit for a king that everyone who loves the game can easily afford.

The par three number seven—180 yards from the blues

Left: The old golf clubhouse in 1928

COURSE #1 "RED/WHITE"

Tees	Par	Yards	Slope	USGA
Blue	70	6124	121	69.4
White	70	5910	119	68.7
Red	72	5451	124	71.0

COURSE #2 "WHITE/BLUE"

Tees	Par	Yards	Slope	USGA
Blue	72	6396	124	70.4
White	72	6082	121	69.2
Red	72	5547	126	72.8

When the 259 acre George W. Price farm was acquired in 1907 by the Buck Hill Falls Company, nine holes were laid out. A widow's dower of $66.35 was involved in the purchase, and not until 1908 could this be paid off. There was no clubhouse nor locker rooms, and no greens fees were charged. The only cost was a fee of five cents a person for transportation by horse and carriage from the inn to the golf course. At the time, some thought this fee to be exorbitant.

When the land for the present course was fully acquired, the total acreage was raised to 1,053, assuring a continued water supply. In 1908, a course was built with a small club-house, and in 1910 a fieldstone shelter was erected, known as the Swarthmore shelter, donated by members of Phi Kappa Psi fraternity.

Over the years, architect Robert White in 1926 and Harry Drennan, the course manager and his staff in 1956, have modified the course. Drennan's work was necessitated by severe water damage to the property following a devastating flash flood in 1955.

A view of the Buck Hill Creek in front with the golf cart bridge, pro shop and Fairway Grille in the back

DONALD ROSS
AND THE KEYSTONE STATE

Pennsylvania caught Donald Ross' eye as early as 1912, when he received his first commission to create a golf course in the Commonwealth at North Hills. It was to be the famed 18-hole Lulu Country Club, also called Lulu Temple Country Club, and he chose to be on site during most of its construction.

From then until 1947, Ross designed 30 courses in the State, of which only three no longer exist. We estimate that he was on site, overseeing construction operations, at 13 or more of these courses. The fact that one of his associates, the engineer J.B. McGovern, lived in Wynnewood, Pennsylvania, contributed greatly to the fact that Ross was able to do so much work in this and surrounding states. No modern-day golf course architect, armed with computers, highly trained staff and the most modern earth moving equipment has come close to achieving what Ross accomplished with pen and paper and a couple of mules.

Tom Fazio was recently asked what he thought Ross would be doing if he were still alive. He said, "I would think that Donald Ross would have a staff of people answering the telephones because there would be so many people calling him to design golf courses, and the rest of us in the industry would be fighting for number two position as best we could."

Source: Sandhills Classics, 1996, *Pine Needles Country Club*

IMMERGRÜN GOLF CLUB

SAINT FRANCIS COLLEGE, BOX 600, LORETTO, PA 15940-0600
(814) 472-3236   FAX: (814) 472-3209

DIRECTIONS: FROM ALTOONA, TAKE RTE. 22 EAST. FOLLOW THE SIGNS TO ST. FRANCIS COLLEGE.

Semi-private, nine holes set up to play 18. Open March 15 to November 15. Rental carts. Pro shop opens 8 AM. Clubhouse and locker rooms. Putting green. Chipping practice area. Teaching pro. Restaurant and snack bar.

The tree-lined fairway on the left stretches over a stream and doglegs right.

Photo by The Tribune-Democrat, *Johnstown, PA*

Immergrün, which means green in German, is located in the beautiful Laurel Highlands area of Cambria County. Formerly the Charles M. Schwab estate and gardens, in the '20s the property had 100 gardeners and farmers, and 15 household servants on staff. It is now Mt. Assisi Friary, Lake Saint Francis and Immergrün Golf Course, complementing the pastoral St. Francis campus.

Steel baron Charles Schwab hired Donald Ross to create a course to be used only for his personal play and that of his guests. Privacy was the key word.

Golf pro Bob Hahn said of this place, "In those days there weren't many designers. Golf was only for the rich and famous. I sat here 20 years ago, and few people realized the course existed. Then all of a sudden, over the

Above: Looking toward the Norman-style clubhouse, built in 1918 at a cost of $21,000

The College Among the Pines.) Founded in 1847, there are 23 buildings on a 600 acre campus with nine residence halls, a student union, athletic center, dining hall, library and chapel. The school is run by the Franciscan friars and a Board of Trustees comprised of friars and community leaders.

Immergrün is a short, yet demanding bent grass course. One of the special joys of playing here is the knowledge that you are playing a Ross course that has not been touched in any way; it is almost exactly as he planned it in 1917. The greens are sloped for water runoff, so it takes a delicate touch because they are quick, and putts tend to slide away toward the mountains. The fairways have rolling hills, adding challenging contours, and are lined with mature woods.

Hole six is the signature hole, a 431 yard par four with an uphill dogleg left. The fairway is straight for 275 yards, then it climbs up hill to a steep elevated green. There is water on seven of the nine holes. The course naturally slopes right to left, and the elevated tees all drop off one way or another. The way the course is set up, ladies use the same tees as the men. The difference is that for nine holes, their par is 40, and the men's is 36.

In the fall the maples, oaks and beech trees are in glorious color. Because of its strict adherence to Ross' specifications, golf architects come from all over the country to study it. The *Washington Golf Times* has called it "The Donald Ross Gem." Curiously, several of the authoritative books on Ross courses have neglected to include Immergrün among the master's works.

Two other noted Ross courses in western Pennsylvania are the Edgewood Country Club and Rolling Rock at Ligonier.

past five or six years, it seems like all the majors (PGA championship events) were played on Donald Ross courses. Everyone suddenly knew who he was. He was always famous, but around here, no one knew who he was."

Hahn dispelled the myth that the course was designed to accommodate the left-handed Schwab's bad slice. As Hahn tells it, "That's not true. In those days there were no bulldozers, no backhoes, no steam shovels, no dump trucks. Everything was done by carts and horses and mules. The work was done by hand, and you designed a golf course with what God gave you. Schwab was fortunate there were no restrictions made by the government in those days. He could go out and do what he wanted with the course. So Ross followed the natural contours of the land. That's what makes it so challenging today."

Herb Werner, in his *Altoona Mirror* column, mentioned an interesting rumor about this course. It is said that Schwab had a ticker tape at every tee, along with a telegraph, so he could keep in touch with his vast business empire. In spite of all that, he went broke in '29 along with millions of other Americans. As a result, from 1939 to 1966, the course lay dormant. Then when the economy had a turnaround, a restoration project took place.

The course's location is in a forest near Loretto, where friars labored to clear the land and then construct the foundations of what would one day become St. Francis College. (The school is alternately called *The Home of the Red Flash* and

Tees	Par	Yards	Slope	USGA
Forward	72	6423	NA	NA
Middle	80	6148	NA	NA

POCONO MANOR INN & GOLF RESORT

1919

EAST COURSE
ROUTE 314, MANOR ROAD, POCONO MANOR, PA 18349
(800) 233-8150 FAX: (570) 839-0708
E-MAIL: PMI02@NOLN   WEBSITE: POCONOMANOR.COM

DIRECTIONS: I-80 TO DELAWARE WATER GAP BRIDGE WEST TO I-380 WEST. AT FIRST EXIT (POCONO #8) TURN RIGHT AND FOLLOW SIGNS TO MANOR.

Resort. 36 holes. Open April 1 to November 31. Rental carts and clubs. Driving range and putting green. Chipping and sand practice areas. Pro shop opens 7:30 AM. Professionals on staff. Golf club dining lounge and restaurant. Tennis/racquetball center, swimming pools (indoor and out), trap shooting, Nautilus fitness center, bicycling, bocci courts, stables, cross country skiing, snowmobiling, outdoor ice skating, masseuse.

The clubhouse

Pocono Manor Inn and Golf Resort features two 18-hole courses and 72 privately owned residences on 3,500 acres. Located on rugged, mountain top terrain, the famed Ross East Course was remodeled in 1919. An equally challenging West Course was built here by George Fazio in 1963. Today, this resort, which has been included in the *National Register of Historic Places,* shouldn't be missed if you love great golf and grand scenery.

Many forms of wildlife, including deer, fox, wild turkeys, pheasants and an occasional bear, make this an interesting golfing experience within easy driving distance of New York City, Philadelphia and Syracuse. It seems to be just about 90 minutes "from everywhere," as its literature claims.

Jimmie Demerest hosted All-Star Golf in 1960/61, and both the PGA Senior Pro Am and an LPGA tournament have been played here. It is the home of the Greg Wall Golf School. Greg is the son of Art Wall, Jr., who won the Masters in 1959 when he was the touring pro from Pocono Manor. He was also PGA

Player of the Year that same year and top money winner.

Golf Magazine has said, "Pocono Manor's Donald Ross-designed East Course is one of the most exciting and enjoyable mountain courses to be found anywhere."

Ross carved a true mountain course with wide fairways, making the very most of this ideal golfing site.

246

History

The first acquisition of 750 acres was made in 1902 by 145 prominent Quakers from Philadelphia and New Jersey, who wanted to create a mountain resort for Quakers. By 1935 they had built 59 "cottages" (massive elegant stone and wood homes), which remain today with minimal alterations. Fifteen have been added since World War II.

The Inn was built in 1902, a wing added in 1904, and by 1908, a heated structure know as Manor Lodge was added to serve visitors over winter months

By 1931, the requirement of member ship in the Society of Friends for managers and directors was deleted, but early Quaker ideals and principles were retained by both cottage owners and innkeepers.

During World War II, the U.S. Navy leased the property for their sailors and commissioned officers as a recreational facility, and in 1966, Samuel Ireland of Atlantic City, a founder of Ireland Coffee and Tea Company, purchased the majority of shares and began renovations. Today, Mr. Ireland's grandson, who is the president, is undertaking more historically conscious renovations.

Pocono Manor has seen some of golf's all-time greats compete on the old East Course, including Tommy Bolt, Jack Burke, Gene Littler, Roberto DeVicenzo, Doug Ford, Jerry Barber and Orvil Moodey.

Art Wall and Arnold Palmer played an exhibition at Pocono in 1961. Jackie Gleason, too, played Pocono. He loved to escape from the pressures of his Manhattan studio and sneak away for a game here whenever he could.

Tees	Par	Yards	Slope	USGA
Blue	72	6565	118	72.0
White	72	6304	116	70.1
Red	75	5977	117	74.0

TUMBLEBROOK GOLF COURSE

3600 Jacoby Road, Coopersburg, PA 18036
(610) 282-0377   Fax: (610) 282-2126

DIRECTIONS: FROM HWY. 78, TAKE HWY. 309 SOUTH.   TURN LEFT AT JACOBY RD. ENTRANCE IS 3/4 MILE ON THE LEFT.

Public. Nine holes, plays to 18. Open March 1 to November 30. Rental gas, pull-carts and clubs. Pro shop opens at 7 AM. Putting green. Snack bar.

Right: The par four eighth hole, the number one handicap, plays 410 yards off the whites, 309 yards off the ladies' tees. Mature trees may cause problems on both the left and right approaches.

Coopersburg was once a leading cattle buying and selling area. Now it is a pretty, quiet town that prefers to stay that way. It is, indeed, a well-kept secret, with very few signs to identify its existence.

All nine holes at Tumblebrook remain the same today as they were almost 70 years ago. The green and white scorecard shows the original plans as laid out by Donald Ross, indicating that there is water running from left to right across the entire property.

The owners have lovingly preserved this small jewel with its bent grass. Located in a picturesque, hill section of Lehigh County, it offers the golfer sometimes troubling lies, sand bunkers and often annoying mounds or hummocks.

Ross really enjoyed hummocks. He had grown up with them on the Dornoch links and believed they were important to test the golfer's skills with irons. As a practical matter, in the early days when Ross built his courses, the moving of large stones and rocks was a serious problem. What better and cheaper way to accomplish the almost impossible than to put in a mound? Ross simply stacked up the rocks and stone that had been removed from one part of the course and piled them up in another location to create one of his troubling mounds, or hummocks. As a very frugal Scot, it seemed logical to Ross, and the practice was commonplace. The result: more interesting and challenging courses, particularly if placed in just the right spots on the course.

Water can be a real problem on two holes. Five of the nine holes have extremely large trees growing in locations that can cause the player to lose a stroke if not careful in shot placement. Tumblebrook may look easy off the first tee, but as one goes around the course, the need for careful shot management quickly becomes evident.

At the time when he designed Tumblebrook, Ross was in great demand. His reputation had spread so far that his company, which sometimes consisted of as many as 3,000 men, were working on 20 to 25 courses at one time. Interestingly, it is said that each of his top aides became course designers in their own right.

Tees	Par	Yards	Slope	USGA
White/yellow	71	6001	96	65.7
Red	68	4608	96	65.7

RHODE ISLAND

TRIGGS MEMORIAL GOLF COURSE

WINNAPAUG COUNTRY CLUB

TRIGGS MEMORIAL GOLF COURSE

1533 CHALKSTONE AVENUE, PROVIDENCE, RI 02909
(401) 521-8460   FAX: (401) 941-5920

DIRECTIONS: FROM I-95, EXIT RTE. 10 EXTENSION TO PLEASANT VALLEY PKWY. EXIT. FOLLOW TO 4TH LIGHT AND TURN LEFT ONTO CHALKSTONE BOULEVARD. COURSE IS 2 MILES ON THE RIGHT.

Public. 18 holes. Open year round. Pro shop opens 6:30 AM. Rental gas and pullcarts and clubs. Driving range. Putting green. Teaching pro. Restaurant and snack bar.

Triggs is owned by the City of Providence and operated by FCG Associates, LP, located at 320 Fall River Avenue, Seekonk, MA. The course was designed and constructed by Donald Ross in the early '30s and officially opened in the spring of 1932.

FCG took over management in 1990. The condition, like many municipal courses, had deteriorated over the years, but has been put back into the excellent condition. In fact, *Golf Digest* has rated this as the "Fifth Best Public Course in the State."

In the restoration, the course has been greatly improved by reverting to the original Ross design, but using modern construction and maintenance techniques. The effort was enhanced by the fact that the original architectural plans were available. The original contours of tees, greens and fairways have been lovingly reconstructed, so the course plays today exactly as it did when Ross created it. No holes have been changed, and, for those purists who must see to believe, Ross' old drawings may be viewed, framed on the wall in the clubhouse.

As in the case of most of Ross' Rhode Island area designs, the bent grass layout follows the natural contours of the site with relatively small, strategically bunkered greens. The front nine is fairly flat, in contrast to much larger changes in elevation on the back nine.

Triggs runs counter to the Ross tradition of "starting simple," with three long, difficult par fours, and then finishes with two more. Indeed, the course is noted for its difficult par fours and relatively short (reachable in two) par fives, as well as four demanding par threes. A careful study of the course reveals Ross' brilliant use of existing topography, contours and bunkers to create character and optical illusions that affect strategy and course management. Water hazards come into play on two holes.

Triggs is located in the heart of the city's

The 462 yard, dogleg left, par five 13th—the shortest par five on the back nine

upper west side in what is now a densely populated area called Mount Pleasant. Originally, it was built on the 140 acre Obadiah Brown farm, but is now bordered by an elementary school, a high school and Rhode Island College.

In September, 1941, Triggs was host to the first and only Providence Open. This three-day event, for a total purse of $5,000, featured many of the country's best and most famous touring pros, including: Horton Smith, Joe Turnesa, Gene Sarazen, Ben Hogan, Tony Penna, Sam Snead, Ralph Guldahl, Byron Nelson and Jimmy Demaret.

Triggs has a long and storied history as the annual host of the Rhode Island Public Links Tournament. In addition, with the dramatic improvement in conditions during the past decade, several major Rhode Island Golf Association tournaments have been held here including: the 1993, '94 and '95 Mid Amateur,

the 1996 and '97 State Fourball and the 2000 95th Annual Rhode Island State Amateur Tournament. The latter is viewed as a great honor, as typically the state amateurs are held at private courses.

Above: The signature par three, 158 yard, well-bunkered hole 14—the easiest hole on the course

Above: Each year at Triggs, Mayor Vincent A. "Buddy" Cianci, Jr. holds a tournament to benefit his college scholarship fund. This money, along with that raised from the sale of his own marinara sauce, helps deserving college students from Providence. Here he is with some of his friends.

All photos by Nanette Goodridge, City of Providence Photographer

Tees	Par	Yards	Slope	USGA
Blue	72	6522	128	72.9
White	72	6302	124	71.9
Red	72	5392	123	73.1

WINNAPAUG COUNTRY CLUB

184 SHORE ROAD, WESTERLY, RI 02891
(401) 596-1237   FAX: (401) 596-0794
(NINE HOLES REMODELED IN 1922. NINE HOLES ADDED IN 1928)

DIRECTIONS: FROM I-95 NORTH, TAKE EXIT 92. GO RIGHT TO RTE. 2 AND GO TO RTE. 78. TURN RIGHT TO TOM HARVEY RD, LEFT TO SHORE RD., LEFT TO COURSE AT END OF ROAD.

Semi-private. 18 holes. Open year round. Pro shop opens 6 AM. Colonial Club restaurant and bar. Gas and electric, pullcarts and club rental. Driving range. Chipping and sand practice areas. Pool room and card room.

Above: From the side of the seventh green looking back up to the seventh tee

At Winnapaug, all holes on the 6,345 yard course, with the exception of numbers 14 and 16, remain the same today as when Ross created them. Number 14 was modified from a dogleg right to a dogleg left. The par three, 179 yard (off the blues) 16th green has also been enlarged and lengthened from 150 yards.

Golf Digest has rated this the sixth "Best Public Course" in Rhode Island. Owner George Buck claims the course has the best greens of any in the state. He maintains they are slower and work better for the average golfer. The trick: mowing the greens to a height of 3/16

inch rather than the lower grasses usually kept on other courses.

The message on the back of the restaurant menu reads: "The course requires a balance of technical skills for the avid golfer. Mr. Ross carved Winnapaug from the natural, picturesque geography of hills, valleys, juniper, oak and pine. The test for golfers calls for long, accurate tee shots and precise handling of the short game." It has been owned by the George Buck family since 1969. George was employed here at age 14 and was once the youngest superintendent in the country. It is a family business dedicated to providing first class golf on a premiere course.

If you are partial to vistas of New England stone walls, this course has them everywhere. And each stone represents the handiwork of a farmer, who worked this difficult soil centuries ago.

Looking back at the fourth green from the fifth tee

Tees	Par	Yards	Slope	USGA
Blue	72	6345	118	70.6
White	72	5914	116	69.8
Red	72	5113	110	69.1

South Carolina

Cheraw Country Club

Fort Mill Golf Club

Lancaster Golf Club

CHERAW COUNTRY CLUB

1601 Cash Road, Cheraw, SC 29520
(843) 537-3412   Fax: (843) 537-0819

Directions: From Cheraw, go south on Hgwy. 52 about three miles. Turn left at sign for course.

Semi-private. 18 holes. Open year round. Pro shop opens 7 AM. For tee times in advance, call one day ahead; earliest calls 8 AM. Course is closed on Mondays during Jan. and Feb. Rental gas carts. Driving range. Putting green. Chipping and sand practice areas. Swimming pool. Tennis courts.

The par three fourth hole over water plays 192 from the blues, but only 100 for the ladies—the second easiest at Cheraw

This is an area of the South Carolina plateau known as the High Hill of Cheraw. Here, during the American Revolution, the 71st Regiment of foot of Lord Charles Cornwallis' command, informally known as Frasers' Highlanders, took up a position as the vanguard of a planned British invasion designed to destroy Washington's army. The brave Scot Highlanders could be easily recognized by the red feathers they sported in their hats. One can only imagine that the Scots, bored with often tedious and always dangerous wartime duty, may have taken up their national sport for recreation in the Sandhills of the Carolinas. If so, the golf course now located at Cheraw may have had avid golfers on the spot a good 150 years before another Highlander, Donald Ross, came to town to create a nine hole course.

In the early '20s, a cow pasture near Bennettsville was the nearest thing for a golf course for enthusiasts of the game in Cheraw. The caddies went ahead of the players, carrying big bags of sticks. After a ball was hit, the caddie would mark its spot with one of the sticks he was carrying. In this way, the golfer could find his ball in the thick meadow grass. The fairways in those days were even more dense than the worst of today's rough, and on dewy mornings, a player went out expecting to "get his knickers wet."

In 1924, the Cheraw Golf Club was formally established. Newspaper reports of the time show that "Forty local citizens put up $100 each to raise the money needed for land laid off by a man named Obenchain on 50 acres of land leased from D.W. Moore." A house was built for the first caretaker, John Wallace. Eddie Kuhn was the course's first pro. At this time, the clubhouse consisted of Mr. Chavis' tool house. A modern clubhouse was finally built in

1938. Thomas Harmon was its architect. During the Great Depression, WPA funds assisted the club for fairway and green improvements and the expansion to 18 holes.

This is a decidedly rural course. From the first tee, if one looks directly to the right, the vista is real farm country—actually a cornfield with corn ready for pickin'. There are no homes on this Chesterfield County Bermuda grass course, and limited cart path areas to interfere with the natural views. The signature hole is the par three number four, where the golfer faces a daunting water hazard that plays 192 yards off the men's tees. The most difficult hole here is not on the original Ross section. It is number 11, a par five, 495 yard beauty with a pond strategically placed right in front of the green. That second shot better be right on the money! Water is found on only three holes: numbers four, 11 and 14. We visited the course on a Saturday afternoon and found it well played by scores of active young golfers whose putting prowess put the authors to shame.

Lots of juniors here

Above: The cornfields behind hole number five, a long par four

Left: The sign at the entrance reads "Originally designed by Donald Ross." Here the management is proud of its Ross heritage, and preservation is a continuing tradition.

Tees	Par	Yards	Slope	USGA
Blue	72	6347	111	70.3
White	72	5891	111	67.2
Yellow	72	4977	105	67.3

A MASTER'S TOUCH

Some golfers have said that if you've played one Ross course, you've played 'em all. But that is to mistakenly believe that minimalism and simplicity are characteristics that must, of necessity, lead to sameness. The master architects who have studied Ross' works by playing the courses have come to recognize his touches of genius, and where possible, have tried to emulate many of them. Pete Dye has said, "He was one of the few designers who was able to put a real purpose into each shot on every hole."

Ross' work began with the land, either that with which he was presented or in some instances, that which he helped select. A born environmentalist, he'd walk the land over and over again to get just the routing that nature and the elements seemed to dictate.

A champion in his own right, he'd select 18 green sites that would demand that the player use every club in the bag. In the early days, players carried as few as five or six clubs, but when Ross was at his creative peak, players literally had a club for every contingency. The 14-club limit, still in effect today, was not enforced until 1938—almost at the end of his professional career.

How would he view today's power clubs and extra-distance balls? Perhaps with disdain or amusement. But history has shown that he knew how to make a course for the modern player as well of those of his own day—that's for certain.

Ross was a founding member of the American Society of Golf Course Architects, a group formed in December, 1947 at Pinehurst. There, a bronze statue of Ross, standing beside his friend and colleague, Richard Tufts was sculpted by Gretta Bader of Stanford, California. She did the life-size piece in 1991, based upon a photo given by golf champion and course operator Peggy Kirk Bell of Pine Needles. Bader's works include over 200 busts and are shown in the National Building Museum in Washington, DC.

There are many words cited in *Roget's International Thesaurus* to substitute for "architect." Some of these are: planner, designer, deviser, framer, enterpriser, functionalist, organizer, tactician and strategist. Amazing, isn't it, how Ross so completely personified all these definitions?

FORT MILL GOLF CLUB

101 COUNTRY CLUB DRIVE, PO BOX 336, FORT MILL, SC 29716
(803) 547-2044   FAX: (803) 547-1081

DIRECTIONS: FROM CHARLOTTE, TAKE 177 SOUTH TO EXIT 85. TURN LEFT TO HIGHWAY 160 TO FORT MILL. LEFT ON MAIN ST., RIGHT ON ACADEMY ST. TO COURSE.

Semi-private. 18 holes. Open 7 AM year round. Rental electric and pullcarts. Driving range. Pro shop. Putting green. Chipping and sand practice areas. Teaching pro. Snack bar.

The 432 yard first hole at Fort Mill—a par four dogleg right, number five handicap, with a large, slightly crowned, elevated green

Formerly Spring Mill Country Club, the front nine of this very fine York County course was created by Donald Ross, and the back nine put in by George Cobb 13 years later, in 1959. The course has very open fairways, which are lined with tall pines and oaks. The holes designed by Ross have his trademark turtlebacked elevated greens with slight undulations. This was one of the last creations of Ross, who died in 1948. Eight of the original nine holes he designed remain today exactly as he designated them: one, three, four, five, six, seven, eight and nine.

Some of the celebrities who have played Fort Mill include: Mickey Mantle, Eddie Payton, Terry Bradshaw and Roman Gabriel.

Tees	Par	Yards	Slope	USGA
Blue	72	6826	123	72.7
White	72	6373	118	70.5
Gold	72	5684	112	67.3
Red	72	5427	125	71.6

LANCASTER GOLF CLUB

1821 SPRINGS CLUB ROAD, BOX 289, LANCASTER, SC 29720
(803) 416-4500   FAX: (803) 416-4500

DIRECTIONS: FROM CHARLOTTE, TAKE HIGHWAY 521 SOUTH 40 MILES TO HIGHWAY 200 WEST FOR FOUR MILES. TURN LEFT ON AIRPORT RD. ENTRANCE ON SPRINGS CLUB RD.

Semi-private. 18 holes. Nine holes in 1935 and nine holes added in 1969. Open year round. Driving range. Rental electric and pullcarts and clubs. Pro on staff. Pro shop opens 8 AM. Snack bar.

This Lancaster County bent grass course (originally Bermuda), offers golfers greens that are known for their speed. Water hazards come into play on three holes.

The signature hole is number seven, a par three challenge that plays to 157 yards off the blues and only 135 off the whites. It is located on an island green and is completely surrounded by water. When Ross laid out this hole, the island green was reached by a small wooden plank the golfers walked over to reach the green. When the hole was improved in 1990, a permanent stone bridge was built, allowing golfers in carts to drive behind the hole, cross the small stream and walk onto the green. The green is sloped forward from back to front, so a good shot will be close and in front of the pin. This hole takes a straight drive to the small green. It is truly outstanding and great fun to play.

Today Lancaster has about 750 members and, together with visitors, about 40,000 rounds are played each year. Because the course is laid out with wide fairways, even when busy, it does not convey the sense of being crowded.

The number one hole features a prominent sign that reads *No Mulligans*, a good way to start the golfers off as quickly as

The dogleg right approach to the second hole—412 yards—the number one handicap at Lancaster

possible. The day we visited, we can report that the course was in excellent shape and very well maintained.

Donald Ross Associates laid out the front nine holes here. Holes seven and eight have been modified since Ross did his initial work. The holes that are still true to his original plans are three, six, nine, ten and 17.

PGA professional Alan Rowsam has developed an active junior program at Lancaster as part of the South Carolina Junior Golf Association. He reports that, during some weeks, as many as 50 boys and girls are on the practice tee learning the game under Al's guidance.

Top: A gorgeous green placement at Lancaster

Bottom: The fine, modern clubhouse has a well-stocked pro shop and comfortable snack bar.

Tees	Par	Yards	Slope	USGA
Blue	72	6538	128	71.8
White	72	6099	124	69.8
Gold	73	5097	105	64.1
Red	73	4967	120	69.4

THE U.S. OPEN TOURNAMENT HAS BEEN PLAYED 20 TIMES ON ROSS COURSES – SO FAR

Shown right: Ryder Cup Matches, Pinehurst, 1951. Jack Burke on the 15th tee, No. 2 Course. Burke and Clayton Heafner beat the British team of Max Faulkner and Dai Rees to win 1 point for the United States.

Photo Courtesy of the Tin Whistles

At the starter's shack at Pinehurst No. 2, there's a large, easy-to-read wooden sign that conveys this message of Donald Ross to each golfer before he or she tees off.

—

I sincerely believe this course will be the fairest test of championship golf I have ever designed. It's obviously the function of the championship course to present competitors with a variety of problems that will test every type of shot which a golfer of championship ability should be qualified to play. Thus it should call for long and accurate tee shots, accurate iron play (and I consider the ability to play longer irons as the supreme test of a great golfer), precise handling of the short game, and finally consistent putting.

—

Because Donald Ross had participated in championship tournaments in the United States and Scotland, it was always his goal to create in each course qualities that would lend themselves to championship play. Some courses, particularly nine-hole efforts, did not allow this to happen. But over and over again, many of his great works met the test—not of club members or managers or professionals, but of the powers to be who selected the courses for the great tournaments of the day. One measurement of Ross' achievement in this area is to look at his record in U.S. Open Championships from 1895 to now. There have been exactly one hundred U.S. Open tournaments. (None were played during 1917-18 and 1942-45—World War I and II.) All the courses listed here, selected as sites for the Open, were designed by the master, himself.

1919 - Brae Burn Country Club, Newton, MA – Walter Hagen
1920 - Inverness Club, Toledo, OH – Edward Ray
1922 - Skokie Country Club, Glencoe, IL - Gene Sarazen
1924 - Oakland Hills C.C., (South Course), Birmingham, MI, Cyril Walker
1925 - Worcester Country Club., Worcester, MA -William Macfarlane
1926 - Scioto Country Club, Columbus, OH - Robert Trent Jones, Jr.
1930 - Interlachen Country Club, Edina, MN, Robert Trent Jones, Jr.
1931 - Inverness Club, Toledo, OH – Billy Burke
1937 - Oakland Hills Country Club, (South Course), Birmingham, MI, Ralph Guldahl
1951 - Oakland Hills Country Club, (South Course), Birmingham, MI, Ben
1956 - Oak Hill Country Club (East Course), Rochester, NY, Cary Middlecoff
1957 - Inverness Club, Toledo, OH, Dick
1961 - Oakland Hills Country Club (South Course) Gene Littler
1968 - Oak Hill Country Club (East Course), Rochester, NY, Lee Trevino
1979 - Inverness Club, Toledo, OH, Hale Irwin
1985 - Oakland Hills Country Club, Andy North
1989 - Oak Hill Country Club (East Course) Rochester, NY, Curtis Strange
1996 - Oakland Hills Country Club (South Course), Steve Jones
1997 - Congressional Country Club (Blue Course) Bethesda, MD, Ernie Els
1999 - Pinehurst Resort & Country Club, Payne Stewart

Notes: Three courses were remodeled by Ross after Open Tournaments were held there: Newport, RI; Minikahda, Minneapolis, MN; and the Philadelphia Cricket Club, Philadelphia, PA, where Alec Ross won the Open in '07 over Gilbert Nicholls.

Tennessee

Brainerd Golf Course

Vinnylinks at Shelby Golf Course

BRAINERD GOLF COURSE

5203 OLD MISSION ROAD, CHATTANOOGA, TN 37411
(423) 855-2692 FAX: (423) 855-9436
WEBSITE: WWW.CHATTANOOGA.GOV/CPR/GOLF

DIRECTIONS: FROM CHATTANOOGA, TAKE I-24 NORTH, TAKE MOORE RD. EXIT, TURN LEFT. TURN RIGHT AT OLD MISSION RD. ENTRANCE ON THE LEFT.

Public. 18 holes. Open all year. Clubs, electric and pullcart rental. Walkers invited and encouraged. Putting green. Chipping and sand practice areas. Teaching pro. Complete pro shop. Snack bar. The newly renovated turn-of-the-century clubhouse is available for special events.

This 6,470-yard, bent grass, Hamilton County course is in very fine shape from recent fairway renovation and improvement. Proudly operated by the City of Chattanooga Parks and Recreation Department, the course is very well-tended. The number of players continues to grow—70,000 are anticipated this year here. Operataing two courses, Brainerd and Brown Acres, the Golf Division now contributes 70% of all earned revenue of the Parks and Recreation Department.

Possibly the oldest course in Chattanooga, Ross designed the front nine holes, and they are very much the same today as when Ross laid them out, with renovations to the greens.

The greens are slightly larger than the usual Ross design, but they are, as ever, sloped and undulating, yet reasonably easy to read. Of course, the golfer can never take a putt on a Ross green for granted.

Water comes into play on four of the Ross holes. The front nine tend to be rolling, and the back nine are on relatively flat land. Mature trees surround the fairways, and many golfers are in awe of the picturesque surroundings as they progress from hole to hole.

The first time you play this Chattanooga course, you may want to have a supply of old balls, because there's more water than usual. Meandering streams cross fairways one, three, four and nine, and may also be found behind the 15th tee and beside the first and 16th greens. A small pond lies, strategically placed, directly in front of the 11th green. Water also runs along the 18th, from mid-point to behind the green on the left. The most difficult hole is

The par four, 419 yard ninth hole—not a particularly pretty bunker—but it can serve its purpose of giving the golfer a bit of misery

the first, a 420 yard, par four, requiring a long tee shot around a dogleg left fairway, and then a good, accurate approach shot to the green. Watch out for the large bunker to the right of the dance floor. There is a separate green fee for those who prefer to walk the course, and many do.

The photographs show that Brainerd has much of the feel of Ross courses of this period in his architectural development. The fairways are open, with plenty of lining trees to keep the golfer honest and no shortage of vexing sand bunkers protecting the slightly elevated greens. It is Ross at his minimalist best, with no homes on the course to detract from the scenery.

The par five number four tee box from the gold tees. Water comes into play, and there are two bunkers that are apt to snare the player's approach shot. A third bunker is placed front right of the green.

Tees	Par	Yards	Slope	USGA
Blue	72	6470	119	69.8
White	72	6118	116	68.1
Gold	72	5536	118	69.9
Red	72	4962	113	67.7

VINNYLINKS AT SHELBY GOLF COURSE

1901 SEVIER STREET, NASHVILLE, TN 37206
(615) 880-3427

DIRECTIONS: FROM I-95 NORTH OR SOUTH, EXIT SHELBY ST AND PROCEED EAST (AWAY FROM DOWNTOWN). TURN RIGHT AT 17TH AND GO 4 BLOCKS. GO LEFT ON SEVIER ST. FOR 2 BLOCKS TO CLUBHOUSE.

Public. A short, 1,358 yard junior course.. 9 holes. Open May 15 to November 1. Rental carts and clubs. Driving range. Open to juniors and any member of the public wishing to play. Course will open in the year 2001.

Below: The new hole number seven as created by the Board of Parks and Recreation

When the Board of Parks and Recreation Department at Centennial Park office in Nashville moved its offices in 1989, the original 1919 Donald Ross drawings for a nine-hole course, to be called Shelby Golf Course, were discovered by Superintendent of Golf Operations Danny Gibson. Found rolled up in a trash can, they had been "put away" for future reference, and remained put away for 70 years! They give an excellent picture of the detailed way Ross worked, and were a good guide to park officials when a new links was created here in the year 2000, albeit one specifically designed for junior players.

It seems that Ross had been hired by the City of Nashville in 1919 to create a nine hole course, but it was never built because of lack of funds. Later, when funds were available, the purchase of additional land for another nine made the Ross plans obsolete.

The original Ross plans may be seen framed in the offices of the Tennessee Golf House at 400 Franklin Road, in Franklin. Walter Hatch, a longtime associate of Ross, "made the plans." In a July 17, 1919, letter to Lee J. Loventhal, found loose in back of Board Minutes Volume Three, Hatch reported that Shelby Park is "good ground for a first city golf course. Will try preserve natural landscape, and is excellent site for a club house. Estimates construction costs at $12,000, not including club house and water lines. Maintenance will require three men. If start building course in Aug. 1919, could be ready for play in

Top: Vince Gill, rear, looks on as The First Tee's $100,000 check is present to Save Nashville Youth by The First Tee's Richard Bowers.
Bottom: Preliminary rendering of VinnyLinks Learning Center

May, 1920. Will furnish the general plan of the course with specifications for greens construction." For this report, Hatch was paid $309.38. There is no record of what Ross was paid for the submitted plans.

In 1923, the board purchased 45 acres of the Hinds tract, north of and adjoining Shelby Park, as a site for a new nine hole course, and it bought five lots for $2500 at the end of Russell Street, adjoining the course on the west side. The new land had different topography from the first site, and therefore the Ross plans were impractical for a course there. For some reason, the board hired Tom Benelow of Chicago to survey a new course and build it instead of continuing with Ross. At this time, Ross was so heavily engaged in course construction, particularly in Florida, that he may have turned down the project. In 1926, 900 citizens petitioned the city to add another nine holes, and in 1927, 60 additional acres of the Martha Tilman property were acquired for $300 an acre to increase the size of Shelby Park golf course.

Junior Golf Comes to Nashville

Now, thanks to Vince Gill, the First Tee Program, Dick Horton, and the Tennessee Golf Foundation, a totally new junior golf course is built on some of the very same land that was originally laid out by Donald Ross for Shelby. When Billy Fuller, the former course superintendent at the Masters, was examining the plans, he suggested, "Why don't we build the greens to the original specifications of Donald Ross' plans?"

And so the idea for a par 28 junior course was born. Hole one will be a par four; holes two through nine will all be par threes. The greens are according to original Ross specifications, but slightly smaller than the originals, and the fairways are much shorter. So what now exists in Nashville is the only "Donald Ross inspired" junior course in the nation. It is named The VinnyLinks, to honor Vince Gill, who has been a force behind the development of junior golf in Nashville.

How would Donald Ross feel about all of this activity taking place so many years after he first drew the plans for a course for Nashville? We think he'd be delighted, because Ross was the first golf professional to encourage course owners to create special links for caddies and young players. He was prescient in realizing that, for the game to become a serious sport, it would need a cadre of youngsters who would fill the ranks as the older golfers began to slow down. At Ponkapoag, he did detailed plans in 1933 for a Pitch and Putt course that was never built, but which he had hoped would develop into a fine little course that would be attractive to young, aspiring golfers. Yes, Donald would be 100% behind Nashville's present program designed to encourage young players.

About Vince Gill

Vincent Grant Gill is from Norman, Oklahoma. His instruments are guitar, bass, mandolin, banjo, fiddle and dobro, and he has been awarded so many platinum, gold, double platinum and quadruple platinum record albums that it would take a book to list them. He has received 18 Country Music Association Awards, more than any artist in history.

When not on the road or in the studio, this one handicap golfer is on the tee. His lowest round shot—65, and his favorite course—Augusta National. He has devoted much of his time and energy to hundreds of charities and benefits and the promotion of junior golf programs through his annual pro-celebrity tournament—The Vinny.

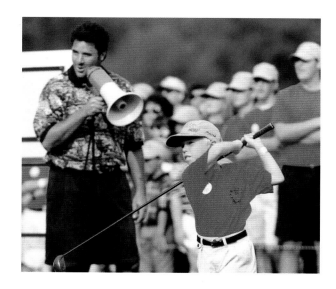

Vince Gill offers encouragement to a young golfer.

Virginia

Belmont Golf Course & Recreation Center

The Homestead, The Old Course

Kinderton Country Club

Sewells Point Golf Course

The Woodlands Golf Course

BELMONT GOLF COURSE & RECREATION CENTER   1922

(FORMERLY HERMITAGE COUNTRY CLUB)
1600 HILLIARD ROAD, RICHMOND, VA 23228
(804) 501-4653   FAX: (804) 501-5284

DIRECTIONS: FROM I-95, TAKE US 1 TO HILLIARD RD. ENTRANCE ON THE RIGHT

Public. 18 holes. Open year round. Pro shop opens 7 AM. Rental electric and pull-carts and clubs. Putting and chipping green. Restaurant serves breakfast and lunch. Snack bar. Tee times advisable. Walking allowed any time.

This Henrico County championship course was remodeled in 1922-23 by Donald Ross, who helped the Hermitage Country Club redesign its greens and irrigation system and convert the greens from sand to Bermuda grass. Some who play the course still call it "Old Hermitage," but today most refer to it as Belmont Park. In 1976, Hermitage Country Club relocated to a larger site west of Richmond, and this location was renamed.

The original design was done by A.W. Tillinghast, six years before Ross was called in. Since Ross did his work, there have been modest changes made to holes one, two (green), nine, 16 (green) and 17.

It was here that native Virginian, Sam Snead, won the 1949 PGA Championship, and All Star Golf was played in the '60s. Since 1976, it has been a public facility operated by the county. Recent improvements have included construction of a clubhouse and a pedestrian tunnel under the widened Hilliard Road.

Belmont is a hilly course, promising the golfer many uneven fairway lies. The fairways are narrow, and the greens are typically Ross—small and challenging. A pond can cause the golfer grief on two holes.

Above: Hole number five during the 1949 PGA. Snead won.

Hole number two with old Richmond-Ashland trolley trestle in background. This is no easy hole; a narrow fairway requires a careful drive to the left to avoid trees and creek on the right. Fairway bunkers are no threat to a well-hit approach shot. The greens measure 30 x 19 and are crested in the Ross manner.

Above: A venerable course that's held its beauty for over 75 years

Par four hole number five, a serious dogleg to the right with a fairway that has enough bumps and valleys (known as "murderer's hollow") to qualify for the Guiness Book of Records. It's the number one handicap.

According to attorney Bruce H. Matson, Hermitage Country Club historian, the Richmond-Ashland Trolley Line actually crossed the first fairway at one time. (See photo on first page.) Now the power lines over the same easement provide a formidable challenge for golfers driving from the first tee.

Matson has written, "If the player can gain a long, straight drive (out-of-bounds on right), usually a long iron is still required to clear the stream fronting the first green, which itself is three-tiered sloping back to front. A stern opener to say the least." He reports that in earlier days the green was actually in front of the creek. And talk about dangerous holes! According to Matson, a caddie was killed by an errant tee shot off the second hole in 1923!

This was one of Tillinghast's very early works. He skillfully routed the course along a narrow property as he faced the task of managing meandering streams that still come into play. Although Donald Ross greatly helped improve the original Tillinghast work here, with all the changes made over the years in modifications and improvements, it is now essentially an amalgam of efforts by many competent hands. The unplanned result of it all is a very mature and fine course which provides great golfing enjoyment to all who visit and play here.

Tees	Par	Yards	Slope	USGA
Blue	71	6350	126	70.6
White	71	5944	122	68.4
Gold	73	5754	119	67.3
Red	71	5436	130	72.6

THE HOMESTEAD THE OLD COURSE

ROUTE 220, HOT SPRINGS, VA 24445
(540) 839-773 FAX: (540) 839-7954
E-MAIL: HOMESTEADRESERVATION@OURCLUB.COM
WEBSITE: WWW.THEHOMESTEAD.COM

DIRECTIONS: FROM I-64 EXIT AT TOWN OF COVINGTON AND GO NORTH ON RTE. 220. AT HOT SPRINGS FOLLOW SIGNS. PRIVATE PLANES MAY LAND AT INGALS FIELD, BATH COUNTY AIRPORT. 17

Resort. 18 holes. Play limited to resort guests and members. Open April 1 to October 30. Pro shop opens 7 AM. Rental electric carts and clubs. Driving range. Putting and chipping practice areas. Professionals on premises. Three day, four night golf packages available, which include the Golf Advantage School. Tennis, swimming, theater, fishing, horseback riding, over 100 miles of trail walking, trap and skeet. 521 rooms. Guests may reserve tee times up to 60 days in advance. Caddies are mandatory for walkers.

Below: The tenth hole, a tough, 381 par four—big dogleg left, 200 yards from the tee—a small green with a big fat bunker on the right. Aim for the target pole 164 yards from the blue tees.

The Homestead—what can be said that has not already been told in superlatives? Three golf courses, the oldest designed by Donald Ross. Called "The Old Course," it actually started as six holes back in 1892. A plaque boasts the oldest first tee in continuous use in the U.S. on hole number one at The Old Course. By 1913, it was enlarged to 18 by Ross and took its place in golf history.

Over the years it has been modified by William Flynn and most recently, a more than million dollar redesign by Rees Jones has restored it to its former glory. New bunkers and tees were added, and hole 18 was relocated.

The other two courses, "Cascades," designed by William Flynn and "Lower Cascades" by Robert Trent Jones, have hosted many tournaments, but it is still the Old Course that brings Ross aficionados from throughout the world to play The Homestead.

If it is your goal to improve your game, you might want to consider attending the Golf Advantage School, which gives individual as well as group instruction with a student-to-instructor ratio of a maximum of four to one. In May, *Golf Digest Woman* magazine offers a four-day getaway with instructional clinics, a tournament and awards banquet with top PGA/LPGA teaching professionals, just for women.

Of the 18 holes on the 6,211-yard Old Course, the greens at holes three, four, five, seven, eight, ten, 11, 16 and 17 have been preserved as Ross designed them almost 80 years ago.

The Old Course is unique in that it has

six par threes, six par fours and six par fives for a par 72. The writers found the fairways as rolling, with uneven lies up and down. Side hill lies make for a greater challenge to hit good shots into the very small greens that are known to be very fast. A stream courses through the property and may come into play on holes one, 15 and 16.

Sam Snead said of the Old Course in 1984, "I got my start at the Old Course when they let me caddie at the age of seven."

The Old Course is very open. It premieres with a 519 yard par five test, with three generously sized sand bunkers left of the green, roughly 100 yards from the flag.

Left: Golfers ascend the Old Course's first tee, the oldest in continuous use in America (1892). This is not an easy beginning—a 519 yard par five with three formidable bunkers to the left of the fairway at the red marker.

Left: The par four 17th green plays 354 yards from the blues to a small green. Here a straight drive is a necessity.

Tees	Par	Yards	Slope	USGA
Blue	72	6211	129	69.7
White	72	5796	125	66.9
Red	72	4852	116	67.7

271

KINDERTON COUNTRY CLUB

799 KINDERTON ROAD, BOX 758, CLARKSVILLE, VA 23927
(804) 374-8822   FAX: (804) 374-5501

DIRECTIONS: FROM HIGHWAY 58, TAKE US 15 SOUTH TWO MILES TO BURLINGTON ROAD. GO LEFT ON ROUTE 122 AND LEFT ON KINDERTON ROAD TO THE COURSE.

Semi-private. 18 holes. Open year round. Pro shop opens 7 AM. Pool and tennis. Snack bar. Rental gas and pullcarts. Tee times may be arranged up to three days in advance. Call after 8 AM.

The par five, number seven hole in the distance plays 498 yards off the blues. Only number ten is longer, at 530 yards.

The town of Clarksville, the home of Kinderton Country Club, sits smack dab on Kerr Lake (known to locals as Bugg's Island Lake) in the middle of Southside Virginia. It boasts over 50,000 acres of fresh water, with 800 miles of shore line. Whether you're looking for boating, swimming, water skiing, fishing, golf or hiking, there is something here for everyone who visits.

It is the home of the "Lakefest," recognized by the Southeast Tourism Society as one of the "Top Twenty Events in the Southeast," held each year during the third weekend in July.

In 1946, shortly after the start of construction of a textile plant by Robins Mills, Carl Robins purchased an adjacent plantatiion and hired Donald Ross to design and supervise the construction of a nine-hole course.

Kinderton is very well maintained, and close to Clarksville's other activities. The front

Above: Teeing up on the par three, 231 yards number eight plays up a steep incline. A mighty pretty sight.

nine (3,247 yards) plays to tight fairways and very small greens. Water comes into play throughout the course, with streams and large ponds in several locations. Hole number six, a par four, 404 yard challenge, is the number one handicap hole. All the front nine are exactly as Ross created them, with the exception of number one, which was changed when the course was modified and enlarged in 1949.

In 1950, when the flooding of Bugg's Island Reservoir covered the main access road to the club, major alterations were made to the front nine, and the back nine was constructed under the direction of Dick Wilson. One of the most modern watering systems was installed under every fairway, green and tee, permitting all tees and greens and half the fairways to be watered simultaneously.

In 1954, the merger of Robins Mills with Textron made it possible for the membership to lease the club property and comply with regulations to join the USGA and VSGA. Burlington Industries later purchased the property and continued to lease to the members until 1968, when the membership bought the facilities. During the years of the lease, the membership ranged from a low of 65 to more than 250.

When 150 families pledged to buy stock, the facilities were purchased from Burlington Industries.

In 1955, a young Clarksville businessman, Sam Davis, Jr. conceived the idea of the Kinderton Invitational. From the beginning, it was a huge success, with 200 golfers on hand for the first tournament. For the next five years the tournament continued to grow, and the 14th annual in May, 1968 drew 244 players. In the early '70s, bad weather caused a drop in player participation, but when the tournament was changed to August, the numbers showed a rapid upswing.

The course record from the middle tees is 64, and is held jointly by Clint Toms of Durham and the late Lloyd Leibler of Chesapeake, Virginia. (Leibler was only 15 years old at the time.) Bill Harvey is the only three-time invitational winner, and three others have won the event twice.

Tees	Par	Yards	Slope	USGA
Blue	71	6414	128	71.5
White	71	6108	123	68.8
Red	72	4984	115	68.5

NAVSTA Bldg. CA-99, Norfolk, VA 23511
(757) 444-5267   Fax: (757) 444-5977

DIRECTIONS: FROM I-64 GOING WEST, TAKE HWY. 564 WEST. GO RIGHT AT TERMINAL BLVD. THE COURSE IS ABOUT 1/2 MILE ON RIGHT.

Military course. Non-military should be accompanied. 18 holes. Open year round. Putting green. Chipping and sand practice areas. Teaching pro. Restaurant. Snack bar. Complete pro shop.

In 1954, The Norfolk Sports Club and the United States Navy co-sponsored *Golf Day* at the Sewells Point Golf Course. Professionals John O'Donnell, the host pro and State Open Champion; Chandler Harper, Mobile Atlantic winner; Ira Templeton and the U.S. Amateur Titlist, a guy named Arnold Palmer, played an exhibition. Palmer made his professional debut that day. Admission was free.

The par 71 course has a colorful history, going in and out of existence from 1898 through 1927, when Donald Ross completed the final design. It was variously called "The Country Club," "Norfolk Country Club" and "Country Club of Norfolk."

In 1907, Norfolk planned the Jamestown Exposition to commemorate the 300th anniversary of the Jamestown settlement and selected the Sewells Point area as the site for the seven-month celebration.

The city wanted the club's land, so the club sold its property in 1906. By 1908, a new site for the club was selected along the Lafayette River. In 1909, the Country Club opened with a new clubhouse, four tennis courts, a magnificent river view and nine holes of golf.

In 1917, upon the outbreak of the hostilities in World War I, the U.S. Navy decided to establish a major base in the Norfolk area, and the government purchased most of the site where the Jamestown Exposition had been held, including a portion of the Country Club's golf course. Ten years later, it sold the remainder of the course. Enter Donald Ross, who was hired to design the new club's course.

It is said that it is possibly the only military course in the country that has civilian members, be-

Sixty acres of trees grace Sewells Point Golf Course—a typical elevated, sloping green surrounded by daunting sand bunkers—Ross as he liked it best.

cause in 1942, when the Navy acquired the facilities, the existing Norfolk Golf Club members were permitted to retain golf privileges. There are six civilian members left. In the '70s, facilities were made accessible to enlisted men as well as officers. The course is open to all active and retired military personnel and their guests.

Recently, the firm of Ault, Clark & Associates, Ltd. has put in new tees, greens and bunkers, which expanded due to the volume of play, but to this day, the Ross course retains its unique routing of a clockwise circle surrounded by a counterclockwise circle of holes, emulating the Muirfield links in Scotland. All holes except four, five, six and eight are exactly as Ross designed them. The fairways are tree lined, and the greens are fast. There is water that comes into play on three holes, and the golfer must watch for the ever-present sand bunkers. The terrain is flat and easy to walk.

Celebrities who have played at Sewells Point include: Sam Snead, Gen. Dwight Eisenhower, Chandler Harper, Doug Sanders, Joe Bellino, Bob Feller, Brooks Robinson, Phil Neikro, Sparky Lyle, Tug McGraw, Catfish Hunter and Harmon Kilibrew.

Above: The clubhouse is a historic landmark, circa 1926. These day, over 50,000 rounds are played here annually.
Below: This pond on six is strategically placed for an additional irrigation source.

Tees	Par	Yards	Slope	USGA
Blue	71	6280	125	70.1
White	71	6027	122	68.9
Red	73	5748	120	67.6

THE WOODLANDS GOLF COURSE

9 WOODLAND ROAD, HAMPTON, VA 23663
(757)727-1195   FAX: (757) 727-1277

1928

DIRECTIONS: FROM I-64 EAST TAKE EXIT 267. GO LEFT AT LIGHT ONTO SETTLER'S LANDING RD. AFTER TWO LIGHTS. FROM I-64 WEST, TAKE EXIT 267 . GO RIGHT AT LIGHT ONTO WOODLAND RD. AFTER ONE LIGHT AT COUNTY ST., GOLF COURSE ON LEFT.

Public. 18 holes. Open year round. Clubhouse open 6:30 AM. Pro shop. Restaurant and snack bar. Electric and pullcarts and clubs. Spacious putting green, chipping area and practice bunker. Seven Hartru tennis courts.

Above: The new clubhouse, opened July 1999, from the 18th fairway, is one of the prettiest in Virginia. Eighteen is a nice finish to the round, playing 385 off the blues for a makeable par four. It plays straight with a large pond to the right of the green.

If Virginia is "For Lovers," then this is just one more reason to love the state. Woodlands is short but outstanding! Located near Hampton University, it is excellently managed by the Department of Parks and Recreation, City of Hampton.

The bent grass greens and Bermuda fairways were originally built in 1890 and, according to *Golf Magazine's* list, was one of "The First 100 Clubs in America." During the Great Depression, it was purchased by R. B. Hunt, who eventually sold the course in 1968 to a developer from Virginia Beach. The City of Hampton would not rezone for a housing development, so the course lay dormant. Formerly Hampton Roads Golf & Country Club, it was bought by the city in 1972, and it was reopened in 1975 as Hampton Golf and Tennis Center, and renamed

The Woodlands Golf Course in 1988.

It is a flat property, with generous-sized trees lining the fairways. Water hazards come into play throughout the course, and greens are well bunkered. There is a handsome new cedar shingled clubhouse and plenty of parking. This busy course, with over 65,000 rounds played annually, is only 25 minutes south of Williamsburg and 20 minutes north of Virginia Beach.

Donald Ross did his work here when he was in his period of greatest activity and creative powers as a course architect. In 1972, the course was completely renovated and expanded at the city's request by Ed Ault of the firm of Ault, Clark and Associates, Ltd. The present scorecard, which is one of the best looking and most functional in our collection of Ross cards, shows yardage of only 5,391 off the blues. (In the original 1928 layout the yardage was 6,072.) Valuable land was lost over the years. In those days, both front and back nines played over 3,000 yards each.

According to Golf Program Manager, Martha Miller, holes five and 13 are the two remaining Ross holes. Both of these holes have permanent boundaries, a road by one and the river by the other; these are the same boundaries on the original map. Thirteen is the only elevated green on the course.

Although only a par 69 course, it more than makes up for shortness of distance with a plethora of sand bunkers—52 of them! And water comes into play on 11 holes, which means one thing: bring along plenty of disposable balls!

This is one of the busiest public courses in the State of Virginia, so a tee time is recommended, and really a "must" for weekends and holidays. Tee times may be reserved by calling, starting at noon, three days prior to day of play.

Above: The 13th tee box, heading out over water 350 yards from the blues. Here the player wants to keep the drive to the left as the hole doglegs right to the flag, half way to the pin.

Tees	Par	Yards	Slope	USGA
Blue	69	5391	113	65.6
White	69	4990	109	63.8
Yellow	69	4467	105	62.0
Red	69	4154	106	62.9

THE ROYAL DORNOCH GOLF CLUB: WHERE IT ALL BEGAN

Above: Overview of the course, beach and, in the distance, the Dornoch Firth

The first three golf links in Scotland of which there is written record are: 1552, St. Andrews; 1593, Leith; 1616, Dornoch. Dornoch lies on the 58th parallel; in Canada you'd be in the middle of Hudson's Bay. It is now less than four hours from Edinburgh by car. Inverness airport is nearby. The golf club was founded in 1877 as the successor to the Suther-land Golfing Society, whose members played at Dornoch and Golspie. At one time it was the fifth longest course in Britain. In 1906 the club was granted a Royal Charter by King Edward the Seventh, and Royal Dornoch Golf Club was born. The superb Carnegie Shield was given to the club by Mr. and Mrs. Andrew Carnegie in 1901 to present for annual competition each August. It is one of the world's most beautiful trophies, with pictures of Dornoch Cathedral,

Skibo Castle and the then Bishop's Palace, now the Castle Hotel.

Donald Ross grew up here, saw the game played here as a child, and in due time was employed at the course as club maker, professional and greenkeeper. He and his brother Alec perfected their game at their home course. It has been written that their swings were noted by ease, grace and rhythm. After his great success in America, first as player, then as course architect, he would return more than once to his beloved town where many of his relatives remained.

He claimed he owed all he achieved in life to his upbringing and professional start in Dornoch. In a 1935 interview he said, "When I was a young man over here I used to think of Scottish village life as very narrow and hard. Life was limited to work and the church. The older I get the more I can feel myself turning back to their way of thinking. At least they never compromised with honesty."

With its North Sea location, Dornoch has never been the most widely known course, but it has hosted the Northern Open, The Scottish Ladies and Scottish Professional Championships. In 1980 Tom Watson had played here before winning the third of five Open championships at Muirfield. Recently Ben Crenshaw, Jack Nicholson, Greg Norman and HRH Prince Andrew have been seen on the famed links.

Golf Magazine's International Panel of Selectors in '93/'94 ranked it the 13th best course in the world. The Royal Golf Hotel is located just ten yards from the first tee.

Donald James Ross, the product of this wonderful golfing environment, was enshrined in the Golf Hall of Fame on August 23, 1977. He had given up golf competition in 1911, but in the previous 11 years in the States he had trophies for victories in the '03, '05 and '06 North And South Opens, with victories in the prestigious American classic, the '05 and '11 Massachusetts Opens.

The first fairway and green at dawn

Photos by Ian Lowe, St. Andrews Studio